The Salesforce Business Analysis Playbook

Second Edition

AF781352

Become a trusted Salesforce advisor through expert business analysis and applied AI skills

Srini Munagavalasa

<packt>

The Salesforce Business Analysis Playbook

Second Edition

Copyright © 2026 Packt Publishing

All rights reserved. No part of this book may be reproduced, stored in a retrieval system, or transmitted in any form or by any means, without the prior written permission of the publisher, except in the case of brief quotations embedded in critical articles or reviews.
Every effort has been made in the preparation of this book to ensure the accuracy of the information presented. However, the information contained in this book is sold without warranty, either express or implied. Neither the author, nor Packt Publishing or its dealers and distributors, will be held liable for any damages caused or alleged to have been caused directly or indirectly by this book.
Packt Publishing has endeavored to provide trademark information about all of the companies and products mentioned in this book by the appropriate use of capitals. However, Packt Publishing cannot guarantee the accuracy of this information.

Portfolio Director: Pavan Ramchandani
Relationship Lead: Alok Dhuri
Project Manager: Divij Kotian
Content Engineer: Esha Banerjee
Technical Editor: Vidhisha Patidar
Copy Editor: Safis Editing
Indexer: Pratik Shirodkar
Proofreader: Esha Banerjee
Production Designer: Alishon Falcon
Growth Lead: Nivedita Singh

First published: November 2022
Second edition: March 2026

Production reference: 2130326

Published by Packt Publishing Ltd.
Grosvenor House
11 St Paul's Square
Birmingham
B3 1RB, UK.

ISBN 978-1-80610-927-2
`www.packtpub.com`

Contributors

About the author

Srini Munagavalasa is a seasoned technology leader with more than two decades of global experience across Salesforce CRM and PRM, SAP CRM, and HR domains. Currently serving as Vice President within the Salesforce Engineering team at MUFG Americas, Srini has built a career rooted in a genuine passion for emerging technologies and a commitment to delivering meaningful business value through innovation.

A thought leader in his field, Srini has authored over 10 articles for **Wellesley Information Services (WIS)** and shared his insights at major industry events, including Salesforce Dreamforce and SAP Sapphire/ASUG. His professional journey includes impactful tenures at world-class organizations such as IBM, The Walt Disney Company, PwC, and CA Technologies. Srini holds a bachelor's degree in engineering and a post-graduate diploma in management.

I would like to extend my deepest gratitude to my wife, Sunanda, and my children, Sravan and Sai, for their unwavering support and encouragement throughout the journey of this second edition.

My sincere thanks go to the team at Packt—specifically Alok, Esha, and the rest of the dedicated team members—for their expert guidance and for keeping me on track during the publication process.

I am especially grateful to my technical reviewer, Andrew Nixon. His meticulous attention to detail and wonderful suggestions provided the technical depth this edition required; I truly appreciate the invaluable advice he shared throughout the review.

Finally, I want to thank my family, friends, and colleagues for their continued support. I also want to extend a special thanks to my LinkedIn community; I have learned so much from our collective insights, and it has been a privilege to share my own journey with you through webinars and personal mentorship. Your engagement and curiosity continue to inspire my work every day.

About the reviewer

Andrew Nixon is a certified Salesforce Application and Systems Architect with over 20 years of experience in software delivery. He has a deep appreciation of all software life cycle management aspects, having progressed through support, Business Analyst, and program management roles delivering tier 1 ERPs and CRMs for global organizations.

In 2016, he took the decision to focus solely on Salesforce and now heads a Salesforce Center of Excellence, managing several enterprise-wide Salesforce instances.

Andrew is passionate about learning, sharing knowledge, mentoring, and upskilling his teams. In his spare time, he also volunteers as a Salesforce administrator for non-profit organizations.

Table of Contents

Preface

In my 20-plus years of leading successful global implementations, I have seen far too many projects derailed by a single, avoidable flaw: the absence of disciplined business analysis. It is a hard-earned lesson that a project's success is not determined by how "high-fidelity" the solution appears, but by how deeply the team understands the true needs of its business users. Those needs are rarely presented in black and white. More often, they are nuanced, layered, and hidden beneath assumptions, legacy processes, and unspoken expectations.

This book is designed to equip you with the tools and techniques to read between the lines—to uncover the underlying business drivers that determine whether a solution merely functions or truly delivers value. Without this foundation, even the most sophisticated and expensive initiative risks becoming just another underutilized system gathering dust.

The Salesforce Business Analyst Playbook provides a practical roadmap for navigating every phase of the project lifecycle with clarity and confidence. You will learn how to define meaningful, value-driven requirements; translate business intent into viable technical solutions; and validate outcomes with rigor and purpose.

Beyond frameworks and documentation, this book focuses on your evolution into a trusted advisor—someone who does not simply gather requirements or deliver features, but who guides stakeholders through change and drives sustainable adoption.

Success in this field does not require magic. It requires disciplined mastery of proven processes, structured thinking, and thoughtful execution. By applying the principles outlined in these chapters, you will ensure that your work delivers measurable business impact—not just another set of documents.

Who this book is for

This book is intended for intermediate- to senior-level professionals with a foundational understanding of Salesforce CRM or similar CRM platforms who want to strengthen their business analysis expertise. If you have participated in CRM projects involving configuration, customization, or integrations, this guide will help you bring greater structure and discipline to your approach. Whether you are a Salesforce Administrator looking to formalize your BA skills or a Functional Consultant seeking to apply deeper analytical rigor in your implementations, this playbook will equip you to deliver measurable and sustainable business impact.

What this book covers

Chapter 1, Identifying Requirements, defines the modern role of the Salesforce Business Analyst and emphasizes the importance of business analysis in uncovering meaningful requirement sources. You will learn how to secure project sponsor support while proactively identifying where true business needs originate by recognizing organizational signals and practical "clues."

Chapter 2, Elicitation and Document Requirements, focuses on the essential skills and techniques for gathering accurate, actionable business requirements. You will learn how to plan elicitation activities effectively, apply proven techniques, and document findings clearly to ensure alignment with business needs.

Chapter 3, Prioritizing Requirements, breaks down the critical process of categorizing business needs to ensure the most impactful work is delivered first. You will learn techniques to map dependencies between requirements, sequence development logically, and manage prioritization meetings to build stakeholder consensus.

Chapter 4, Process Flows—As-is Versus To-be, guides you through reviewing existing process flows and capturing the "as-is" state using proven techniques. You will learn how to identify gaps and uncover opportunities for improvement or automation, then develop a clear "to-be" future state.

Chapter 5, Business Requirements Document, User Stories, and Acceptance Criteria, moves from discovery to formalization, emphasizing the precision needed to communicate effectively with a diverse project team. You will learn how to capture user requirements, functional and non-functional needs, and use cases at the right level of detail—ensuring clarity for developers, stakeholders, and executives alike.

Chapter 6, Solution Design and Functional Documents, bridges the gap between the "what" and the "how" in Salesforce projects. You will learn how to leverage process flows to identify both functional and non-functional requirements, ensuring solutions are flexible, maintainable, and scalable. The chapter also covers data conversion and transitional requirements—such as migration and user training—and guides you in developing a functional requirements document that translates business needs into actionable technical specifications while aligning stakeholders and the development team.

Chapter 7, Navigating Declarative versus Programmatic Salesforce Solutions, explores the spectrum of Salesforce development approaches, from no-code declarative tools to fully programmatic solutions. You will learn when to choose declarative, programmatic, or hybrid approaches based on business requirements, complexity, and scalability. The chapter demonstrates how combining declarative and programmatic techniques can deliver efficient, maintainable, and impactful solutions.

Chapter 8, Demonstrating Functionality Using Prototypes, highlights the power of visualization in bridging the gap between written requirements and the final solution. You will learn how to transform functional specifications into interactive prototypes and wireframes, creating a "sandbox" where stakeholders can provide meaningful feedback. This phase helps uncover hidden challenges and test alternatives before development begins.

Chapter 9, Exploring Conference Room Pilots, explains the purpose and value of CRPs in validating Salesforce solutions before full-scale deployment. You will learn when to schedule CRPs, identify the right participants, and facilitate sessions effectively.

Chapter 10, Technical and Quality Testing, explains the Business Analyst's pivotal role in bridging the gap between a "finished" build and a truly functional solution. You will explore testing tiers—from unit and system integration testing to **User Acceptance Testing** (**UAT**)—and learn how to assemble and guide an effective testing team. The chapter emphasizes scenario-based testing, strategic use of test data, and best practices to ensure comprehensive coverage.

Chapter 11, Requirements Traceability Matrix, highlights the importance of linking business requirements to design, development, and testing activities. You will learn what information to capture in an RTM, explore different types of traceability, and review a sample template.

Chapter 12, User Acceptance Testing, focuses on identifying the right participants and guiding them to test Salesforce solutions effectively. You will learn how to gather actionable feedback on usability, understand the purpose and benefits of UAT, and leverage Agile techniques to make testing iterative and collaborative.

Chapter 13, Communication and Knowledge Management, focuses on the human element that ultimately determines a project's success. You will learn about strategic communication frameworks, diverse knowledge management methods, and how to make knowledge artifacts and in-app guidance accessible exactly when users need them. The chapter highlights how effective communication and structured knowledge management improve adoption, reduce support requests, and build confidence.

Chapter 14, End-User Training, serves as the final, critical hand-off between the project team and the business. You will learn how to plan, prepare, and deliver high-impact training programs, including bite-sized video tutorials and structured materials that respect users' time while maximizing competence. The chapter emphasizes the value of in-person or live virtual sessions, highlighting what to include—and what to omit—to keep participants focused and confident.

Chapter 15, Post-Production Support and Super Care, focuses on the critical "Day 2" operations that sustain long-term Salesforce success. You will learn how super care and production support build trust, using a one-to-two-week cadence to deliver enhancements and fixes that show users their feedback is valued.

Chapter 16, The Salesforce Productivity Tool Kit, explores modern tools and strategies to enhance efficiency, streamline maintenance, and improve Salesforce adoption. You will learn how to leverage automation, guided workflows, and processes such as Guided Selling and Guided Service to optimize business operations.

Chapter 17, Salesforce Business Analyst Certification, provides guidance for professionals pursuing formal recognition of their Salesforce business analysis expertise. This chapter is intended for BAs working on Salesforce implementations or enhancements, functional consultants focused on requirements and stakeholder engagement, product owners or solution leads involved in delivery, and professionals transitioning into Salesforce-focused BA roles. You will learn how the certification validates your skills, prepares you for real-world project challenges, and enhances your professional credibility in the Salesforce ecosystem.

Chapter 18, Career Opportunities and Related BA Roles, explores the Salesforce Business Analyst role in practice and the various paths to enter this career. You will learn about common entry points, opportunities for career progression, and related roles within the Salesforce ecosystem. The chapter also highlights the key skills and competencies that enable long-term success, helping aspiring and experienced BAs plan a strategic, growth-oriented career.

Conventions used

There are a number of text conventions used throughout this book.

Bold: Indicates a new term, an important word, or words that you see on the screen. For instance, words in menus or dialog boxes appear in the text like this. For example: "The **component-level design process** is also known as **low-level solution design**."

> Note
>
> Warnings or important notes appear like this.

> Tip
>
> Tips and tricks appear like this.

Download images and screenshots

We also provide a PDF file that has all the images of the screenshots/diagrams used in this book. You can download it here: `https://packt.link/gbp/9781806109272`

Get in touch

Feedback from our readers is always welcome.

General feedback: If you have questions about any aspect of this book or have any general feedback, please email us at `customercare@packt.com` and mention the book's title in the subject of your message.

Errata: Although we have taken every care to ensure the accuracy of our content, mistakes do happen. If you have found a mistake in this book, we would be grateful if you reported this to us. Please visit `http://www.packt.com/submit-errata`, click **Submit Errata**, and fill in the form.

Piracy: If you come across any illegal copies of our works in any form on the internet, we would be grateful if you would provide us with the location address or website name. Please contact us at `copyright@packt.com` with a link to the material.

If you are interested in becoming an author: If there is a topic that you have expertise in and you are interested in either writing or contributing to a book, please visit `http://authors.packt.com/`.

Share Your Thoughts

Once you've read *The Salesforce Business Analysis Playbook*, we'd love to hear your thoughts! Scan the QR code below to go straight to the Amazon review page for this book and share your feedback.

`https://packt.link/r/1806109271`

Your review is important to us and the tech community and will help us make sure we're delivering excellent quality content

Free benefits with your book

This book comes with free benefits to support your learning. Activate them now for instant access (see the "*How to Unlock*" section for instructions).

Here's a quick overview of what you can instantly unlock with your purchase:

Online Exam-Prep Tools

Ace your certification exam with exam-ready online resources

DRM-Free PDF Version

Download DRM-free PDF and ePub copies of this book.

7-Day Packt Library Access

Get 7-day unlimited access to 8,000+ books and videos. No credit card required.

Available for first-time Packt+ trial users only.

Next-Gen Reader Access

Read this book on Packt Reader with progress sync, dark mode and note-taking.

How to Unlock

Scan the QR code (or go to `packtpub.com/unlock`). Search for this book by name, confirm the edition, and then follow the steps on the page.

UNLOCK NOW

Note: Keep your invoice handy. Purchases made directly from Packt don't require one

Part 1

Planning and Analysis – Building the Right Foundation

We begin where every successful project begins: with clarity. In this part, you will master the art and discipline of uncovering true business needs through structured stakeholder engagement. You will learn how to prioritize requirements based on measurable value, establish a well-governed product backlog, and craft a phased roadmap that aligns technology delivery with strategic objectives. We also address common pitfalls that derail projects early, and explore how AI can enhance analytical rigor without replacing foundational business judgment.

This part has the following chapters:

- *Chapter 1, Identifying Requirements*
- *Chapter 2, Elicitation and Document Requirements*
- *Chapter 3, Prioritizing Requirements*
- *Chapter 4, Process Flows – As-Is versus To-Be*
- *Chapter 5, Business Requirements Document, User Stories, and Acceptance Criteria*

1

Identifying Requirements

A successful Salesforce implementation is built not on technology, but on a deep understanding of business needs. Skipping this crucial first step risks building a technically perfect solution for the wrong problem—one that fails to deliver real value or drive meaningful outcomes.

This begins with requirements identification: the disciplined process of moving beyond surface-level requests to uncover the core business drivers. It demands strategic stakeholder engagement, a systematic analysis of current processes, and proven techniques to reveal both stated needs and hidden opportunities for improvement.

In this chapter, we will discuss the role of a Business Analyst and different types of software requirements. Then, we will review some important factors that will help gain project sponsors' confidence and trust. Finally, we will explore common sources to look out for that help us spot and identify business requirements. We will also touch upon, at a high level, some business analysis lingo that you should be aware of to be able to facilitate business analysis activities. Remember, we wish to identify requirements at a very high level. We will do a deep dive into understanding requirements in more detail and from different perspectives during the elicitation phase, which will be covered in the next chapter.

In this chapter, we will cover the following topics:

- The role of business analysis in identifying requirement sources
- Securing support from the project sponsor
- Common sources where you can identify business requirements
- Real-life scenarios with examples
- Practical tips for success

By the end of this chapter, you will have a good idea of where and how to find requirements that will help you with requirements gathering. You'll also know what you should do to understand current processes and observe the inefficiencies, roadblocks, and opportunities surrounding them. As AI continues to evolve, its capacity to assist in business analysis will undoubtedly expand, and we will explore some of its beneficial applications within this chapter.

> Note
>
> **Your purchase includes a free PDF copy + exclusive extras**
>
> Your purchase includes a DRM-free PDF copy of this book, 7-day trial to the Packt+ library (no credit card required), and additional exclusive extras. See the *Free benefits with your book* section in the *Preface* to unlock them instantly and maximize your learning.

Identifying requirement sources

Before we get into the details of the **business analysis role**, let's quickly review what some common terms mean, which will be helpful in our upcoming discussions:

- **Business analysis**: Business analysis is a practice that involves understanding the current capabilities and needs of the business users, identifying gaps in the current processes, and enabling desired future capabilities to derive efficiencies, competitive advantage, and business benefits.
- **Business Analyst**: A Business Analyst is someone who practices business analysis while utilizing various tools, techniques, and resources. The goal is to help businesses move from their current state to a desired future state by understanding business needs, pain points, opportunities, and gaps in processes, and providing robust, efficient, and effective solutions that are simple and usable.
- **Customer relationship management** (**CRM**): CRM is the practice of helping customers manage sales, service, and marketing processes effectively and efficiently so that they can grow their business and provide excellent customer service.
- **Salesforce**: Salesforce is a cloud-based CRM technology platform that helps organizations serve their customers with CRM functionality.

With this basic understanding, let's discuss business analysis in detail.

Business analysis work starts with planning; there is no one cookie-cutter approach that works for every project. Business Analysts need to know and understand the context and characteristics of the project to ensure that the planning activities are scoped accordingly. Prior planning and spending time on identifying the user requirement sources will lead to a better understanding of the scope of business analysis work, stakeholders' expectations, and the amount of analysis work that needs to be done in subsequent phases of the project. We need to create a well-thought-out business analysis roadmap so that the analysis process is effective and successful.

As a Business Analyst, the first and foremost task to focus on is identifying business needs. Business needs are the gaps between the current state of a business and its expected goals. Business needs analysis is also referred to as gap analysis – the current "as-is" state versus the desired "to-be" state. Needs are the basic drivers of change. By understanding needs, the Business Analyst can document requirements. This activity happens during the project planning or pre-project phase. As an analyst, you will use this data as a starting point for requirement gathering and elicitation or to create a business plan and provide findings for management decision-making.

Before you get into the requirements, you need to plan and identify where you can get the business needs and requirements. What are the good quality sources, and where can you find them? These can be from stakeholders, documents, existing processes, observations, interviews, and so on.

I have worked on multiple global projects where the projects started at different stages. Most of the time, the majority of the functions that are needed are on existing systems – enhancing or adding more capabilities. I got the opportunity to work on a few projects where, as a Business Analyst, it was I who would guide the business, identify requirements, tools, and systems, and provide a system that the business can benefit from and value. This is very stressful as well as rewarding when you have to guide stakeholders and help them understand their requirements and needs. I will touch upon various examples along the way that may benefit you.

There are three possible business requirement scenarios that I would like to cover:

- The system is already in use, and business users would like to request enhancements. Here, you must add additional features to existing functionality. This can be your minor enhancement release or a production support item, such as a defect or maintenance item.
- The system is already in use, and business users would like new functionality. This can be a brand-new functionality and addressed via a project.
- You must add new capabilities to address usability and adoption issues. This can be a complex requirement where multiple stakeholders are involved.

Based on these scenarios, let's explore our analysis process. Examples for each of these scenarios have been provided with screenshots in the *Real-life scenarios with examples* section.

Project teams and IT teams most often blame the business users, stating that they do not know what they want. That is the very reason why we have project managers, Business Analysts, IT teams, QA teams, training teams, and so on. Business users do not need to know what they want. It is up to the project team, especially the Business Analyst, to identify the right stakeholders, pull ideas out of users, and get agreement from everyone.

Stakeholders, even though they know the problems in most cases, do not know how to articulate their needs. On the other hand, few users can articulate, anticipate, and lay out their needs, wants, and desires, and pretty much want everything their way. You need to be cognizant of both and watchful for the latter.

In reality, only a few requirements are documented in some form. Most of them reside in the heads of stakeholders, end users, and process flows that are yet to be understood and developed.

For a project to be successful, understanding and documenting requirements accurately is one of the key success factors. Failure to understand and capture requirements accurately will lead to project delays, false expectations, broken promises, blame games, and stressful situations. So, let's focus on learning, understanding, discovering, and getting the right requirements by focusing on extracting the ideas, issues, wants, and needs of the users.

> **Note**
>
> I will be covering real-life practical scenarios – successes as well as failures and lessons learned. We will use many existing Business Analyst tools and techniques. As needed, I will explain them at a very high level. I will not be providing definitions or procedures; instead, I will explain the scenarios with practical examples based on my experience.

Let's delve into what it takes to identify business needs and wants. Our ultimate end goal here is to identify a set of requirements that are consistent, non-redundant, and complete. In this chapter, we shall concentrate only on the extent of learning problems and/or opportunities to sufficiently understand the situation and not perform a complete requirement analysis, which shall be explained in future chapters. Ensure that you're not subjective and judgmental; you are here to understand business needs, not design solutions. As Business Analysts, we must make every effort to understand business needs and wants, how they align with the vision/ strategy, and how this enables us to achieve our strategic end goal.

As Business Analysts, we need to get as much information as possible by exploring all possible avenues and areas. You need to know what information you must get and where to find that information. For that, we need to ask six questions (five *Ws* and one *H* – *Who, What, When, Where, Why*, and *How*) iteratively to completely understand the full scope and intent of the business needs. When asking these questions, you should know the rationale for every question and be able to explain to stakeholders why that question is relevant.

By understanding different types of requirements, you will be able to manage the requirements process effectively at all project stages. Remind yourself that we are here to gather information to identify the real problem or opportunity and not to provide our opinions or solutions.

Types of requirements

There are four main types of requirements, as listed here:

- **Business requirements**: An example of this is if you are implementing a new system or functionality. These requirements are the most complex to understand, as there are too many unknowns. These requirements describe the high-level functionality that the business needs.
- **Stakeholder requirements**: Also called user requirements, these are features and functions that the users need and specify how they interact with the system. Getting to know the stakeholders' needs and wants is critical because, often, they may not be able to articulate them clearly. This is very critical as stakeholder requirements are later translated into system requirements. Any flaws here get amplified at later stages and result in rework.
- **System requirements**: These requirements describe the characteristics of the solution. There are two types of system requirements:
    - **Functional**: Describes a specific set of capabilities
    - **Non-functional**: Describes the characteristics
- **Transition requirements**: These are transient requirements and are needed for a short period. Make sure that you discuss and get details around transition requirements. They are essential and critical to project success.

The most notable requirement is **data migration**. In the **extract, transform, and load** (**ETL**) process, data may be rendered useless if data migration is not done diligently. I have seen many instances in projects, including the one I worked on a few years ago, where, after converting HR data, the team was unable to run the payroll on time. You know what's going to happen if employees are not paid on time.

Knowing and understanding different requirement types and establishing goals and timelines for identifying requirements will help pave the foundation for the next step of our business analysis. Here, we are trying to understand the current state and the desired future state. Analyzing business needs and wants will help us provide the right solution or address the right problem during our design phase.

In the past 18 years, I have worked on multiple Salesforce implementations: Sales Cloud, Service Cloud, and Partner Relationship Management. I employed more than one method to get to know and understand business needs. It all depends on your implementation methodology, people, culture, IT team maturity, and so on, and you need to tailor and use a combination of the methods discussed in the *Common sources where you can identify business requirements* section, later in this chapter.

Securing support from the project sponsor

Securing support from a project sponsor is another important factor for any project to succeed. The business analysis process and the Business Analyst play a vital role in securing confidence and trust with the project sponsors. Business analysis involves defining the requirements, designing the solution, communicating, validating the solution, and training activities so that they are well-positioned to assess and identify project impacts. They can act as the eyes and ears of the project sponsor. The project sponsor often depends on project managers and Business Analysts for all key decision-making. Just like gaining confidence and trust from **subject matter experts** (**SMEs**), project team members, and super users, we have to gain the project sponsor's confidence and trust, too. One of the most important activities is to keep the sponsor in the loop at all times.

As a Business Analyst, you can gain project sponsors' trust and confidence by assisting them with information and the decision-making process. This is possible through good planning and communication. Let's outline what you should be doing to help the sponsor:

- Present information accurately and concisely at the appropriate level.
- Issues are bound to arise, so be prepared with the information and facts to facilitate smooth decision-making.
- At each stage of the project, provide a summary of the business analysis work while highlighting achievements and any risks.
- As a key resource, be prepared and provide recommendations with pros and cons.
- Be truthful, transparent, and courageous to deliver unpleasant information. Be able to say "No."

Gaining confidence and trust will empower Business Analysts to navigate their work smoothly, efficiently, and productively. This will help the project team and you, as a Business Analyst, in areas such as the following:

- Resource availability for SMEs and other project resources
- Timely decision-making

- Providing direction – defining the scope, prioritizing requirements, and so on
- Influencing escalations, resolving conflicts, and motivating

Now that we have learned how effective business analysis begins with meticulous planning and a deep understanding of business needs—not solutions—we can see how this foundational work sets the stage for all subsequent phases. With this strategic context in place, let's now explore the common sources of requirements.

Common sources where you can identify business requirements

Now that we understand how to identify requirements and why it is important for a business, let's review the various sources where we can gather these requirements.

- **Document analysis:** Document analysis involves getting your hands on any relevant documentation: scope documents, project initiation requests, business plans, knowledge transfer artifacts, manuals, presentations, minutes of past meetings, user guides, and so on.
  AI-driven tools such as Otter.ai, Grammarly, Grok, and so on can greatly improve document analysis by rapidly processing large document sets, pinpointing key terms, extracting pertinent data, and highlighting inconsistencies or gaps for further review.
- **Identifying key stakeholders:** Who will be impacted by the change directly or indirectly? You can start with a business sponsor and a program manager. Find out the scope and range of the project implementation in terms of various **business units** (**BUs**).
- **Navigating the organization:** Get to know SMEs, data captains, planning team members who focus on analytics and management dashboards, and a few enthusiastic end users.
- **Current system usage:** Find out how current systems are used to perform their job and how they are integrated into other systems in the company.
  This is a great opportunity for you to observe and find opportunities to enhance and simplify the processes and save time and frustration.

  An example would be users struggling to access the system due to login issues (incorrect password or system lockout due to too many incorrect password attempts). This can be easily addressed by enabling **single sign-on** (**SSO**), which is available out of the box for almost all cloud applications. With SSO, users need to click on one bookmarked URL to access an application.Consider how you might boost productivity with the help of an assistant. By examining user behavior and data, AI can identify areas of inefficiency or common challenges and recommend solutions or automation opportunities based on how the system is used.

- **Identifying the key end user:** Users who are passionate about the change and who are direct beneficiaries understand existing work practices and existing unaddressed problems. I listed them separately as they are not identified as part of the project stakeholders. They can be your level 1 support or call center representative.
  Plan brainstorming sessions by facilitating the conversation and allowing key participants to openly debate and speak out. Take notes and make sure you let the conversation flow freely; your job is to facilitate the conversation and ask questions as appropriate.

  Use AI-powered transcription services during sessions to capture all details, enabling the Business Analyst to concentrate on facilitation. After sessions, AI can organize discussions, detect recurring themes, and summarize key decisions and action items.

- **Needs decomposition:** Try to get as much information from whatever source possible via decomposition, breaking down needs into smaller needs until they can no longer be decomposed. This way, we are breaking down a complex requirement into multiple small and simplified individual components of need.
- **Getting a system walkthrough:** Understand firsthand how end users normally use the system regularly. Be an observer and let the user navigate and walk through their process in the system from end to end. This user journey helps you understand and identify missed elements and any usability requirements.
- **Active participation:** Listen attentively and actively, acknowledge, ask questions, and rephrase what you heard and understood. This is to ensure that an accurate understanding of what has been communicated is agreed upon by both ends. Also, avoid judging what you hear so that information flows freely. Focus on business needs and do not get into designing the solution.
  Most often, the stakeholder assumes that the Business Analyst already knows or is aware of the business needs and provides high-level information only. Business Analysts need to make sure that information is provided in enough detail.

  Let the participants debate and vent their frustration. You get facts and truth from this kind of conversation and are able to grasp stakeholders' perspectives on business needs.

  Different stakeholders may have different perspectives; it is your job to explore them and resolve any conflicts.

Make sure you keep the discussion aligned to the agenda and manage it so that it doesn't get out of control.

- **Existing systems:** Find ways to get access to current systems and be able to run some key reports and dashboards. This will help you identify and get reports and stats on end users who use the system.
  During one of my first implementations, I was able to run a few reports and find out who the power users were. I ran stats and saw why usage dropped from quarter to quarter (or over a period). By doing this, along with the data and facts I had gathered, I was well prepared to ask the users the right questions.
- **Risk, actions, issues, and decisions (RAID) log**: Another great source of information from previous projects is the RAID log. This project management tool offers a wealth of context for a current implementation. Reviewing it can provide key insights into the previous project's objectives, mitigating actions, and the critical decisions made throughout its life cycle. Understanding these past pain points and resolutions helps us anticipate gaps and validate assumptions, leading to more complete and accurate requirements.
- **Note-taking:** Take notes, prepare minutes, and share them with the participants on the same day, and solicit feedback. Clarify any open queries individually with specific participants.
  When taking notes, make sure that you tag the requirement type as business, stakeholder, solution, or transition. By understanding the requirement type, you can fine-tune and facilitate the conversation effectively and efficiently.

  AI tools such as Microsoft Copilot or Notion AI can assist in real-time note organization, automatically tagging requirement types based on keywords or context, and even highlighting potential ambiguities for immediate clarification.
- **Assumptions:** Avoid and eliminate all assumptions around requirements. Business needs must be verified, and assumptions, if any, need to be confirmed and documented.
- **Meeting minutes:** Prepare and share a list of simple, clear, consistent, and complete high-level requirements. This will help you provide the steps that must be taken.
  Now that we have learned where and how we can identify and gather business requirements, let's learn how to implement them with some real-world examples. These will be covered in the next section.

Real-life scenarios with examples

Business needs vary from very simple to extremely complex. While there are many different types of business requirements and needs, for this discussion, we will focus on three distinct and practical scenarios. Using these examples, I will explain the various needs and discuss how they are addressed and implemented. A strong understanding of business needs will help us in the elicitation phase.

Scenario 1

This is a simple scenario where users know what they need. It could be an existing pain point where we are looking for improvements. This case is true when users are already using the system, and they can easily point out the gaps, be it defects or enhancements to the application.

For example, in Salesforce, duplicate leads, accounts, and contact records cause multiple issues down the line. These types of requirements are very straightforward. As a Salesforce-savvy Business Analyst, I can provide a quick solution. Here, I could suggest that users use the available duplicate management functionality.

By understanding the business needs, we can fulfill this requirement quickly by using existing out-of-the-box features from Salesforce. We will be able to find a quick solution for the majority of simple requirements. The key is to understand the business needs.

This is an example where elicitation is straightforward, as business needs can be articulated easily and clearly.

> Note
>
> You may have to do a one-time cleanup of existing data to implement this solution.

Duplicate management functionality on the contact record

Here, we shall implement a rule where the Salesforce system will prevent users from creating duplicate contacts if the last name and email combination match.

A duplicate rule with matching criteria can be quickly implemented. Whenever any user tries to create a duplicate contact, the system should prevent the user from creating one. The following screenshot shows a duplication rule being created:

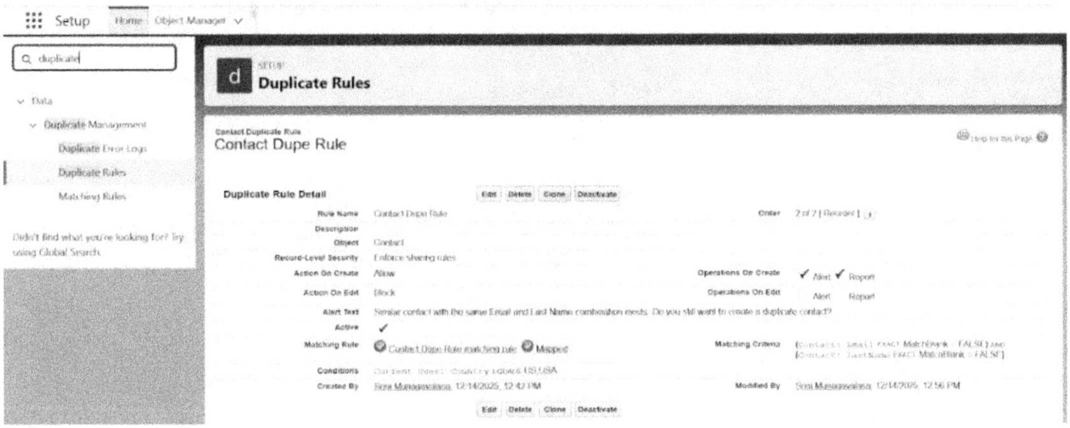

Figure 1.1 – Creating a duplicate rule

In the following screenshot, I tried to create another contact with the same last name and email address. By implementing a simple duplicate rule, the system should prevent duplicate contact records:

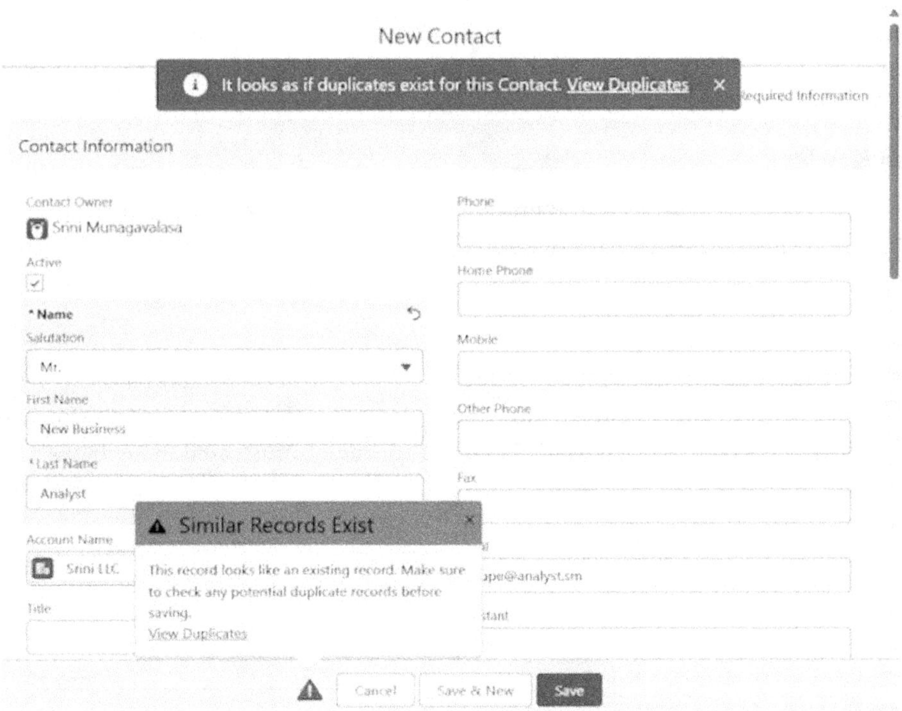

Figure 1.2 – Salesforce system preventing users from creating a duplicate contact

You can view the duplicate as shown. Here, users will be able to make any updates as needed to the existing contact record:

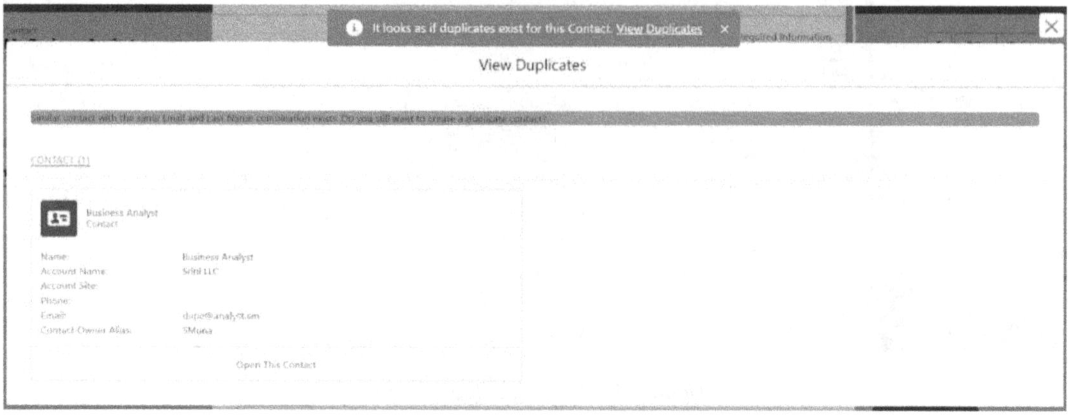

Figure 1.3 – Option to view the existing duplicate contact record

You can also propose a more robust solution using AppExchange packages such as **Demand Tool**, which is an excellent tool for keeping your data clean and relevant. This is a managed package, and there is a subscription fee per user. There are many paid and free tools on AppExchange. Do your research and try them in a sandbox before deciding to use them in your production environment.

Scenario 2

In this scenario, the business need is to improve data quality by ensuring that related records are consistently updated. Specifically, we aim to automate data changes on the `Account` record onto all related `Contact` records. By automating this synchronization, the data remains accurate, current, and relevant across the system.

For example, when the account billing address is updated, the new address must automatically populate the mailing addresses of all related contacts. In a platform such as Salesforce, this type of automation is typically achieved via **Flow Builder**, as illustrated in *Figure 1.4*.

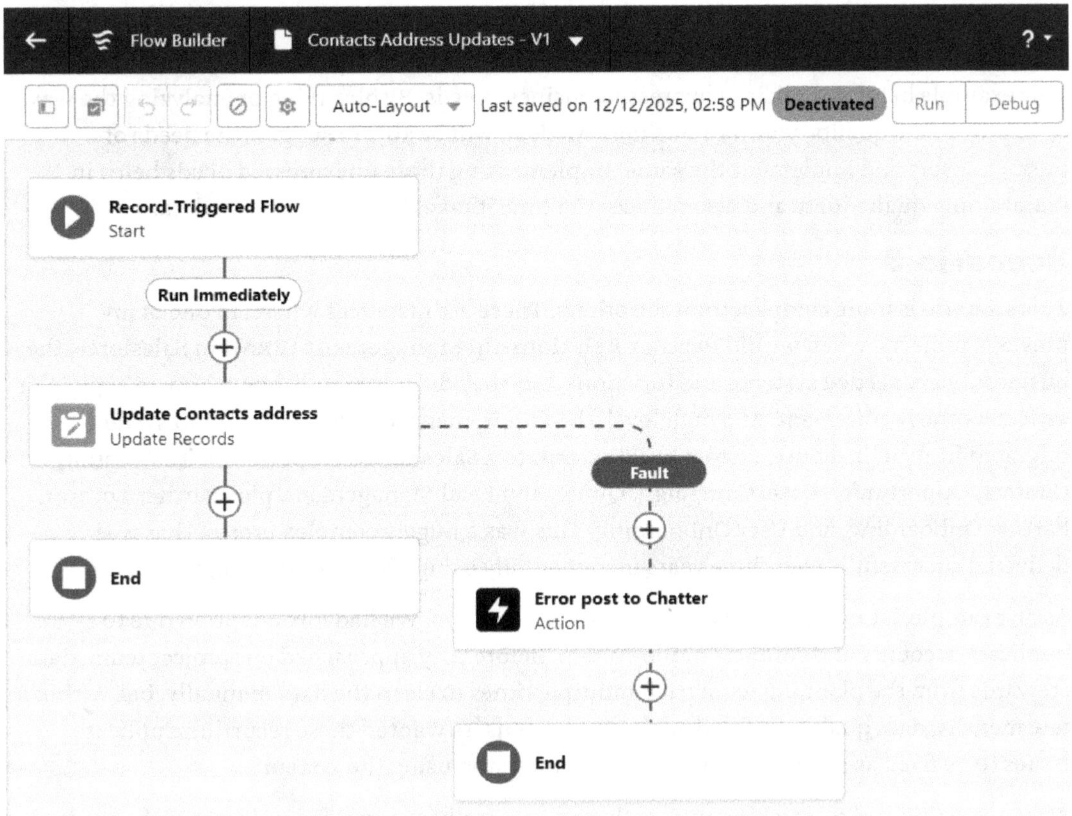

Figure 1.4 – Using Flow Builder to automate address updates on the contact record

Let's look at another example. In Salesforce, the sales team would like to see certain fields from the `User` record and `Account` record defaulted on the **Opportunity record** page. This requirement requires some level of analysis.

To simplify this, let's look at a simplified requirement. A specific BU user would like to default certain field attributes from the `User` record (such as `Region`, `Country`, `Division`, and `Department`) and `Account` record (such as `Account Owner`, `Industry`, `Account Type`, and `Rating`). The rationale for this requirement is to have information available on the same `Opportunity` record and also be able to create list views from the **Opportunities** tab. To simplify further, let's assume that you, as a Business Analyst, socialized this with other BU stakeholders and got confirmation that they would like to have the same functionality extended to all.

You can have multiple solutions in Salesforce. Here, you can go with flows, but the simplest and easiest solution is to create a formula field. In our case, this is the preferred solution as users need data with view access; any updates that are made to user or account attributes are immediately reflected on the **Opportunity record** page.

This example helps you elicit unexpressed business needs. By observing or analyzing the ways to improve data quality, you, as a Business Analyst, will be able to suggest the needs of business users and implement the same. Implementing these unexpressed needs helps in maintaining quality data and also reduces the time it takes the user to create data.

Scenario 3

This scenario is more complex than the others. These are instances where, in one of my previous projects, when we did **Partner Relationship Management** (**PRM**) in Salesforce, the business users needed systems and functions, but they did not exactly know how to explain or articulate the requirement. At a high level, the requirement was to have the PRM system migrated from an in-house custom build system to a Sales Cloud for partner with Account, Contact, Opportunity, Case, Campaign, Quote, and Lead Management, plus Partner Locator, Partner Onboarding, and User Onboarding. This was a hugely complex project that was delivered successfully over three years incrementally using Agile methodology.

As an example, let me explain a relatively simple scenario. We had low adoption due to duplicate accounts and contacts in the system. Before they approached our project team, data stewards from the planning team tried multiple times to clean the data manually, but within a few months, data quality suffered again. Business users wanted these recurring duplicate issues to be fixed as soon as possible, as users may stop using the system.

After analyzing and researching internally and externally, we could identify the right product for our business. This not only enabled us to capture good-quality data but also enriched the data records by synchronizing the right data at a specific set frequency. This saved a lot of time, and our business could have accurate, complete, and meaningful data. We used a popular tool that is completely integrated with Salesforce. As Business Analysts, we need to be open-minded, understand business needs, and find the right solutions. In this case, rather than developing the Salesforce platform in-house, we found external tools to get the job done with minimal resources. The tool we used was an AppExchange product called **D&B Hoover**. This is a paid subscription managed package that is seamlessly integrated with Salesforce. Once synced up, the tool can update more than 100 account and contact attributes and add a D&B identifier:

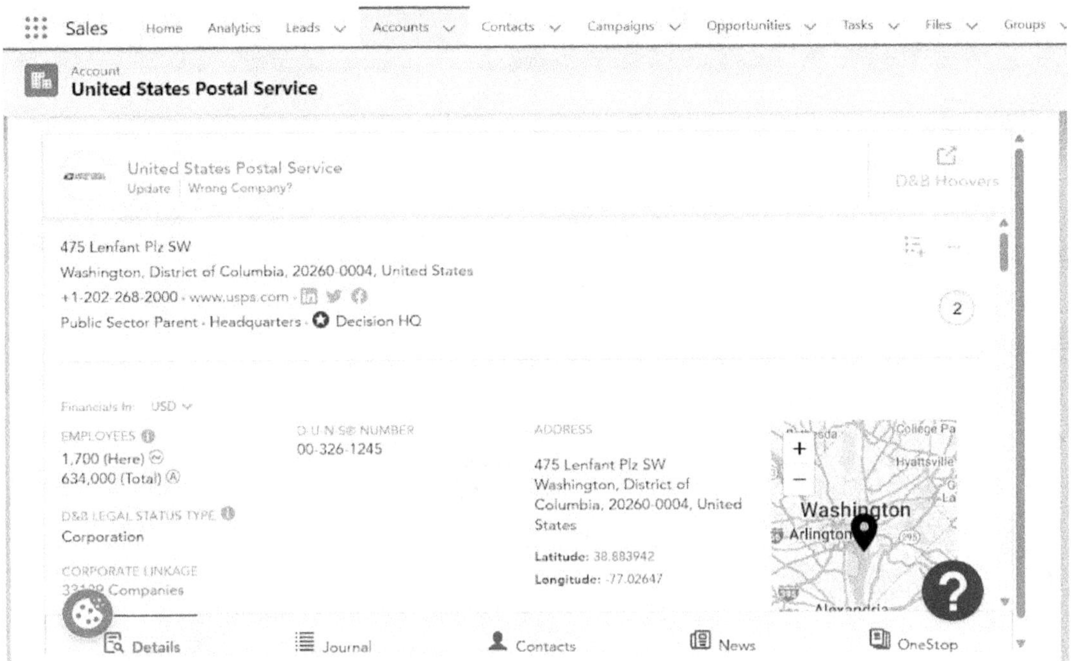

Figure 1.5 – D&B tool integrated with Salesforce on the Account Management page's layout

Since this tool is embedded seamlessly into Salesforce **Accounts** and **Contacts** pages, users can access this tool without the need for a separate login. In addition to customer and contact data, sales teams will be able to get innovative analytical features:

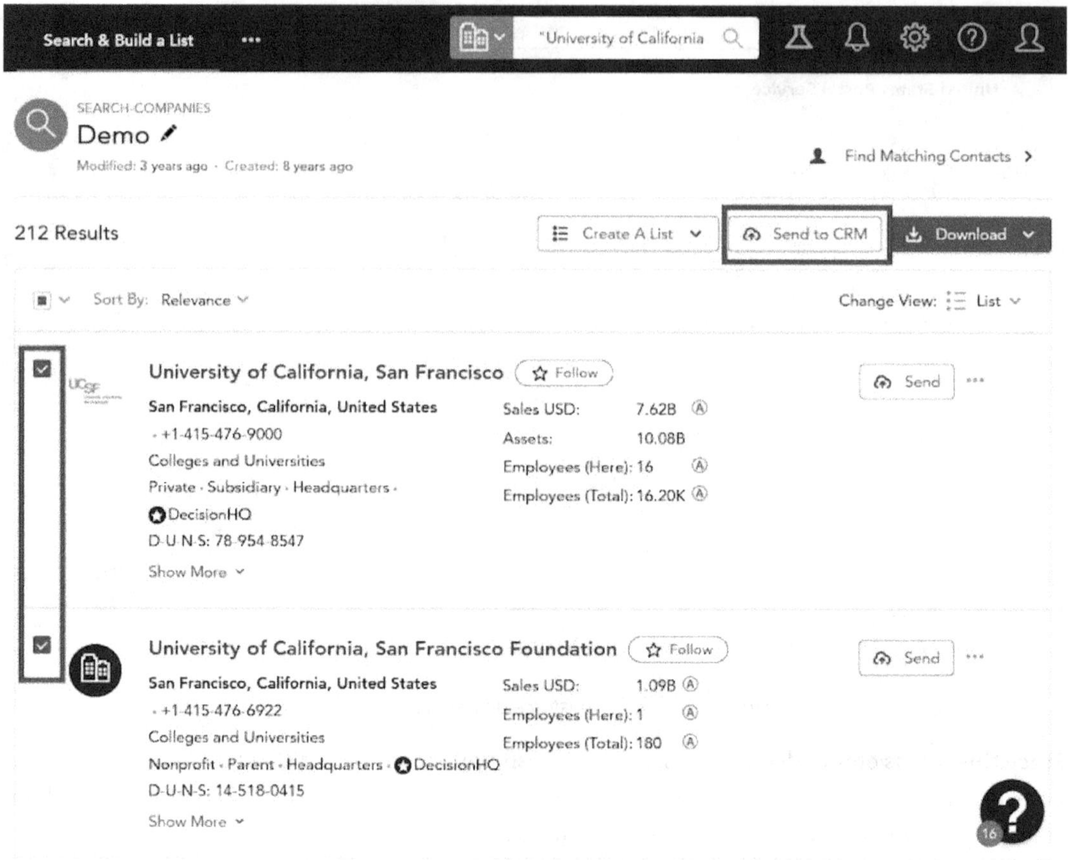

Figure 1.6 – Example where users can search for companies and sync them to Salesforce with one click

This example helps us see that business needs are not always obvious. In this case, the business user did not even state their needs. By analyzing the root cause of low adoption, we interacted with many key stakeholders and SMEs to understand the needs. Then, we explored internal and external tools and found the one that best fits our needs. Sometimes, the end goal will help us with eliciting and drawing forth a business need that can have a positive impact on our business users.

Now, let's look at some practical tips that I found useful.

Practical tips for success

I would like to outline a few pointers that you can use when you do business analysis tasks. These are relatively simple tasks that helped me tremendously. The simplest and easiest-to-do items are always overlooked. You can avoid common causes of missing out on understanding business needs by taking note of the following pointers:

- Understand the goals and objectives of the business analysis work that you plan to perform. You should be in a position to explain in simple terms why you are performing these activities.
- For any business analysis effort to be successful and to be able to identify needs, analysts need to gain trust from stakeholders. This is a long process, and trust needs to be earned. I would encourage you to start it early.
- Get to know the stakeholders. You can get information from organizational charts or social profiles.
- Schedule meetings in advance. Make sure that you find the right time and location/medium and block time in advance.
- Provide an agenda. Prepare and communicate it a day or so before the meeting.
- Facilitate the meeting and make sure that you encourage everyone to contribute. Your job is to facilitate discussion and mediate any conflicts.
- Capture notes (assign one of your team members who is good at note-taking) and send out the minutes. Consider using AI-driven meeting assistants that automatically transcribe and summarize meetings, helping you focus on the conversation while ensuring accurate documentation.
- Follow up as needed until you and the stakeholders understand and agree on high-level requirements.
- Do not get into designing solutions. Understand the business requirements. If you're savvy with Salesforce and CRM technologies, if you know a requirement is not feasible because of design constraints, say so and place it in the parking lot. Being open and honest will help build trust in the long run.
- Approach with a design-thinking mindset. Look for people and their needs before feasibility and viability. This automatically maximizes usability and user experience. Your goal should be to gain a good understanding of the complete situation and not provide options or solutions.
- Ask end users and stakeholders how their needs benefit them and their business unit. If this need is not fulfilled, do they have a workaround?

With this, we have completed this chapter on how to identify sources of requirements.

Summary

In this chapter, you learned where to find the sources of business user needs. By doing so, you learned how to get the requirements at a very high level and the key sources where you can plan to elaborate by eliciting more granular details. You also understood the key terms and ways to prepare yourself for the next stage of the requirement elicitation activity by utilizing the skills you learned in this chapter. Consider using AI as your assistant to greatly improve your productivity during the identification of requirements.

In the next chapter, we will discuss various ways to draw out the users' business needs and wants from various sources that we've identified so far. We will cover different techniques and extract information to accurately understand users' requirements.

Questions

1. Explain the difference between functional and non-functional requirements in one sentence.
2. Name a few non-functional requirements.

Further reading

- *Business Analysis Body of Knowledge (BABOK®) Guide*, by IIBA, Lightning Source Inc.
- *The PMI Guide to Business Analysis*, by Au Project Management Institute
- *Trailhead*, by Salesforce: `https://trailhead.salesforce.com/`

Get this book's PDF version and more

Scan the QR code (or go to `packtpub.com/unlock`). Search for this book by name, confirm the edition, and then follow the steps on the page.

UNLOCK NOW

Note: Keep your invoice handy. Purchases made directly from Packt don't require an invoice.

2

Elicitation and Document Requirements

In the previous chapter, you did all the planning in identifying the sources from which you can elicit the business needs. In this chapter, we will discuss various methods to draw out those needs and requirements from various sources. We will dive deep into various sources, and you will learn a few cool tips that you can implement during your elicitation phase. Our end goal here is to extract sufficient information to understand users' requirements.

We will also look into best practices to efficiently and effectively document these requirements. As we process elicitation iteratively, we document them right from the start, and we keep refining them as we understand them more and more. Our goal here is to document all requirements—needs, wants, nice-to-haves, and assumptions—and come up with a solid list of all requirements that can be understood by stakeholders.

Requirement elicitation is an iterative loop: you plan, prepare, conduct, and document. Elicitation is the art of discovering the real problem to be solved.

We will cover the following topics in this chapter:

- Elicitation planning
- Requirement elicitation techniques
- Requirement documentation
- The art of elicitation
- Actionable tips for success
- Leveraging AI responsibly in business analysis

By the end of this chapter, you will understand elicitation planning, process, and techniques, and be able to produce high-quality documented requirements.

Elicitation planning

Before you start elicitation, you need to plan and prepare. Consider the following tasks and any other tasks, and do as much research as possible so that you can maximize the outcome:

- **What information do I need to elicit?**: Make a list and always have options and alternatives.
- **Where are the sources of information?**: You already know this from the previous chapter.
- **How do I extract information from these sources?**: What techniques do we utilize?
- **What order to elicit**: You need to follow a logical order for the free flow of discussion. Be flexible as the order can vary based on stakeholders and the situation.

Explore AI-based assistants such as ChatGPT and Copilot to summarize existing documentation or stakeholder communications, providing a head start in identifying potential areas of concern.

Note

For effective elicitation or, as a matter of fact, for any business meeting/discussions, do the following:

- Know the players—learn about the participants
- Secure commitment and set up meetings
- Prepare an agenda
- Facilitate meetings
- Capture notes
- Summarize and send out a recap

Elicitation tasks

The following are the elicitation tasks that I follow religiously. You need to plan and prepare to utilize time and resources effectively and efficiently. This means you need to spend lots of time doing your homework. In my opinion, for every 1 hour of elicitation sessions with users, be prepared to spend approximately 5 to 6 hours of pre- and post-work. Time spent on preparation pays for itself by accurately capturing true business requirements. Leverage an AI tool such as Copilot to organize stakeholder lists, identify missing roles, or create pre-meeting summaries based on data from previous sessions. Any incorrect requirements will result in solutions that do not meet business needs:

1. **Prepare**: This step involves the following activities:
    a. Set your goals for the elicitation
    b. Prepare the required material/artifacts
    c. Identify and prepare a stakeholder list
    d. Collect supporting material (where AI tools can assist in organizing vast amounts of data and identifying patterns)
    e. Set out the techniques you plan to use, and so on
2. **Conduct**: This is when you perform the elicitation activities. You have to use a combination of tools, techniques, and styles to keep stakeholders engaged and collaborative. You can employ research, collaborative, or experimental types of elicitation. Like any good meeting, you need to structure the elicitation sessions with an introduction, the main content, a closing summary, and a follow-up.
3. **Confirm/validate**: In this step, you are at the end of the elicitation session and summarizing business requirements. You verify with participants that the information you gather is understandable, complete, accurate, and consistent.
4. **Communicate**: Utilize intelligent tools such as AI to summarize meeting minutes, list out all the requirements elicited and agreed upon during the session, and capture the discussion around open items, assumptions, and gaps. This communication shall go to all stakeholders: the business as a whole, SMEs, and technical, project management, and quality assurance teams.
5. **Collaborate**: Managing stakeholder/SME collaboration is a very important activity. You can get great input from them if you can get their time and effort. Getting commitment with their busy schedules will be a challenging task. The purpose of the collaboration is to get stakeholder participation, contribution, consensus, and agreement. There will be

disagreement and heated discussions, which when handled adroitly, yield productive, innovative out-of-the-box thinking.

Elicitation is an iterative process that progressively refines business requirements. With each iteration, you extract more granular details, identify gaps, and discover new requirements, ensuring a comprehensive understanding early on.

Requirement elicitation techniques

There are multiple techniques that you can use for your elicitation activity. There can be multiple factors why you may have to choose one technique over another. As a Business Analyst, you pick the one that meets your objectives within the given resources and constraints. We will discuss some of the techniques that my team has utilized with great success. The techniques you use depend on many factors. I have used many and some of them never worked in my project scenarios, while others worked very well. What technique we use depends on the context and you need to have a complete awareness of the context in which you are doing elicitation. For example, doing an elicitation activity for an existing production system is different from the one you plan to do for a completely new implementation.

Since Salesforce CRM is a cloud-based SaaS solution, the way to gather requirements varies greatly compared to one that is an on-premise application. As an example, with cloud applications such as Salesforce, we do not need to worry about scaling the system based on data volume or user base, as long as we follow Salesforce guidelines. The Salesforce SaaS platform has a governor limit that prevents the system from crashing.

In this section, we will cover the following techniques with examples. There are more techniques than those listed here, so you can use techniques that you are comfortable with and that work best for you:

- Observation
- Brainstorming
- Surveys
- Interviews/focus groups
- Conference room pilots/requirement workshops
- Prototyping
- Process models
- User stories

Let us go through each technique in greater detail so that you can get a better understanding and tailor your elicitation process by using the right technique.

Observation

This technique may be the easiest one if you have in-depth business and system knowledge. However, remember that the success of observation is built on trust. Before you begin, take the time to build a rapport with the user so they feel confident and comfortable sharing what they do and why they do it. You can go to your trusted superusers and ask them to walk you through their daily process—a day in the life of their daily activities. For example, consider a service agent handling customer complaints and how they utilize the current system: navigation steps to be able to access and create cases and find customer accounts and contact information; the ability to find knowledge articles and link to similar issues, routing important cases to level 2 or the supervisor; and so on. By observing each step, taking notes, and asking the right questions, you will be able to understand their needs and pain points or identify opportunities to make the process simpler and better. This technique removes the communication barrier as the agent does not need to articulate their issues verbally. In some cases, screen recording tools enhanced with AI, such as Scribe, can also assist by capturing user flows and surfacing repetitive steps or pain points that might not be obvious during manual observation.

Your job is to capture and take notes, ask questions, and confirm each step. Why not take the help of AI-assisted transcription for comprehensive details? Make sure to observe any gaps in the flow and ask questions to find out how they handle those gaps and the pain points around them. Do not provide or even think of designing a solution.

Brainstorming

This method helps you when you are working on completely new functionality, and no one knows exactly what they want and how they want it. You involve SMEs from business, functional, and technical teams. Brainstorming, when facilitated well, will help each individual to speak out loud and dump all their knowledge, relevant or irrelevant. This technique will help you gather a vast amount of information that can provide you with a good sense of direction. Coupled with other techniques, you can better your understanding of the requirements.

Your job here is to make sure you do the following:

- Occasionally provide insight with thought-provoking queries
- Encourage everyone, especially the shy ones, to speak out freely
- Encourage healthy conflict to generate ideas and manage conflict if it tends to get out of control

Surveys

A survey is another useful technique that you can use to elicit requirements in a structured manner in a short period of time.

This technique is helpful to gather information and opinions from a large number of people, and from diverse groups and business units across your organization or business unit. You can also use this to validate the information that you gathered from workshops or focus groups and find agreement or disagreement. This validation task helps you in the long run with better user adoption.

Surveys are a set of questions that you can send or ask identified stakeholders, groups, subject matter experts, end users, and so on. Their responses are collected, documented, and analyzed to get knowledge about their interests or issues. Survey questions should be designed in a logical manner to ensure the information needed is obtained efficiently and effectively.

Survey techniques include the following:

- **Questionnaire**: Participants can individually answer a set of questions. This is quick, but the response rate will be low, and responses may be vague.
- **Interviews**: This involves asking questions one-on-one, following up with more questions based on the responses. This technique is time-consuming, but the outcome is often much better than the previous one.

To obtain good participation from respondents, you'll need to do the following:

- Define your objective so that the respondent understands why they are spending time on the survey.
- Use a wide range of question types to keep your participants engaged. Keep survey questions mixed (closed-ended, open-ended, and multiple choice). If the survey is for new functionality, open-ended responses will provide you with innovative responses.
- Tailor survey invitations and distribute them in a way that best fits the participant's needs. There are many tools you can use to plan, create, distribute, collect, summarize, and report surveys. If you use a CRM tool such as Salesforce, you can use and manage surveys from that tool.

Analyze responses by generating reports and metrics from survey responses. You can use AI tools to cluster common responses, identify sentiment in open-ended answers, and summarize key takeaways to accelerate your review process. Based on your analysis, you will be able to identify and understand the needs. This data can be further distilled and can be used for a new level of elicitation using a different technique.

Interviews/focus groups

This is when you set up meetings with individuals or small groups. Wherever possible, it will be beneficial if interviews or focus group sessions are done in person or via live video chats. The key stakeholders that you would usually interact with are SMEs and power users, such as Sales Operations or Planning teams. If conducted well, by asking the right questions, you will be able to gather a wealth of information. Remember to go to the sessions well prepared, as you may not get more than a few hours. SMEs and power users mostly have a wealth of knowledge, so we need to be careful when asking questions. Make sure you understand what you are asking and elaborate as needed, and ask the right, relevant questions.

I've seen many business analysis books/videos saying *keep asking questions repeatedly till you get a defined answer*. Believe me, it will not work. You need to know the business area well and, to a very good extent, understand the system too. Being knowledgeable and asking intelligent questions with supporting facts and figures will help gain their trust, and they need to believe that you know what you are doing. Again, you need to use your judgment, as there may be scenarios where something may sound silly, and you may not be fully conversant in a specific area. In this situation, if you know the users from before and if they trust your knowledge, you can go ahead and get clarifications; otherwise, you can note it down, do some research, and take it offline with specific users.

Wherever possible, try to record the conversation. Nowadays, it is very easy to do it on many collaboration tools, such as Teams, WebEx, and Slack. This will offer you a chance to be able to replay and review the conversations/transcriptions and even leverage AI-enabled meeting assistants that can transcribe these sessions in real time and provide summaries or highlight key themes—freeing you to focus more on the conversation itself.

The follow-up conversations need not be as formal. I prefer to take people out for a coffee or business lunch and have conversations.

Conference room pilots/requirements workshops

Conference room pilots/workshops are usually three- to four-day workshops offsite or in a conference room without any distractions and full-day sessions. In my experience, for these sessions to be effective, I recommend three sessions (for medium- to high-complexity projects). For simple enhancements or additional functionality on an existing system, a session duration of a few hours should be fine.

For my complex to medium-complexity projects, I usually schedule three sessions as follows, so the team as a whole understands and evolves the needs into full-fledged requirements:

1. The start of the analysis phase

2. The start of the design phase
3. Toward the end of the design phase and a few weeks before **User Acceptance Testing (UAT)**

The start of the analysis phase is when you are planned, prepared, and ready to start elicitation activities. You have identified the right stakeholders (limit the number of participants from 10 to 12, excluding the IT team). As much as possible, have an in-person session in a good-sized conference room. Participants being present in one location helps you understand clues from their non-verbal communication and helps everyone focus on the task at hand.

Plan the sessions and provide the agenda to all participants in advance. Set expectations for the session, and as a group, what you are all trying to get out of it. Make sure you keep slots for breakout sessions. Remember, not all sessions need all stakeholders.

During the start of the analysis phase, schedule the first session. The agenda and rules of engagement have to be very clear. As a Business Analyst, your job is to facilitate the conversation, manage conflict when things get out of control, and ask the right questions. You have to rephrase and ask questions till you and the participants understand the response and the need. There will be conflicting viewpoints on some requirements, which is natural. You can pause there and go on to the next requirement. During the breakout session, you can have a conversation with individuals with conflicting views and hash it out. Sometimes you have to escalate it to project and functional managers if a consensus is not reached. You are here to understand business needs, not to please everyone.

The team can use whiteboards/flip charts to put their ideas in visual form. It is an iterative process, so let it keep going. Remember not to let conversations get sidetracked. Time is of the essence here, and you need to manage it well. Once a requirement is understood, rather than putting that directly onto your tablet or into your book, I advise you (or one of the scribes) to write it on a flip chart, so that everyone can see it. Keep adding agreed requirements one after the other on the flip chart and let it be legible and visible to all during the duration of the session.

On the last day, make sure you sum up and read through the requirements loud and clear, and see if anyone has questions or concerns. Their body language will offer great clues, and you can speak to them offline and clarify any concerns they have. Summarize the session and thank them for their participation and invaluable input. Provide a high-level agenda and schedule for the next session. Within the next business day, make sure you create a document with all the agreed requirements for all the participants and their managers. As needed, any open queries around any of the requirements are to be addressed in the next one to two weeks.

Prototyping

This technique will be most suitable for developing completely new processes/systems with brand new features and functions. The users may not be able to conceptualize exactly how they want the end product to be. **Prototyping** helps with a mock-up – an early sample of a build to test the concept, which helps identify early what it should not be.

Prototyping can be as simple as whiteboarding. The complete process is a screen flow on a whiteboard/flip chart with integration and automation captured in swim lane diagrams with various actors. This is an excellent collaboration technique where every team member should be given enough opportunities to comment and edit. Here, too, leveraging AI-based design assistants such as Figma or Uizard can help transform rough whiteboard sketches or ideas into basic mock-ups, giving stakeholders a tangible way to refine their vision.

As an example, in one of my past projects, **partner relationship management (PRM)** was a brand-new functionality in Salesforce. We were one of the first companies to implement PRM. Our channel partner business wanted a tool for customers to be able to search for partner contacts from the company website. The requirement was very vague at that time, as we could not get much help from the vendor or the consulting company we employed.

There are two types of prototypes:

- **Low-fidelity**: These are quick and easy ways to visualize the outline of the proposed solution. Examples are wireframes, screen mock-ups, whiteboards, and flip charts.
- **High-fidelity**: A mostly finished product with most of the features and functions. These can be utilized for pilot programs and later can be incorporated into the actual solution. In software, this evolves into the final design solution.

Process models

Process models help business analysts understand the current business processes and help model the future desired "to-be" processes. This model helps the stakeholder understand their current business process model. You can do it on a whiteboard or flipchart, either by drawing with markers or using post-it notes. This will help stakeholders pitch in and point out or rearrange post-it notes if any activity is misarranged. Unless we understand the current "as-is" process flow, we will never be able to understand or identify the gaps. Once you and the stakeholders get to understand the current process clearly, you can start building the desired process flow models with the stakeholder, so that both parties agree on the desired model.

After you create the quick and dirty models, you can refine them and transfer them as permanent artifacts using the tool of your choice. I prefer to use the **Visio tool** to create the process flow and then socialize the Visio process flows in PDF format to stakeholders and get their feedback and agreement. These artifacts will be extremely useful for future projects and for creating and developing test scripts for testing.

User stories

User stories are a popular technique to write user requirements from the actual user role perspective. There are three main elements to a user story: who, what, and why. User stories are most often used in Agile project methodology:

- As a *<Who = user role>*
- I want *<What = to do something>*
- So that I can *<Why = achieve a specific need or goal>*

The user role represents a type of user (for example, sales specialist, employee, investment banker, etc.). What is the action that the user wants to perform (for example, submitting a timesheet)? The last part of the user stories is the purpose of the action (for example, I can get paid).

The benefit of a user story is that the business, as well as the technical team, shall be able to understand and have a good idea of the requirements.

We should make sure user stories are written clearly and have no ambiguity. Every user story should have clearly defined and mutually agreed-on acceptance criteria and the definition of done. Verify and validate that each of your user stories is independent of other user stories, is negotiable, adds value to your stakeholders upon implementation, can be estimated by your technical team, is small enough to be contained in itself, and contains enough information that it can be tested. Employ AI writing assistants to polish user stories, ensure clarity, and generate acceptance criteria from initial drafts. AI writing tools streamline user story development by improving narrative quality, recommending acceptance criteria, and ensuring clarity. Tools such as **Grammarly** or **Jasper.ai** can transform vague requirements such as "As a user, I want to log in easily" into more specific, actionable statements such as "As a user, I want to log in with single sign-on to access the platform seamlessly."

Let me share with you a few examples.

The first example is partner registrations in the Salesforce system. Partner users should be able to register and gain access to their account, and be able to access the Salesforce Partner portal. The business need, in this case, is to automate the complete process of Partner user creation. I drew this with workshop participants' input on a whiteboard. We refined it until we all agreed on what the business wanted. Later, we documented this in MS Word and added it as a document requirement addendum. This simple flow helped stakeholders. Project team members understood this complex business process in very simple visual terms.

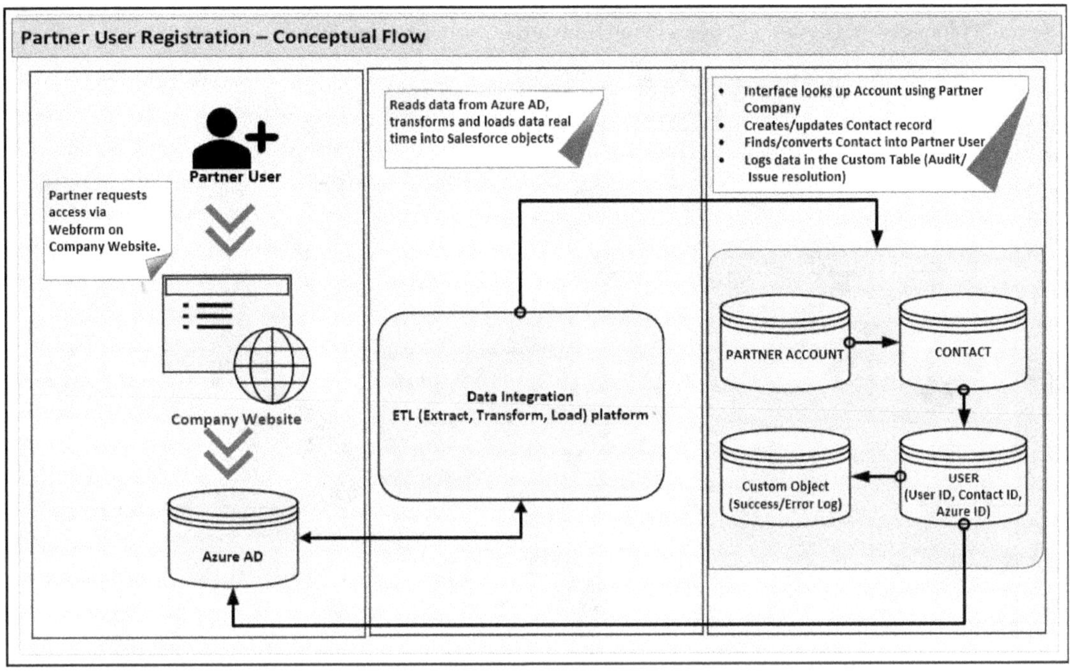

Figure 2.1 – Partner user registration process – conceptual flow

This second example is the account registration process. This was done during a conference room pilot session where we had stakeholders and technical team members. We captured all our thoughts collaboratively and came up with the swim lane diagram on a large whiteboard. Our team loved this process flow so much that they requested that I take a copy of the drawing "as is." The following flow was hand-drawn and copied into a Visio format for distribution, and you can do the same, too. I found this process very collaborative, and it excites participants as they are part of developing the process.

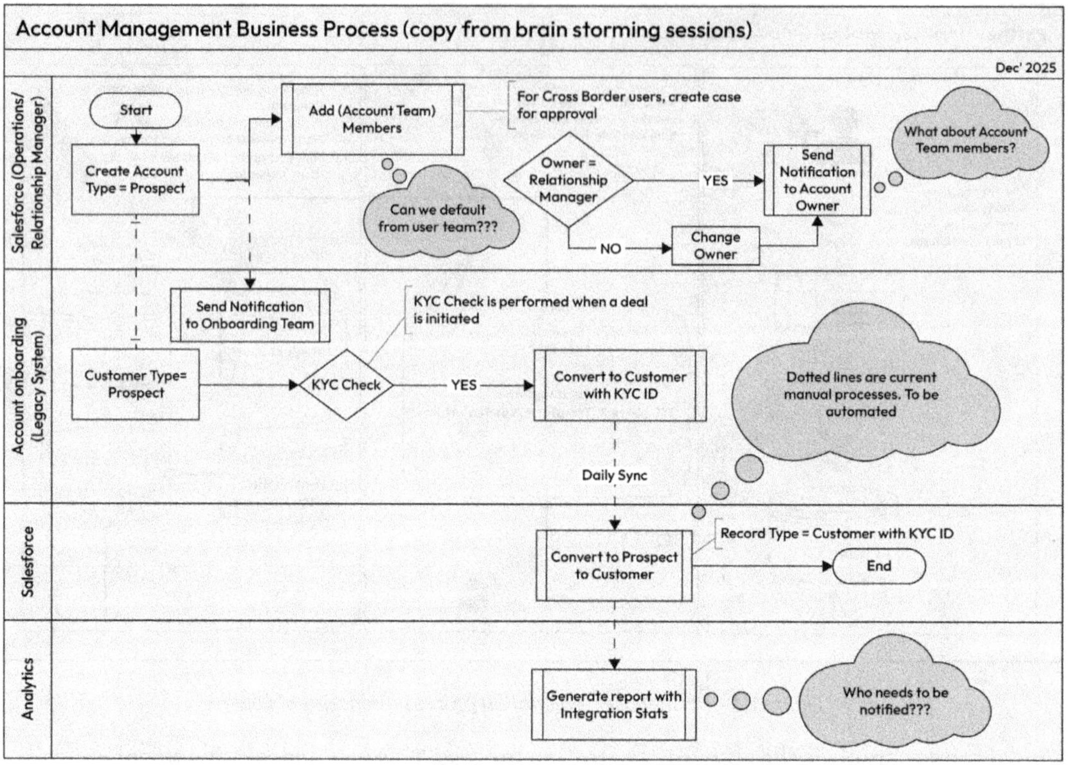

Figure 2.2 – Account registration process swim lane diagram

Example 3 (shown in *Figure 2.3*) shows a process flow where users will be able to create multiple product opportunities under one global opportunity. The production opportunities can be created by multiple product teams.

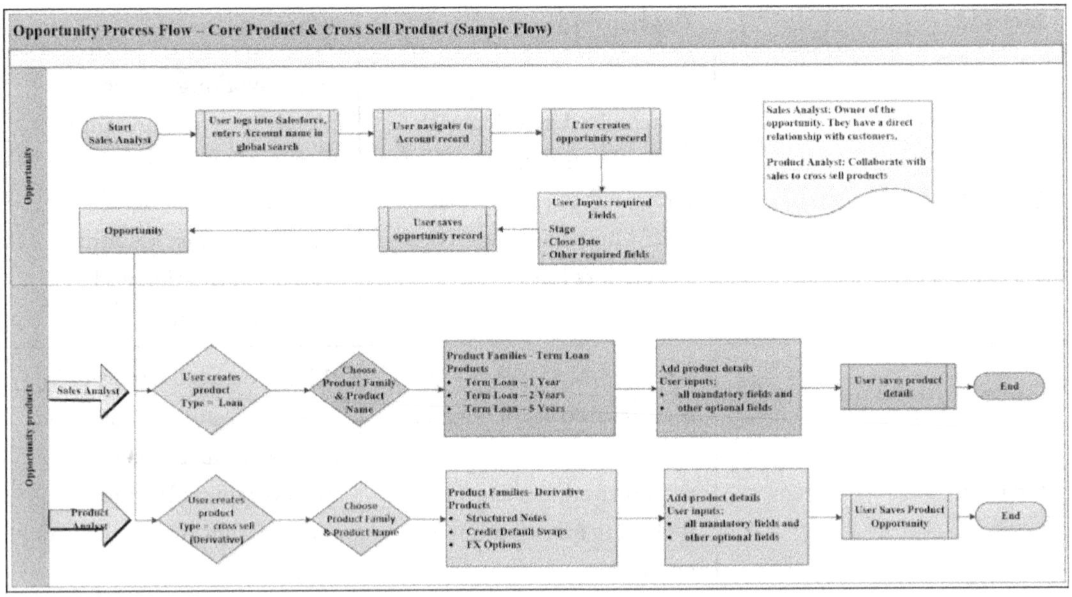

Figure 2.3 – Salesforce opportunity process flow

So far, we have discussed a few elicitation techniques that I found very helpful for my elicitation activities. There are numerous techniques available, and you can use ones that suit you. To draw out the needs of users, you have to use more than one technique. As needed, you conduct more elicitation activities to gain a complete, detailed understanding of the requirements.

Let's summarize and matrix key information, providing a simple, reader-friendly recap of our elicitation techniques. This is a good example where we can leverage generative AI's assistance.

Method	Description	When to Use
Observation	Going to superusers and asking them to walk you through their daily process, taking notes, and asking clarifying questions.	When you have good in-depth business and system knowledge, and want to understand the current system utilization, needs, and pain points without relying on verbal articulation.

Method	Description	When to Use
Brainstorming	A facilitated meeting with SMEs (business, functional, technical) to speak freely and "dump" all knowledge to generate ideas.	When working on completely new functionality and no one knows exactly what they want; helpful for gathering a vast amount of initial information and a sense of direction.
Surveys	A structured set of questions sent to target groups to gather information and opinions, including questionnaires and interviews.	When you need to gather information and opinions from a large number of people or diverse groups/business units in a short period, or to validate information gathered in workshops.
Interviews/Focus Groups	Structured or informal meetings (one-on-one or small groups) with key stakeholders such as SMEs and power users.	When you need to gather a wealth of detailed information by asking follow-up questions, it requires you to be well-prepared and knowledgeable in the business area.
Conference Room Pilots / Requirements Workshops	Focused, multi-day, off-site, or dedicated-room sessions with stakeholders and IT to collaboratively evolve needs into full-fledged requirements.	For complex to medium-complexity projects, to reach a group consensus, understand non-verbal cues, manage conflict, and agree on requirements (often scheduled at analysis and design phases).

Method	Description	When to Use
Prototyping	Creating a mock-up or early sample (low-fidelity, such as wireframes, or high-fidelity, such as a finished product) to test a concept.	Most suitable for developing completely new processes/ systems with brand new features, where users may not be able to conceptualize the final product.
Process Models	Visually mapping the "as is" (current) business processes and collaboratively building the desired "to-be" (future) processes.	When you need to understand the current process flow, identify gaps, and get stakeholder agreement on the desired process flow for a new system or change.
User Stories	Writing user requirements from the user's perspective, following the format: "As a [Who], I want [What], so that I can [Why]."	Most often used in Agile project methodology to create clear, unambiguous requirements that are easily understood by both business and technical teams.

Table 2.1

So far, you have captured a wealth of information from various sources; now it is time for you to distill all the information and capture the essence of the needs and wants into documented requirements. Let us explore what you can do from your end to create this artifact.

Requirement documentation

So far, you have captured notes on the users' needs and wants. These are all the potential requirements—they are still vague and need structure so that they can be understood by both the stakeholder as well as your technical, testing, and training team. Our job is to transform and document them into high-quality, well-formatted requirements. The final documented requirements we produce will be well-written, clear, concise, and descriptive enough to avoid conflicts and confusion. Use AI tools to assist you in identifying ambiguous phrasing, redundancies, or inconsistencies in large requirement sets, ensuring a consistent and professional standard.

For stakeholder and project team members to be able to understand the requirements consistently in the same way, the requirements shall be written to conform to the following attributes:

- Unambiguous
- Testable
- Original stakeholder understands and agrees
- Conforms to fit criteria
- Provides rationale
- Reviewed and agreed for completeness by technical and test leads

For documenting requirements, there are many templates available, and your organization may have standard templates. The key attributes that you need to make sure you capture are the following:

- Requirement ID
- Objective
- User role
- Description
- Rationale
- Alternative scenario
- Assumptions
- Acceptance criteria
- Fit criteria
- Requestor name
- Document date
- Business unit

We've covered the science of elicitation techniques; now let's understand what it takes to apply them effectively—the art behind the practice.

The art of elicitation

Elicitation activity is a combination of art and science: science in the sense that you need tools and techniques to keep you organized and help you identify, capture, and understand what the users want and need; art in the sense of subtly getting the true essence of the business requirements that provide meaningful information that adds anticipated short- and long-term benefits.

Incorporating problem-solving and **root cause analysis** (**RCA**) methods in the business elicitation phase is crucial for transforming vague symptoms into concrete requirements. Here are a few methods (some of them are explored in greater detail in future chapters) and how they can help with business analysis activities:

- **"Five whys" technique (RCA)**: This involves repeatedly asking "Why?", also called five whys, to drill down past symptoms and identify the foundational cause of a business issue, ensuring requirements address the actual root problem. We use this to stop fixing symptoms and start solving real issues.
- **Fishbone/Ishikawa diagram (RCA)**: This visual tool helps categorize potential causes of a problem (such as people, process, system, environment) into a structured diagram. It leads to a comprehensive exploration of all contributing factors during interviews or workshops.
- **Gap analysis (problem solving)**: By comparing the current "as-is" state with the desired "to-be" state, BAs can precisely define the gap. This gap then translates directly into the functional and non-functional requirements needed to close it.
- **Prioritization techniques (problem solving)**: Methods such as **MoSCoW** (**Must have, Should have, Could have, Would have**) force stakeholders to make trade-offs. This is key to preventing scope creep and ensuring high-value requirements are elicited and delivered first.
- **Process mapping/flowcharting (RCA/problem solving)**: Visually detailing the current process allows BAs and stakeholders to spot bottlenecks, redundant steps, and points of failure. These findings become opportunities for new, streamlined requirements.
- **Use case analysis (problem solving)**: This method describes how an actor interacts with the system to achieve a specific goal. We use it to effectively turn identified problems (e.g., "The system fails to process X") into detailed, actionable solution requirements.

Getting the facts requires planning, practice, discipline, skill, and, of course, a lot of hard work. Let me list a few of the skills that I feel you may find useful:

- **Understand your stakeholders**: Get to know their strengths, influences, likes, dislikes, hobbies, and so on. You need to connect with the users to be able to gain their trust.
- **Plan well in advance**: Go with a purpose. You need to understand the culture, business, technology, and how they operate.
- **Prepare and plan your conversation tailored to the participant's style**: Have the right set of questions and prepare scenarios on how to ask the questions intelligently.

- **Listen actively to both verbal and non-verbal clues**: You need to be comfortable with periods of silence when interacting with participants so that they can formulate their business needs, and allow them to fill in the blanks.
- **Ask the right questions and show interest in learning from the users**: If you show interest in their area of expertise, they will not be able to stop their urge to share their knowledge.
- **Structure your conversation and try to see the big picture before getting into details**: Try to facilitate an intelligent conversation.
- **Make sure your elicitation sessions flow smoothly without any interruptions or distractions**: It is all about the flow of what is in the minds of users. This means keeping note-taking activity to a minimum but taking enough notes to jog your memory later.
- **Some end users will try hard to convince you of their requirements to get into the limelight**: They will exaggerate and embellish. You need to be observant of these users and make sure these requirements are verified and agreed upon by other users.
- To become good at elicitation, you need practice. Keep practicing, and it becomes second nature. These are the soft skills that make you better at understanding your true needs. During some elicitation sessions, you may not get any meaningful information, and this is perfectly fine. Keep calm and stay focused. You usually get the most insight just before concluding a good conversation. The three most important questions you should ask just before concluding the elicitation session are the following:
- What else can you tell me?
- What else did I miss?
- What else do you know?

You will be surprised by how much valuable information and insight you will be able to obtain. Investigate AI tools to support your work. While AI cannot replace human connection, it can help by generating questions, summarizing prior discussions, and identifying overlooked perspectives from past sessions.

Practical tips for success

Here are some tips that will help you with elicitation activities. I make a checklist of these tasks so that I remember to implement them as much as possible.

- Be an active listener – be able to understand the meaning behind the work and the user's intentions.
- Understand the user needs in the context and be technology-agnostic.

- Avoid stakeholders telling you what to do (solution) rather than what they need.
- Adopt incremental approaches where possible to foster innovative solutions and better solutions.
- Take notes... lots of them. Tag the source where you got the information. At a later date, if you need clarification, it will help you identify the source easily.
- Use visuals as much as possible to bring everyone to a common understanding.
- Communicate – send the minutes to all stakeholders, including the visuals, and solicit feedback.
- Thank your stakeholders and team members for their participation. A good way to thank people is to take them out for a team outing or dinner. This helps with team building too.
- Provide feedback to participants' managers if someone went above and beyond. Recognition is a very strong tool, and it motivates and encourages participation.

As we embrace these analytical techniques, it is also imperative to consider the evolving role of technology, specifically how we can leverage artificial intelligence to enhance our effectiveness without compromising the human-centric core of our profession.

Leveraging AI responsibly in business analysis

AI is fast developing, and it's going to stay with you. While AI excels at data processing, human judgment remains essential for interpreting emotions, building trust, and making strategic decisions. AI may produce generic outputs without sufficient context or detailed project information.

As the famous adage reminds us, "With great power comes great responsibility."

Here are some implementation guidelines:

- **Tool selection**: Match tools to specific needs (Otter.ai for transcription, Grok for questions, Grammarly for writing)
- **Quality input**: Provide structured data such as meeting agendas and user stories for better results
- **Human validation**: Always review AI outputs to ensure accuracy and context alignment
- **Strategic focus**: Let AI handle routine tasks while you concentrate on relationship-building and strategic discussions

There are many tools available; I found some of the following useful for business analysis work. (See *Figure 2.4*). Numerous excellent tools are available, and even more are emerging. Select the one that best suits your requirements.

Elicitation Task	AI Tool Suggestion	Purpose
Auto-tagging of requirements	ClickUp AI, Confluence AI	Classify and track requirements
Domain-specific questions	ChatGPT custom GPT	Generate elicitation questions by stakeholder
Interview note automation	Fathom, Notion AI	Action item and highlight extraction
Interview transcription & tagging	Fireflies, Otter.ai	Real-time notes and summaries
Process flow from text	Lucidchart + GPT, ScribeHow	Generate diagrams from narratives/screen recording
Prototyping aid	Uizard, Figma + Genius	Convert ideas/sketches into UI mockups
User story refinement	StoriesOnBoard, Craft.io	Suggest clear, testable user stories

Figure 2.4 – Sample AI tools helpful for business analysis activities

Summary

In this chapter, we covered elicitation planning. You learned about different tools and techniques of elicitation, and that you have to use more than one tool and technique to bring forth requirements. Now you know that you need to take as many notes as possible so as not to lose any valuable information, and then take all that knowledge and write great requirements. This chapter also equipped you to transform business users' expressed and unexpressed intentions, thoughts, and ideas, and document clear, crisp, formalized requirements that eventually add value to all your stakeholders. You also saw how AI can support your efforts by assisting with tasks such as transcription, summarization, and pattern recognition, helping you stay focused on meaningful stakeholder engagement.

In the next chapter, we will take these requirements and work on prioritizing them. We will cover techniques that you can use to help you prioritize your requirements so that the technical team can add value during solution design and development activities.

Questions

1. How often do you do requirement elicitation?
2. What are some of the most important tasks during elicitation?
3. Can you recollect different tasks to perform during the elicitation phase to make it productive?

Further reading

- The PMI Guide to Business Analysis, PMI (`https://www.pmi.org/pmbok-guide-standards/foundational/business-analysis`)
- Designing and Conducting Survey Research: A Comprehensive Guide, 4th Edition, Louis M. Rea, Richard A. Parker

Get this book's PDF version and more

Scan the QR code (or go to `packtpub.com/unlock`). Search for this book by name, confirm the edition, and then follow the steps on the page.

UNLOCK NOW

Note: Keep your invoice handy. Purchases made directly from Packt don't require an invoice.

3

Prioritizing Requirements

In the previous chapter, we learned about elicitation planning and the different tools and techniques of elicitation. You got the opportunity to transform the business user's expressed and unexpressed intentions, thoughts, and ideas into formalized requirements. You have a complete list of clear, consistent, complete, and validated requirements. Now, we need to review and sift through this huge list of requirements and work on prioritizing them. We have limited resources, and we cannot deliver everything. To enable businesses to realize optimum business value by addressing the most pressing and important requirements, we need some kinds of prioritized requirements. For this, we need to identify the requirements that are valuable and group them.

In this chapter, you will learn about the process of managing requirement prioritization based on urgency and relative importance. You will work with the stakeholder/subject matter experts and rank requirements that are identified during the requirement identification phase. You will learn about the methods to identify important tasks that provide business value. You will also learn about the dependency map between various requirements and how to prioritize dependencies without creating gaps in the requirements flow. We will conclude this chapter by reviewing proven techniques for managing meetings, resolving conflicts, and getting consensus and agreement from stakeholders.

We will be covering the following topics:

- The importance of requirement prioritization
- Reviewing various prioritization techniques
- Creating a dependency map between requirements
- Managing prioritization meetings and getting consensus
- Practical tips for success
- Simple CRM requirement prioritization and roadmap scenario

By the end of this chapter, you will understand the concepts, techniques, and dependencies of requirement prioritization and be able to effectively facilitate prioritization discussions and create a practical CRM requirements roadmap.

The importance of requirement prioritization

Requirement prioritization enables you to identify the most important business needs so that the next phase of the project can work on these important requirements. The most challenging task is how, as a business analyst, you manage conflicting priorities based on stakeholders having different goals and priorities. It is highly recommended to initiate ranking or staking requirements from the elicitation phase itself. From my experience, by starting early, you can often easily identify about 50% of the top priorities that you think may go into the first release. Prioritization helps you plan the implementation and layout of the roadmap.

Any project has a limited budget, definite duration, and finite resources. Prioritization helps with managing requirements and the allocation and utilization of resources effectively and productively. It helps us focus on putting our efforts into implementing the most critical requirements that matter most. By prioritizing, we are identifying and defining when requirements get addressed and implemented. This helps us improve communications and keep everyone transparent. Many times, I have experienced that the prioritized list keeps changing. When socialized with stakeholders, they rethink and redefine what they need now versus later. This helps us move requirements around and prioritize them to get the most benefit for everyone.

Prioritization activity should be iterative; at our workplace, we revisit this list every 3 to 6 months and adjust it based on the needs at that point in time. New requirements will be added, and they may take higher priority, whereas the existing prioritized ones may be dropped as we found a new way to better address the needs, or the value of the feature may have already been met, therefore making the requirement in the backlog redundant. This list also helps us in creating project/product roadmaps. You can group them into various releases, such as numbers 1 to 10 from the prioritized list go into Release-1, numbers 11 to 20 go into Release-2, and so on. Sales and service team members do not have the patience to wait for years to see the solution, especially with Salesforce implementations. After we get the agreed prioritized list, we create a roadmap for the next 12 to 15 months, spacing releases every 3 to 6 months depending on the complexity of the deliverables. Good prioritization helps us build these roadmaps, and this, in turn, helps us plan project activities and keep stakeholders informed on when they can see the finished working product.

Reviewing prioritization techniques

To enable effective requirement prioritization processes to happen, we need to use objective consensus methods to remove any bias. Let us look at some of the frameworks that we can utilize. Sometimes, you have to use a combination of frameworks to achieve results.

These frameworks will aid you and your stakeholders in better decision-making. None of the techniques can work in isolation, and it needs to be a collaborative effort. Understanding the available techniques will help you pick one that provides the most actionable results.

The following are some of the techniques/frameworks. Use the ones that work best for you:

- **The MoSCoW method**: Used to identify and action important requirements.
- **Multivoting**: Voting requirements based on an established set of rules/voting ranks that are point-based/cumulative.
- **Weighted ranking/staked ranking**: Ranking requirements based on established risk factors and weightage.
- **SWOT analysis**: Prioritizes based on **strengths, weaknesses, opportunities, and threats**.
- **RICE scoring**: Prioritizes based on scoring each requirement against these four factors: **reach, impact, confidence, and effort**.
- **Value versus effort**: Compares scores based on value, benefit, impact to cost, risk, complexity, and effort.
- **Story mapping**: Orders requirements on a grid in a logical manner to describe the activities end to end. This offers simplicity and is easy to understand.

With the advent of AI-powered requirement analysis tools, teams now have additional assistance in analyzing requirement clusters, identifying hidden dependencies, and even predicting implementation complexity based on historical data. While these tools don't replace business judgment, they can serve as a second opinion or a validation mechanism when used alongside traditional methods such as MoSCoW or RICE. AI tools such as **ClickUp AI** can help auto-summarize requirement lists and suggest priority clusters using sentiment and frequency.

You need to employ more than one method to get to the correct prioritizations.

I often use the MoSCoW method, weighted ranking, and story mapping for prioritizing my requirements. This is what I prefer to do:

- Use a combination of methods to bucket them into three groups: High, Medium, and Low (or you can call them Red, Blue, and Yellow). This task can be achieved fairly quickly in a day or two, provided it is done properly with the right set of team members in the session.

- Get consensus and agreement from everyone that the requirements prioritized are categorized in the right bucket.
- Next, we go through each one of the high-priority bucket items and use one or more of these prioritization techniques to rank them from 1 to N (with 1 being the highest priority).
- Review them again after they are ranked collectively and agree on the ranking priorities. Do the same for Medium and Low. See the following diagram for more information:

Prioritized Buckets					
Priority 1		Priority 1		Priority 3	
Bucket 1 (3 Month Release)		Bucket 2 (6 Month Release)		Bucket 3 (3 Month Release)	
Priority	Requirement	Priority	Requirement	Priority	Requirement
1	Function -A	1	Function -D	1	Function -H
2	Function -B	2	Function -E	2	Function -I
3	Function -C	3	Function -F	3	Function -J
		4	Function -G		

Figure 3.1 – Prioritized requirements with each priority subprioritized

For prioritization, high-level effort estimates are typically required for each requirement to assess feasibility and determine whether a set of features can realistically fit into each delivery bucket within the available timeframe. Next, we lay it on our roadmap. Based on time, budget, and resource availability, we pick *X* number of prioritized requirements for each release. In practice, some of the high-priority requirements will fall in Release-2. This is when the team needs to work collaboratively and see which ones are needed during Release-1 and which ones can wait until Release-3. Most conflicts arise in this kind of situation, as reality does not meet the perceived expectation. You, as a savvy business analyst, with the help of the project sponsor and project manager, need to show your negotiation skills and get everyone on the same page to agree. It's not that these techniques or methods produce a well-prioritized list; it is the team that does that collaboratively. You can use one or more of these techniques or your own techniques.

The following figure shows an example of a multi-year roadmap for a sample of prioritized requirements. Adding a roadmap element to your requirement prioritization activity sets expectations with stakeholders and project team members and keeps the overall requirement process transparent:

Project Roadmap -FY22/FY23								
	FY2022				FY2023			
Roadmap	Q1	Q2	Q3	Q4	Q1	Q2	Q3	Q4
Release -1	Priority 1 Function A,B,C							
Release -2		Priority 2 Function D,E,F,G						
Release -3				Priority 3 Function H,I,J				
Release -4					Priority 4 Function K,L,M,N,O			
Release -5							Priority 5 Function P,Q,R	

Figure 3.2 – FY2022/FY2023 Multi-year project roadmap

Let us review some of these techniques. We would not be getting into details, as that is not the aim of this chapter.

MoSCoW analysis

The **MoSCoW analysis** categorization (or **MSCW** excluding vowels) stands for **must have**, **should have**, **could have**, and **would have**:

- **Must haves**: These requirements are needed, and without these, the project does not exist. Enabling these helps the business unit achieve its goals. These are the core functionality and capabilities of the system. For example, an account management functionality where users can create and edit customer records in a system. Furthermore, any requirement that addresses a security risk or fulfills a compliance mandate is automatically classified as a must-have, as they are inherently non-negotiable.
- **Should haves**: These requirements are important and valuable, and can wait a little longer. You will need them soon, but not immediately. Examples are workflow notifications, automating processes, and so on. Users can still utilize the system, but may need to rely on manual processes, which is inconvenient but possible. These requirements are also important and need to be followed after all the must-haves are completed.

- **Could haves**: These requirements pose a minimal impact on the project at this time. For example, a user would like to see their attributes (such as the owner's region/country/division/department) in account and contact records. Most of the time, these are simple requests and can be clubbed with one of the previous two categories to get synergy by saving time during the design, testing, and deployment. Of course, you still need to develop and do some level of design work.
- **Would haves**: These requirements have no impact for now and do not impact the project. These are more ideas that may eventually morph into more important requirements and move up the chain. Examples are cosmetic changes to the UI or email templates.

Story mapping

In this technique, we arrange user stories for an end-to-end process in a sequence in a specific order of importance. By reviewing the stories along the process from start to finish, both the critical paths and possible alternate paths, we will be able to identify gaps as well as stories in the wrong position or undesired stories along the way. This will help during the prioritizing session in rearranging the stories for a more effective future state. This is like connecting all the dots to make a complete picture. When you see the end-to-end big picture, you can easily see the missing, misplaced, and redundant dots.

This method also lets us map the dependencies, such as the connection between the stories in the sequence of flow. Story mapping helps us find missing or unwanted events, which, in turn, helps us to refine prioritization. If managed well, story mapping gets the best outcome by complementing each other with other techniques.

A sample story mapping event flow is shown in *Figure 3.3*:

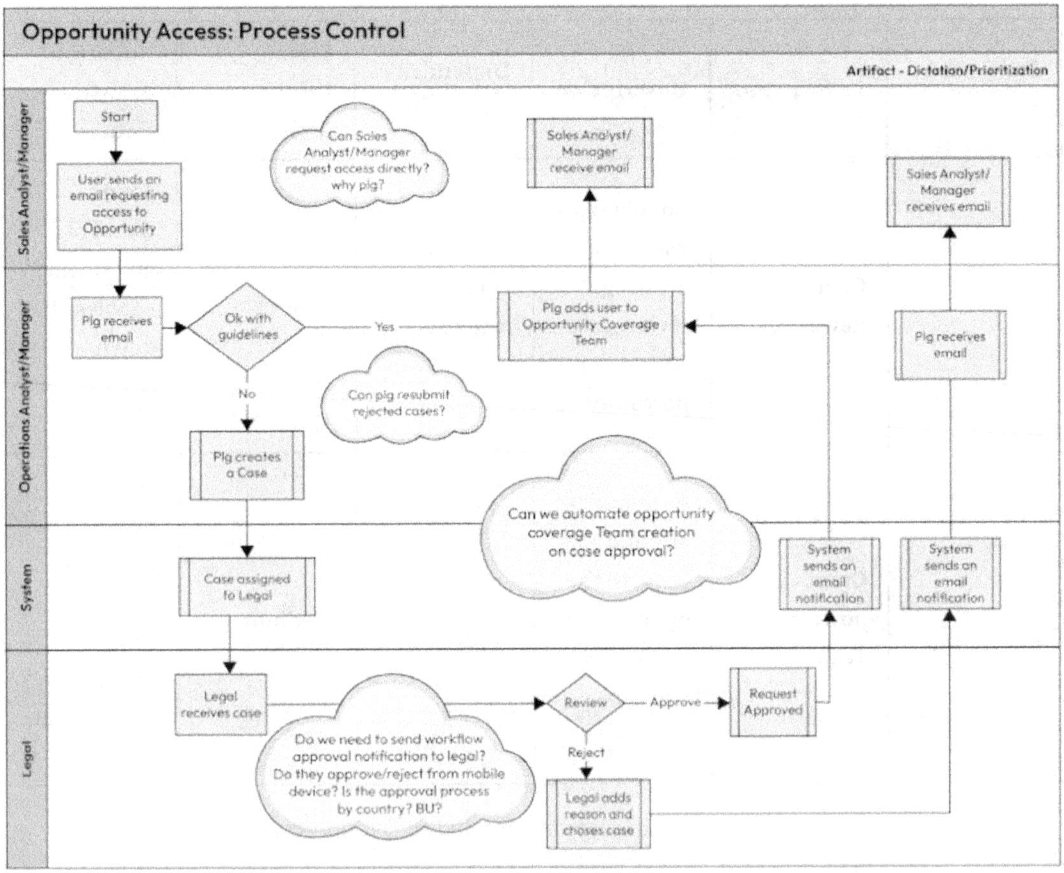

Figure 3.3 – Story mapping business event flow with missing requirements

For simplification purposes, we added only the story name and depicted this in the process flow format. When discussing with stakeholders, you can write each event on a story card and rearrange the story cards until you have the optimal story that fits your business needs. You can think of each activity as a story card. This rearrangement will automatically give you the right priority for each of the story cards.

The following is a focused example using only the initiating and ending story cards, showing how high-level effort estimates help determine whether these features can fit into a delivery bucket:

Story card #	Story name	Description	Dependencies	Effort (high-level)	Notes for prioritization
1	Create Legal Review Case	Enable sales users to create a legal review case from an opportunity	Opportunity exists	Low	Foundational requirement; enables all downstream stories
7	Grant Opportunity Team Access	Automatically add users to the opportunity team after legal approval	Legal case approved	Medium	Delivers primary business value, but cannot be implemented without Story #1

Table 3.1: Example using initiating and ending story cards

These two stories can be captured on index cards to facilitate review with the team. This approach allows participants to physically shuffle and rearrange the story cards during prioritization sessions, making dependencies, effort, and delivery sequencing more visible and easier to agree upon.

```
Story Card 1: Create Legal Review Case

As a sales user,
I want to create a legal review case for an opportunity
so that legal approval can be formally requested.

Dependency: Opportunity must exist
Priority Rationale: Entry point to the flow
```

```
Story Card 7: Grant Opportunity Team Access (Post-Approval)

As the system,
I want to automatically add users to the opportunity team after
legal approval
so that collaboration can begin.

Dependency: Legal case approved
Priority Rationale: Business-critical outcome of the process
```

Figure 3.4 – Story cards

Now, you know that there are different prioritizing techniques, and you can pick the ones that suit your project. In the next section, let us review and see how we can establish dependencies between requirements.

Dependency map between requirements

There exist functional dependencies between requirements, either from the same projects or from other project initiatives, and this will lead to reprioritizing requirements. We need to identify cross-functional dependencies and prioritize requirements to align them by understanding dependencies between processes, systems, and teams.

You can identify requirements dependencies by reviewing or creating end-to-end process flows, function and system diagrams, and conceptual flows.

In this example, let us assume we have requirements from **A** to **J**, as listed in *Figure 3.5*, with priority values from **1** to **10**. We stack-ranked them in our first iteration, and in the second iteration, we used the dependency mapping technique and discovered that two specific requirements are linked together and need to be implemented at the same time; if not, neither will work:

Option 1	
Priority	Requirement
1	A
2	B
3	C
4	D
5	E
6	F
7	G
8	H
9	I
10	J

Option 2	
Priority	Requirement
1	A
2	B
3	C
4	D
5	E
6	F
7	G
8	H
9	I
10	J

Option 3	
Priority	Requirement
1	Ax
2	B
3	C
4	D
5	E
6	Ay+F
7	G
8	H
9	I
10	J

Figure 3.5 – Requirement prioritization options

Let us analyze this step by step.

Option 1 is our first draft of prioritized requirements. We discovered that requirements **A** and **F** are interdependent. Implementing this option makes **A** unusable unless **F** is implemented.

We have multiple ways to address this dependency. For simplicity reasons, let's say we came up with two other options.

Move *F* next to *A* and implement priorities *1* and *2* together as one unit. Now, you are knocking others down. This is **Option 2**.

If feasible, split **A** into **Ax** (independent part) and **Ay** (dependent part with F), so that **Ax** can be done now, and **Ay** and **F** later. This is **Option 3**.

As an example, look at the following two separate requirements:

- **Account management functionality**: Sales analysts shall be able to create, update, and transact with the customers (High priority)
- **Integrate customer identity verification so that sales analysts can verify customer identity**: Sales analysts shall be able to access identifying information from the different systems without the need for a separate login (Medium priority)

On further analysis, we discovered that sales analysts cannot transact with customers without verifying customer identification. There is a dependency between these two requirements.

A possible solution is that we can make it into two parts:

- Enable user-friendly customer identification hyperlinks on the customer page. When the user clicks on the link, it opens up a window requesting them to add their credentials to access the system.
- Enable **single sign-on (SSO)** functionality shortly after release and make the hyperlink SSO-enabled.

We can identify this kind of dependency issue by using prioritization techniques such as dependency maps and be able to find workarounds. After addressing the dependency, we can reprioritize and adjust requirement priorities to get the most benefit.

Managing prioritization meetings

We reviewed various prioritization techniques, and now you are equipped with different prioritization tools. In this section, let us look at how to make the process better by effectively managing the prioritization meetings.

For the requirement prioritization meetings, only key members need to be present in this meeting. Examples include the lead business analyst, technical lead, architect, project manager, cross-functional leads, key SMEs, project sponsors, and stakeholders. The technical team, architects, and project managers will be observers and will need to contribute when their expertise is needed for confirmation and clarification. Usually, the team size should be approximately 10 to 12 people, and it's highly recommended that they are co-located in a conference room. However, this model should be scalable, with the number of participants adjusted based on the size, complexity, and criticality of the project. This is not an elicitation session, and you do not need to have all team members present.

These are key decision-making events where leads/managers decide what is needed, when it is needed, and how it is needed for the business unit. The management can greatly benefit as this prioritized list will be the input for an implementation roadmap for the next 1, 2, or 3 years.

You can make prioritization meetings meaningful and effective, as follows:

- Engagement rules should be communicated
- Prioritization meetings should be well planned and communicated
- A clear agenda and goals should be communicated
- Ground rules for conflict resolution should be established
- Educate and give an overview of the tools and techniques the team plans to use
- Define the criteria for prioritizing factors and their weights
- Set up a good conference room with a large wall-to-wall whiteboard, flipcharts, and a projector to display previously created process flows, conceptual flows, and so on

Note

Business analysts (BAs) can use AI summarization tools before meetings to highlight requirement conflicts, summarize stakeholder comments, and receive priority suggestions based on historical data. Tools such as Confluence AI allow BAs to quickly summarize documents, flag repeated requests, and generate proposed priority categories, ensuring that they come to meetings thoroughly prepared.

Factors you need to take into account while prioritizing are as follows:

- **Statutory/regulatory**: As an example, if it is mandated by the regulatory authority, these have to be prioritized very highly. For example, data encryption at REST for PII data on account and contact records in Salesforce.
- **Policy-related/audit findings**: These are required by the company. It may be a policy to restrict emails from going to external users when sending notifications from the Salesforce system. Or it can be related to an audit finding that needs to be remediated at the earliest.
- **Cost to implement**: This can be any reason, such as consulting costs for specific skills being too high. Specific vendor software can be easy to implement and use.
- **Time to implement**: Can this be implemented quickly in 3- to 4-month windows, or does it need a long time?
- **Value to users**: Does it add value? Can it save users time, help them do things better and faster, or give them a better user experience?
- **Benefit to organization/business unit**: Does it meet regulatory requirements or get a better ROI?

- **Ease of technology use**: Can the system be used by end users relatively easily with minimal training, or can it be scaled for more users?
- **Skills availability**: Do we have skilled team members? If we have to customize a specific function, do we have that skill set? For example, to create a complex function, do we have a skill set in Salesforce Apex and knowledge of Tableau CRM?
- **Conflicting requirements**: Implementing one will prohibit the other from being implemented.

Based on your project, you can use combinations of these factors. Also, the relative importance of each factor may vary between projects and between companies. During the elicitation phase, plan and obtain agreements on the prioritization procedure to make decisions on what takes priority. Make every effort to see whether you can move forward constructively and negotiate a compromise with stakeholders with conflicting priorities or requirements. Establish a conflict escalation and resolution mechanism. Justify why a specific requirement is prioritized as High and another one is rejected. Be open, truthful, and transparent, and communicate the decision as early as possible to all stakeholders.

Based on the project, culture, stakeholders, and other parameters, rather than ranking, prioritize them in groups. All requirements that belong to a group will have the same rank, and they will be implemented and released together.

Practical tips for success

Let us take a look at a few pointers that might help you with your prioritization activities.

These practical tips, drawn from my experience, are designed to save you significant time and effort:

- Manage expectations by progressive prioritization and by being transparent.
- Set expectations with stakeholders that not all requirements may be implemented.
- Ask the right question:
    - What problem are we trying to solve?
    - What happens if we implement it?
    - What happens if we do not implement it?
- Involve the right stakeholder who is relevant to a specific session. For example, if you are discussing the account management process, there is no value in inviting all quote/contract management stakeholders.
- Not all stakeholders are the same. Some have a bigger say on what to prioritize because of their rank, knowledge, role, and so on.

- Whenever you reprioritize, make sure you are not breaking something else. You need to rerun whatever technique you used before, plus at least one more technique.
- Some requirements have to be prioritized as High because they may differentiate your product compared to other competitor products for political reasons (such as you want to release the feature for a major conference), and improve adoption/usability (if adoption and usability are already an issue).
- Prioritizing high-risk requirements early will help you mitigate the risk and find alternative options in the event that it does not work out.
- You have to implement some requirements that may have a lower priority. We create a **minimum viable product** (**MVP**) and implement only the core functionality with minimal effort, which can be enhanced later. This effort will help you gain their trust and create excitement and interest. Do it wisely. Your main opposition will be your project manager.
- Start prioritizing efforts early. Start tagging them as High, Medium, or Low. Keep reviewing them iteratively and keep the document current. Priorities change as the requirements age.

Let's explore how these practical principles apply through real-world scenarios in the next section.

Simple CRM requirement prioritization and roadmap scenario

Here is a real-life scenario that will help you get an idea of how to keep the stakeholder informed and set expectations. I simplified the functions so that it will be easier for you to understand and get a gist of it. The following screenshot is our documented requirements at the end of the elicitation activity. In these scenarios on the left, we have functionality for account management, contact management, and opportunity management in groups:

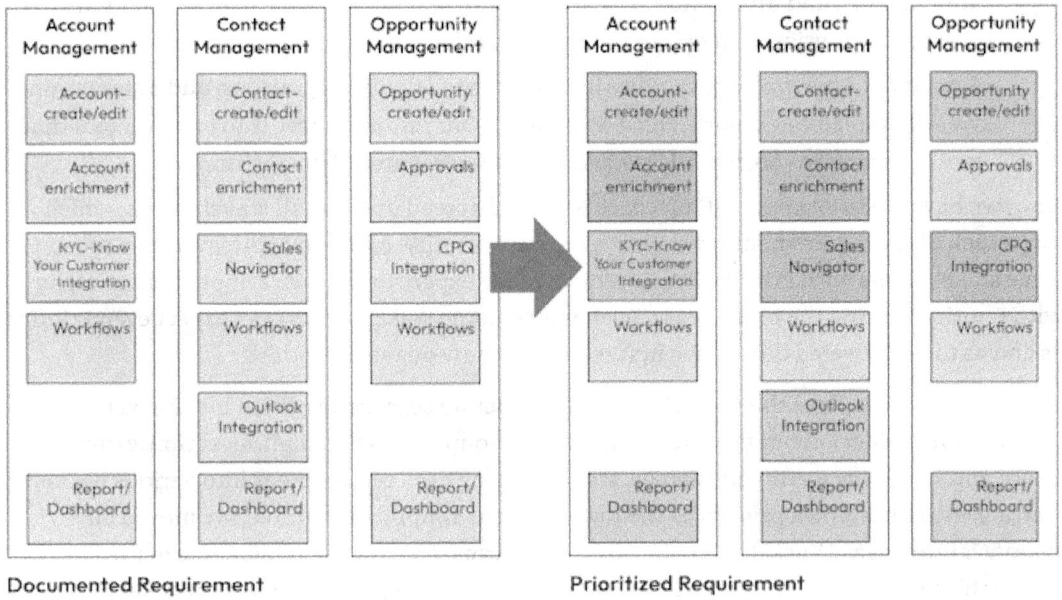

Figure 3.6 – Prioritizing requirements [before --> after]

Now, we took the documented requirements and color-coded priorities during prioritizing sessions with key stakeholders. We used ranking and story mapping techniques and came up with bucket ranking (Red – Priority 1, Aqua – Priority 2, Gold – Priority 3, and Green – Priority 4) on the right-hand side.

Let's review the rationale:

- **Priority 1**:
  - Core functionality, such as account, contact, and opportunity management, is our main goal. Without these, we cannot implement anything else.
  - Compliance and regularity requirements, such as **Know Your Customer** (**KYC**), identify customer confirmation, and this is a complex process that resides in the external system.
- **Priority 2**: Workflows (automation, notifications, and approval) are our next business priority to get informed and take timely action. This will enable us to have a better user experience and better adoption.
- **Priority 3**: Data enrichment tools (for example, D&B Hoovers, PitchBook, and DemandTools), sales navigators (for example, LinkedIn sales tool for contact

enrichment), and integration. These tools and integrations automate and simplify data creation. Our priority here is to keep the data clean, usable, and relevant.

- **Priority 4**: After we have the core functions, good data, integrations, and automation, we will implement reports and a dashboard. Our rationale here is to enable a tool that works accurately. So, it made sense for us to have it after data enrichment.

Now, we have the prioritized list, nicely colored and agreed upon by all stakeholders, which maps each of the requirements to their appropriate priority. All is well with everyone so far, as some stakeholders with Priority 2 requirements may expect to get theirs implemented along with Priority 1 during the first release. Even worse, some stakeholders may expect even Priority 3s and 4s to be delivered during the first release. So how do we solve this?

Your next task is to place them in release buckets. Before segregating them into buckets, educate stakeholders about the release timeline, resource capacity, high-level time estimate, effort, and so on. Once everyone agrees, start dropping each requirement into various buckets, starting with the highest priority to the lowest. In our simplified example, we moved all *Priority 1s* into release bucket 1. If you still have the capacity, you can move some of the *Priority 2s* into this bucket. Finally, you will be able to assign all requirements to various releases after long conversations, agreements, and disagreements. The following figure depicts the roadmaps for your requirements. This gives a glance at when a user can expect to see their requirement implemented:

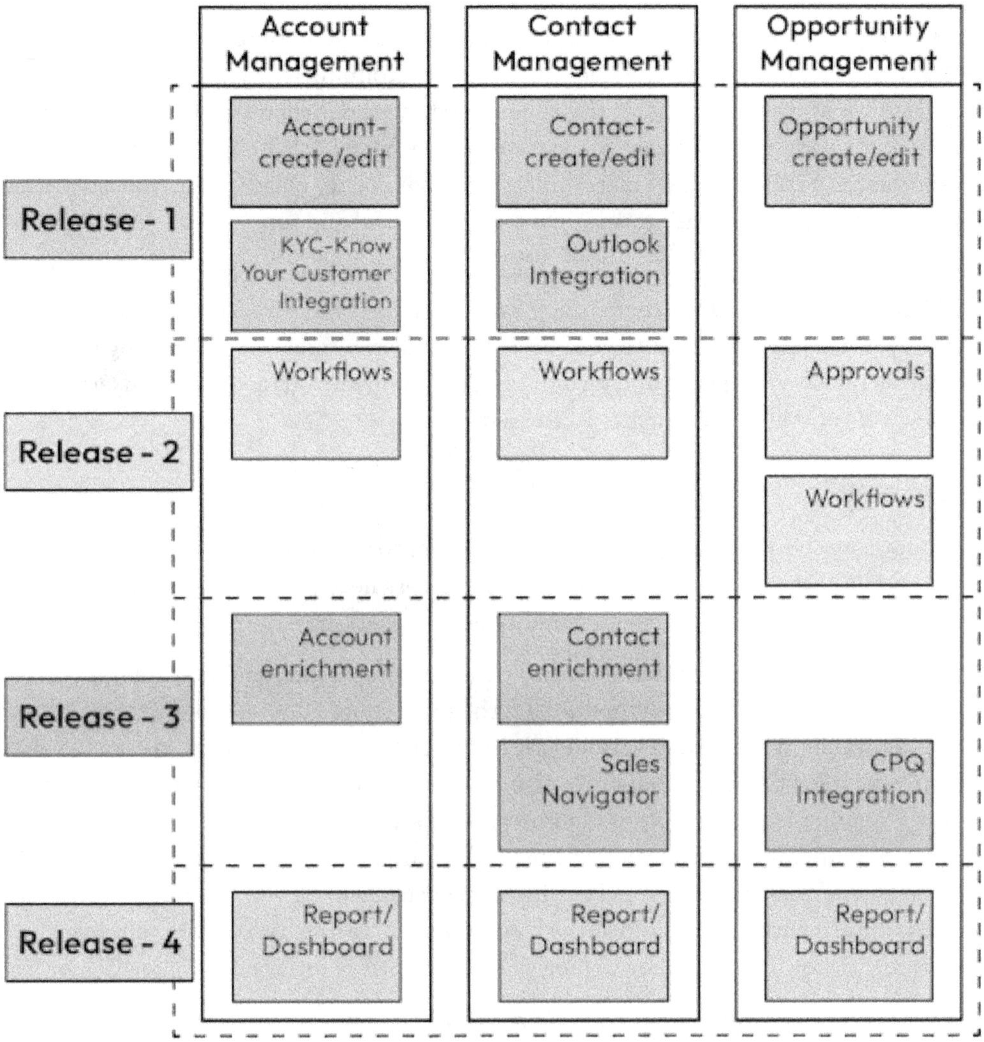

Figure 3.7 – Requirements roadmap

This analysis is specific to the project. Your priorities may be different from the ones we have, even though we both have similar Salesforce implementations. As a BA, you have the knowledge and experience of navigating your organization and getting requirement priorities that fit your requirements.

Business analysis and project management, in a true sense, go by strict rules and are very stringent on what is in scope and what is not. On paper, this is all well and good, but in real work, this is not the way it works. I have seen many requests prioritized as low, and these are requested by influential stakeholders and end users. 80% of these requests take only 20% of the time. Rather than wasting time on negotiations, I would go with reprioritizing and tagging this 80% with other higher-priority items. By logically grouping them, you save time during testing, training, and deployment. At the end of the day, we deliver more with a little bit more effort, but at the same time, we gain the trust of stakeholders. This helped me tremendously in my later projects, as these stakeholders understand that you do what is best, and since they trust you, the business analysis process gets more impactful and fun.

While some may argue that project managers are responsible for project roadmaps with input from all key players, I would say there is no harm in business analysts initiating and creating one. Later, you can hand this over to your project manager. By creating this during the prioritization phase, you are not only prioritizing requirements but also letting users know when they will get their requirements addressed.

Summary

In this chapter, we covered techniques that you can use to help you prioritize your requirements so that you can accurately capture business needs in the right order of priority, keeping the process transparent for all stakeholders.

You got a good idea of why requirement prioritization is important and how it helps you to identify the most important requirements that the team should address to fulfill the business need and add value. We looked at various prioritization techniques that can be used to enable the team in the prioritization process. We also showed you how to create a dependency roadmap of requirements to help you identify any gaps and opportunities to improve by adding new requirements or rearranging existing requirements. Finally, we learned about managing prioritization meetings and getting consensus, helping you manage conflicts, obtain consensus from all participants, and keep stakeholders up to date with the requirement priorities.

In the next chapter, we will cover process flow. We will review how to capture the current state of business and what the gaps and opportunities are, and then develop a process for the desired future state. We will also capture ways to automate processes so that users can have a great user experience.

Questions

1. What are conflicting requirements, and can we implement these requirements?
2. What are the advantages and disadvantages of the MoSCoW technique?
3. Why is requirement prioritization important?

Further reading

- *Requirements Management: A Practice Guide by PMI*: `https://www.pmi.org/pmbok-guide-standards/practice-guides/requirements-management`

Get this book's PDF version and more

Scan the QR code (or go to `packtpub.com/unlock`). Search for this book by name, confirm the edition, and then follow the steps on the page.

UNLOCK NOW

Note: Keep your invoice handy. Purchases made directly from Packt don't require an invoice.

4

Process Flows—As-Is Versus To-Be

In the previous chapter, we learned about the importance of prioritization, various prioritization techniques, mapping requirements dependencies, and finally, managing requirements prioritization meetings. We can successfully create a list of prioritized requirements that accurately reflect our business needs in the optimal order of priorities so that the most valuable needs are addressed first.

This chapter focuses on the journey from understanding current business processes to designing future, more efficient ones. You'll learn how to visually represent "as-is" flows to pinpoint weaknesses and then develop streamlined "to-be" flows, incorporating automation to improve information flow. Building upon this understanding of business needs, we will also learn to craft effective user stories and their corresponding, measurable acceptance criteria, ensuring that the envisioned "to-be" processes are translated into actionable development requirements. Finally, we will explore how business process value mapping can significantly contribute to user adoption.

You'll also learn how to craft user stories and acceptance criteria, ensuring that AI supports the BA in translating process improvements into actionable requirements.

In this chapter, we will cover the following topics:

- Reviewing the process flow
- Understanding and capturing the current state, "as-is"
- Proven techniques to capture the current state
- Identifying gaps and improvement/automation opportunities

- Developing the future state – "to-be"
- Business value mapping to improve overall process and user adoption

By the end of this chapter, you will have learned effective ways to capture process flows, starting with the current state, "as-is," and then morphing this into the future "to-be" state process flow while understanding various steps and their dependencies and sequence. You will be equipped with the knowledge, tools, and techniques through real-life practical examples so that you can adopt these practices while creating your process flows.

Reviewing the process flow

A process flow is a workflow diagram of all the tasks/steps and their interconnection in a visual format. Depicting various steps in a process visually will help all stakeholders get a common understanding of the needs and, hence, the requirements.

Defining process flows is iterative: you start from the elicitation phase with very high-level process flows and keep refining during the prioritization phase until they are socialized and agreed upon by the stakeholders, SMEs, and technical team members. This business process flow will capture enough details in business terminology so that it is a process flow that all stakeholders understand. During the design and development phase, these flows can be refined so that the technical team and testing team can understand them in greater depth. The first thing we must do when we develop a process flow is have the right set of stakeholders and SMEs with in-depth knowledge of their current process. We do not invite all stakeholders like in the elicitation phase. We can use any fancy tools to capture the process flow, but for now, let us stick with our good old whiteboard (or flip charts). This will help with excellent collaboration. Later, once it is finalized, you can take a picture of the finalized drawing and create the flow in the Visio tool or any other **Business Process Mapping** (**BPM**) tool of your choice. Documenting the final version of the process flow will serve as an excellent project artifact that will be helpful to current and future users. You can make this even more productive by exploring AI-enhanced diagramming tools that help you identify potential improvements based on flow patterns or simulate process changes to visualize their impact. For example, tools such as **Lucidchart** with Lucid AI provide intelligent suggestions as you build your process diagrams. To further automate your BPM efforts, process mining tools are becoming increasingly common for their ability to link directly to existing systems and automatically generate "as-is" process diagrams. A specialized example is **Elements for Salesforce**, which derives live processes into editable diagrams, ensuring that your documentation reflects actual system behavior and metadata rather than just manual theory.

Process flows help identify inconsistencies, repetitions, roundabouts, missing steps, bottlenecks, and so on that are involved in a process. A methodical analysis of the "as-is" process flow helps a Business Analyst with the opportunity to think analytically, creatively, and innovatively about what the business user needs so that they can develop an effective "to-be" future state.

There may be times when part of the project (or the entire project) may be put on hold after the analysis phases due to other priorities, or a specific process map may not be adding intended value to the project. This means that, as a Business Analyst, you did your job well and helped the management decide upfront and save resources that can be utilized on other tasks. Documenting and storing these artifacts will result in saving project time and resources when management decides to reinitiate the project scope at a future date. You can then use this artifact as a foundation to revalidate the process flows against any subsequent system changes, ensuring that your documentation accurately reflects current system behavior. It also helps existing users understand their process steps as well as the entire process flow.

Let us start with the current process—the "as-is" flow. If you have an existing flow, you can use that as your starting flow and develop it. However, if you do not have one, you can start from scratch. Do not worry about where to start. Start from somewhere, anywhere, and then keep adding steps. After you add a few boxes and the interconnections, when the workshop participants see the process coming to life visually, this will fuel creativity among the participants, and they will keep adding more details. Keep the momentum and excitement going. From here, your job is to ask the right questions and encourage the team to collaborate. Do not stop or question the flow of user thoughts and their kindled creativity. We are here to capture the essence of the business process, and who else would be better at this than the users who perform those tasks? Give all the credit to them; this will be a great motivator for them to bring out their tacit knowledge. In the first iteration, have them draw anything and everything they can think of. You have time to query and get clarifications in subsequent iterations. It will take a few iterations before it falls in line with what you want to see and makes sense.

A **process** is a sequence of activities. Each activity can be one or more tasks or steps. For simplicity, capture each task/step as a box and add lines with arrows to depict the interconnection between various steps.

Process flow types

Let us look at some of the important types of process flows that you can develop. Knowing about them and understanding their purpose will guide you in picking the right process flow type. Remember, we are not creating these process flows for documentation purposes; they go way beyond and help us achieve better user adoption. Our goal is to come up with a good process that your workshop participants understand and relate to:

- **Macro process map**: This provides understanding for the executive team and provides a management view of the process. This is very high-level and should not contain any technical jargon. Use business jargon such as your company-specific terms so that business users can relate it to their business.

- **Business process flows**: These are the "as-is" and "to-be" process flows and can be understood by the business stakeholders and the end users. Refrain from using technical jargon as much as possible and use business-specific jargon as much as possible.
- **Architectural process flow**: These process flows are complex and highly technical, and mostly cross-functional and integration-related. This helps the technical and enterprise architecture teams understand the flow from a technology perspective so that they can capture the non-functional and non-human interface needs and requirements.

Note

Standard Operating Procedures (SOPs) are not process flows. They are step-by-step instructions for the end users to perform operational tasks in a production system. You can use various process flows and other artifacts to develop SOPs, whose goal is to make the process clear, efficient, and effective.

Understanding and capturing the current state, as-is

To understand business needs, you need to understand how they are operated. What is the current process, regardless of whether you have it documented or not?

Let us start with a clean slate, assuming that we do not have any existing artifacts. Each user knows their tasks and the process related to the task very well, but they do not have the bigger picture—that is, how other users do their tasks or how all related tasks are interlinked.

So, where do we start? The process of documenting any process appears to be complex and confusing, and you may not know where to start. The simplest way is to get the right set of people and start drawing the process on a whiteboard or a flip chart. At this juncture, do not worry about what tool to use and what technique you need – just start drawing it. You need a few cycles before you can get a good process flow that is well understood and approved by all stakeholders.

In the first trial, you may not even go much further, but at least you will be able to lay out a simplified one from start to finish. Let all team members contribute to the flow. Capture any questions/queries/clarification/assumptions as your team collectively develops the flow. Make sure you keep a guardrail so that the discussion sticks to the intended agenda topic while resolving any conflicts that arise along the way.

Let us look at the following example flow. This is one of the functionalities we implemented as part of **Partner Relationship Management** (**PRM**) on the Salesforce Sales Cloud platform. Before the implementation, this registration process was performed using multiple legacy systems, including Excel, and many manual processes. To help you understand this, I have simplified this process and changed it:

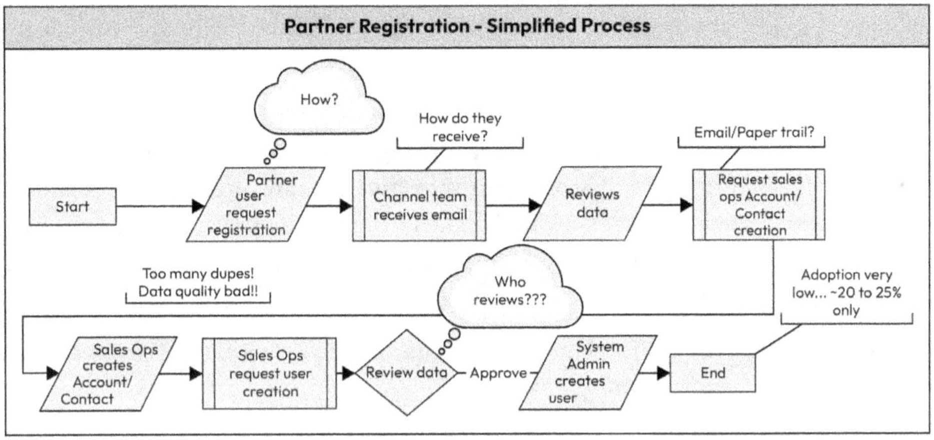

Figure 4.1 – Simplified process flow

This flow is for a partner user to request access and be able to get access to your system so that they can access the customers and related information:

1. Your partner (channel partner) requests registration to your PRM system so that they can access customer data and do so collaboratively with your sales team.
2. The channel team receives a registration request from partners via manual email or over the phone.
3. A review process is involved before you can proceed with this information. During the first iteration, we do not know what this is, but we capture it so that we do not lose track. In subsequent iterations, we will refine this and add more meaning to this step.
4. The next step is requesting sales operations to create Account and Contact records (we do not have any details on who informs Sales Ops or how they are notified).
5. Sales Ops created the data. Since this is a manual entry, and as we do not have any processes defined, this team often creates duplicates, which results in bad data quality.
6. Again, we have a review process, and none of us know who does what, as the process is not defined clearly. It takes too long for the process to complete, and this is a concern that was raised by almost all stakeholders, as it is the major cause for delays in the overall process time.

7. Since user creation is an admin's job, Sales Ops requests the admin to create a user and provide access to the account and related information, such as contacts, opportunities, cases, quotes, and so on.
8. The process ends after creating a partner user record.

We can take these steps and start drawing boxes/arrows. During these phases, do not worry about what shape of box or line you use. Let your imagination flow freely, and you can pretty much capture it in square boxes with some text and comments so that everyone participating understands them.

We also captured discussion items on this topic. During the first few cuts, let information and ideas flow. I have seen this process become more effective as more boxes and lines are added. Our users get excited when they see how their contribution impacts others, the process flow, and the business as a whole. This is like an "Aha!" moment for the users, where they see the complete picture for the very first time.

We will discuss how and why this technique helps us in many ways in the *Benefits of creating process flows* section.

You may be wondering when and how to start this activity. The answer is the sooner the better, and this is intertwined with all other activities. You take small steps and progressively build them with the help of various stakeholders and project team members. I usually start this activity during my elicitation phase, and progressively review and improve it during each phase. At this phase, we did not define who does what and the true dependencies. We merely captured all the business and functional tasks and sequenced them from start to finish. I usually do this during my workshop or conference room pilot sessions. At the end of the session, walk through the process from start to end, and along the way, capture comments. Use different colored boxes, lines, and text to add clarity and to make the process flow more interesting.

Later, after the meeting is over, as soon as possible, take some time and capture exactly what was documented by the team on one of the BPM tools (or you can neatly draw them on white paper). Reflect on the whole meeting and the notes you captured, and check for overlooked tasks or steps. I prefer to use Microsoft Visio since I've been using it for a long time and find it easy to use and very useful. You can save this as a PDF file and send it to all the participants so that they can review it and come prepared for the next iteration. I mentioned PDFs here so that the users cannot modify and make multiple versions where it is difficult to track. Assign one person who will be responsible for creating the process flows so that you can communicate changes based on suggestions to all participants.

I find it very useful to take a screen capture on my mobile device and send it to the participants. Since they are the ones who contributed and drew various steps, they feel proud and motivated to see their drawing. They tend to look at it more often and share it with their team.

> Note
>
> This process flow is conceptual. You get the concept of the process from end to end. Using this as a starting point during requirement activities will help you during elicitation, documentation, and prioritizing requirements. They are easy to draw and easy to visualize and follow through.

Current state swim lane process flow diagram

At this point, we are trying to capture how the end users use the system to perform their business tasks—that is, the existing end-to-end process flow. We are trying to find out what they do now in the present scenario, the essence of what they do, and why they do it that way. This can span boundaries, such as multiple systems and multiple cross-functional teams. We capture everything here, such as duplicates, redundancies, efficiencies, inefficiencies, automation, manual processes, gaps, opportunities, and so on. Remember, you do not have a say in the current process, and it is what it is. Collaboratively, we are trying to understand how it operates.

Now, let us refine this further. We will use the simplified process flow diagram we developed earlier as the starting point for our more refined process flow. My choice of preference is a **swim lane diagram flowchart** to document who does what in the process flow. You can have vertical or horizontal swim lanes, and you can pick whatever way works best for you and your team. If you do not prefer swim lanes, go with the simplified flow and keep refining it as you progress through the project phases:

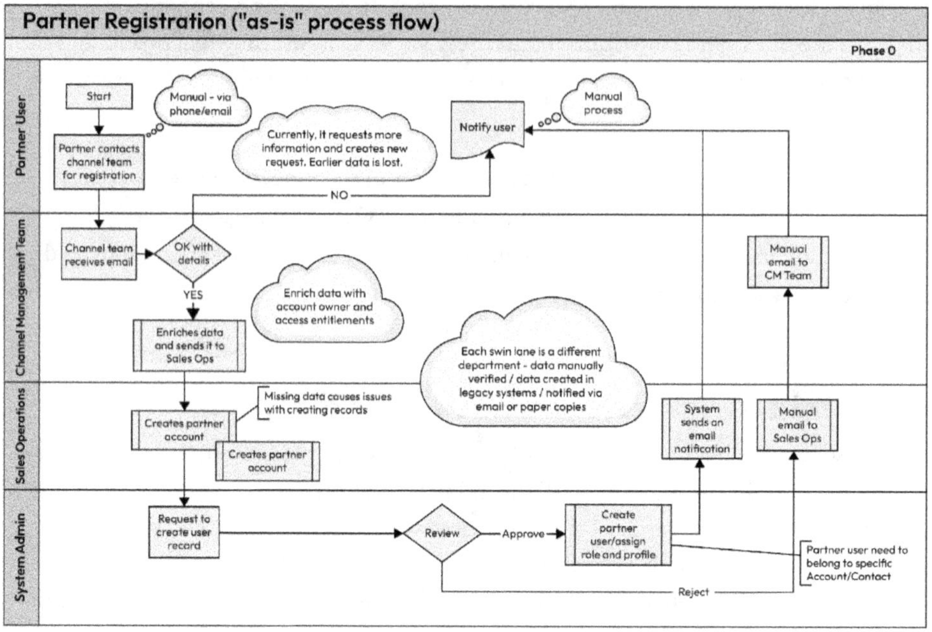

Figure 4.2 – Partner registration "as-is" process flow

In this diagram, we have a horizontal swim lane diagram. Each lane is tagged to a user role – the "who" part of it. For example, who does this task/step? The partner user requests registration and, at various steps, gets notifications/confirmations. We take our simplified flow and start stacking them in a sequence of tasks, as well as the user role, which is responsible for the activity. You cannot just jump from an earlier simplified process flow to this one in one swoop. It takes a few iterations and detailed reviews with stakeholders to come to this point. Our end goal is to capture every possible activity, how each respective role performs the activities, and the sequence of those activities from start to end. Socialize this flow with an extended team member and see whether they have the same understanding as the team that prepared it. Accurately understanding and capturing these process flow steps helps stakeholders and project team members understand and elicit requirements in greater detail, and then turn them into a robust solution that meets the expectations of the business.

Do not look for 100% perfection and accuracy. Resources are limited, so you cannot keep on refining forever. We stop at a point where everyone agrees on some assumptions and constraints. With the given and available resources and timeline, we can come up with a process flow. It can certainly be improved, but we stop here and don't move unless we see a major glitch in the flow. You will get the opportunity to refine this further in the next phase of the project.

Proven techniques to capture the current state

Understanding the current state helps us understand how things work now concerning existing opportunities and pain points, and helps us enhance and optimize processes for improved outcomes. We utilize this current state process flow and optimize it to create a future flow. Let us see what techniques we can use to create process flows.

There are many techniques, some of which were discussed in *Chapter 2, Elicitation and Document Requirements*. I use the following techniques when developing process flow with my stakeholders:

- Observation
- Interviews/focus groups
- Conference room pilots/requirements workshops

My preferred method is workshops/conference room pilots, where you invite knowledgeable stakeholders who know their current ways of doing their business and have a wider knowledge of the industry. Engaging the right stakeholders and getting well prepared for the sessions with an agenda and goals, commitments from stakeholders, and open and honest collaboration will make the workshops/conference room pilots very effective.

From these workshops, we can get very good start-to-finish process steps. You can supplement the process flow we've created so far by observing end users working through the steps in real life, and see whether those steps map to the developed process flow steps.

Also, for some complex to highly complex process steps, it will be beneficial for you to meet with experts in a focus group setting, where you can use your elicitation skills to understand the true need and essence of the process steps. The team may perceive certain steps to be redundant or duplicated, but the true essence is that those steps are required as a part of country-specific business requirements and regulatory or legal requirements. Not understanding these will affect the project adversely, as you will have missed a critical pre-existing business need.

As a Business Analyst, I found this sequencing very helpful:

1. Plan and schedule these sessions in such a way that you schedule them logically. This depends on how much time you have and the availability of your stakeholders.
2. I prefer to start and end with a workshop. This is where we invite all key stakeholders, and their validation and confirmation are key success factors.
3. In between the workshops, plan the focus groups and observation sessions. You need specific experts who are responsible for performing specific steps and who only know that territory.

4. The first session starts with the larger group of key stakeholders. Collectively, you all create the high-level process steps.
5. Study the process steps that you created with the stakeholder group, analyze and research, and come up with the right set of questions about items where you need clarification or a better understanding.
6. Take up these questions with the smaller groups or by actually watching end users perform their jobs.
7. Take plenty of notes and make sure you understand the process thoroughly.
8. Facilitate a final session with key stakeholders (our original first session group) and walk them through the process. Update the group as needed based on findings from the focus group/observation.
9. Finalize the current "as-is" process flow. After you finalize it, lock and publish this approved version to all project team members.

Your elicitation skills and collaboration with the right set of skilled stakeholders, coupled with these steps, will help add structure to capturing the current state process flow accurately.

Identifying gaps and improvement/automation opportunities

So far, we have created the current "as-is" process. We have a pretty good understanding of how things work. Now, let us see how we can identify bottlenecks and improvement opportunities in our existing process and refine the process flow.

Before we finalize the prioritization of this list of requirements, we have another iterative task of mapping them to the process flow steps that we created so far. Let us see how we can do this:

- Map each requirement to one or more of the activities from the "as-is" process flow.
- Sometimes, one requirement may map to more than one activity or set of tasks. For example, creating an account record generates an email to the owner of the record, as well as sends the data via a web service call to your backend KYC system.
- Not all requirements will map to the current process. This is expected as the new requirements mean new functionality that the business needs, and we need to add new boxes to the flow diagram.
- Some requirements require the addition of cross-functional connectors. For example, we want to send a quote on approval to the SAP system for contract generation. After

the contract is generated in SAP, we must update the Salesforce quote with the contract ID before we can close it.

- You may find duplicate steps on current process flows, which need to be deduplicated. Whether you add or remove a step, make sure you run through the whole process flow from start to finish so as not to break any functionality.
- If you outrun all your requirements and still have some activities on process flow, you need to revisit requirements gathering. This means you missed some obvious requirements.
- If you see dependent activities created by different teams on the process flow, this is the time to automate the specific activity. Automating helps keep the data clean and relevant. For example, when creating an opportunity from the Account record, let's say we would like to default the industry, sub-industry, owners' country, owners' region, and account type so that users can view these fields on the opportunity list view controls in Salesforce. List view controls let users choose fields only if they are on that object. Rather than users keying the same data from an account on to opportunity, we can easily automate it.

As you walk through the process flow, you'll notice multiple notifications and emails being sent to various user roles. This is a great opportunity to leverage AI-based process mining tools to uncover recurring bottlenecks or manual handoffs that are slowing things down. Tools such as **Celonis**, which offers AI-driven process mining, can help surface inefficiencies, deviations, and automation opportunities across your systems. As an example, Celonis can ingest Salesforce data, such as opportunities and cases, to help businesses identify inefficiencies, bottlenecks, and gaps, enabling them to optimize and improve existing processes (see the *Further reading* section for the link). This is a good opportunity for us to enhance the usability of this notification. For example, we can add a URL link to record the notification. By doing so, users can access records via email, where the URL will be provided, with a single click, without the need to search for the record.

You can find a multitude of considerations that can add value. Can we use web calls to update data in real time rather than batch jobs?

As we can see, there are many benefits to visually representing the process. By combining this with other tools and techniques, stakeholders can understand and contribute more openly and honestly. In the next section, we will learn how to use this knowledge to identify gaps and opportunities and come up with a future state "to-be" process flow.

Developing the future state—to-be

Previously, we took the "as-is" process flow and identified some gaps and a few areas of improvement. We can add those sets to the process flow to create a "to-be" future state. When developing a "to-be" process flow, you and your stakeholders should be very clear on what future state you want to develop. Is this for phase 1, the project, or the entire project roadmap? If the roadmap is too long, you need to evaluate it and see whether it makes sense to do so in digestible chunks. For example, you could create a future flow for phases 1 and 2. After these two phases have been implemented, based on users' feedback, you can start the next version of the process flow. This is especially true when you're implementing completely new business processes on a new software platform.

Remember to scope and think of usability and user experience. Better user experience translates into better usage and adoption, and this translates into greater value to the projects.

At each step in the process, think about some of the usability elements from the user's perspective:

- **Simplification**: How can we simplify this step in the process flow?
- **Automation**: Do we need the user to perform this step, or can we automate this task?
- **Intuitiveness**: Is the screen flow designed in such a way that the user can intuitively perform the tasks with ease? Does the process guide the user?
- **Accessibility**: Does the user get a complete picture of what they do? For example, do they have a 360-degree view of the customer page?

Future state swim lane process flow diagram

Some of the enhancements/improvements we can add based on prioritized requirements are as follows:

- We can add functionality for users to request registration from the company website rather than requesting via email.
- On submitting the web registration form, we can store the data in a custom object. This adds value if the partner has to submit more/corrected information or needs to resubmit the form with additional requested information.
- We can automate many workflow rules originating from the system.
- We can provide a confirmation ID to partners for future reference so that they can use this ID to obtain the status of their request.

- In case more data is required from the partner, we can provide a link in the workflow notification so that the partner user can update the existing registration web form and resubmit the data.
- We can use table functions that potentially go into future phases/releases. These are placeholders and help stakeholders and project team members think about what is on the horizon.
- To improve adoption and usability, we can highlight the auto-creation of user records based on the domain address and enable a **single sign-on (SSO)** feature.

Now, let us take a look at the future state "to-be" process flow after incorporating the necessary changes into the current state flow. A sample future flow with more streamlined and connected steps with automation is shown in the following diagram:

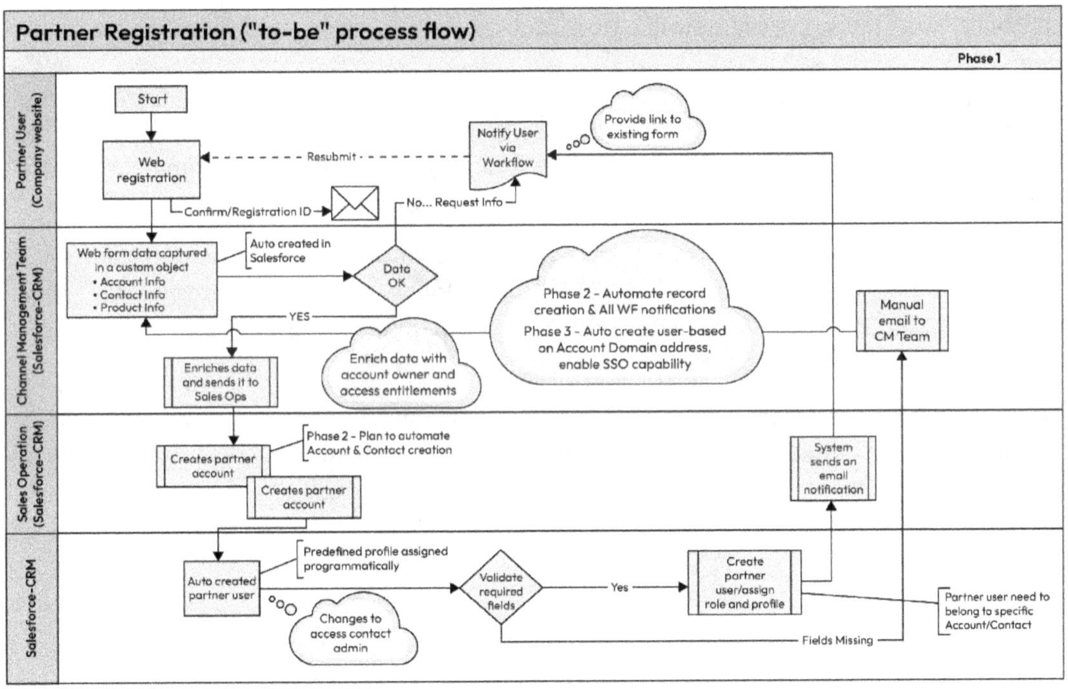

Figure 4.3 – Partner registration "to-be" process flow

If you look at *Figure 4.3*, in addition to implementing new features as defined in the project requirements, we can collaboratively enhance the future state by considering enhancements such as:

- Sending a confirmation email to the partner user
- Capturing web form details in a custom object, if it makes sense for data management

- Providing a link to a web form when additional information is needed, allowing the user to make updates directly
- Programmatically assigning predefined profiles
- Automating partner account and contact creation (as part of the next project phase)
- Exploring automation for user creation and enabling SSO capabilities (in a future phase)

This future state "to-be" process flow provides us with a smooth flow of steps from start to finish, with key prioritized requirements planned for phase 1 of the project roadmap. More functions and automation will be added in later phases of the project.

I used Visio to create the process flows in this chapter, as it's a tool I'm already comfortable with. While AI-generated visuals are still evolving and I'm continuing to explore their capabilities, the following example illustrates how AI can assist in creating visual process flows.

Sample process flow using Lucid AI

I started with a simple prompt: "Draw a process flow diagram for steps to automate the quote approval process in Salesforce with two levels (Sales Manager, VP) based on the discount %."

Lucid AI instantly generated a draft process flow. I then refined it further by adding another prompt: "Update the approval workflows to reflect the following discount thresholds: discounts under 10% are auto-approved; 10% or higher require Sales Manager approval; and 25% or higher require additional VP approval."

With just these two short prompts, the AI produced a working process flow within minutes. This can be used as a high-level draft that can be iteratively refined into a detailed, demo-ready flow. See *Figure 4.4*:

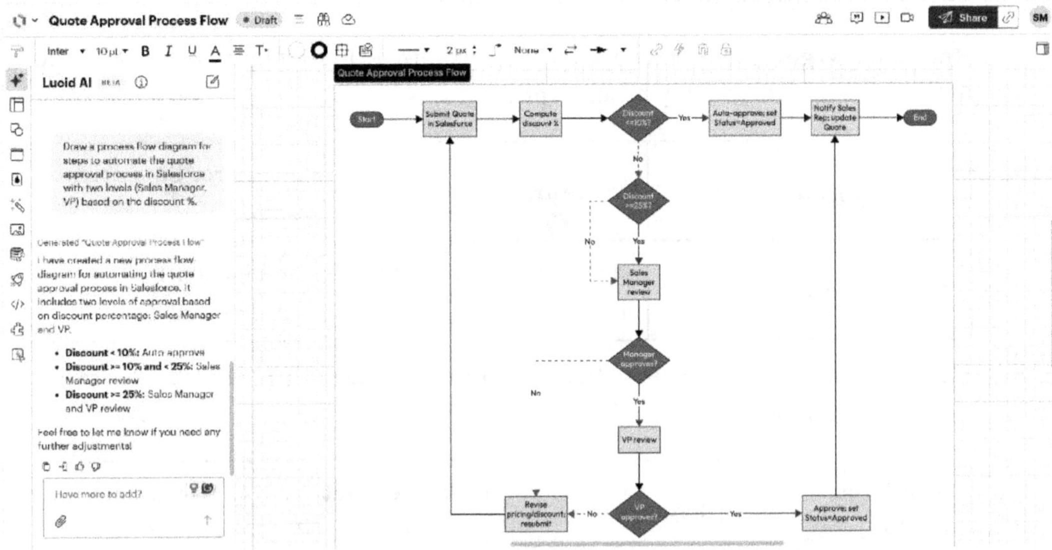

Figure 4.4 – Lucid AI-generated process flow using simple prompts

Now that we have a clear understanding of visual flows and their benefits, let's shift our focus to business value mapping—an essential step in connecting process improvements to measurable business outcomes.

Business value mapping to improve the overall process and user adoption

Business Value Mapping (**BVM**) is a strategic framework used to align business initiatives, processes, and technology investments, such as Salesforce, with the tangible value they deliver to the organization. It allows stakeholders to visualize how day-to-day activities and system capabilities contribute to key business objectives such as revenue growth, cost optimization, customer satisfaction, and competitive advantage.

Why BVM matters

Using BVM helps organizations do the following:

- Align Salesforce features with strategic business goals
- Track measurable KPIs such as revenue, cost, and operational efficiency
- Ensure stakeholder satisfaction and adoption
- Prove and communicate ROI to secure executive sponsorship

Let's look at the key components of BVM:

1. **Key business goals and value drivers**: To maximize ROI, start by clearly defining how Salesforce supports your top business priorities.

Business goal	Value driver	Salesforce CRM contribution
Increase revenue	Improve sales productivity	Automation, lead scoring, pipeline visibility

2. **Mapping Salesforce features to business outcomes**: Identify how each Salesforce module delivers specific capabilities that drive measurable business results.

Salesforce module	Key features	Business outcome	Measurable impact
Sales Cloud	Opportunity management, lead nurturing	Faster deal closure	20% increase in win rate

3. **Stakeholder value mapping**: Understand how each stakeholder group benefits from Salesforce. CRM systems create value across departments by addressing their unique challenges.

Stakeholder	Value delivered	Example
Sales team	Shorter sales cycles, reduced admin work	40% less manual data entry, more time for selling

4. **Quantifying business value (ROI calculation)**: To justify and sustain your Salesforce investment, translate outcomes into numbers:
    - **Revenue impact**: Higher win rates (e.g., 20% improvement through better pipeline visibility)
    - **Cost savings**: Less manual work (e.g., 30% reduction in admin tasks)
    - **Efficiency gains**: Faster access to insights (e.g., 80% improvement in reporting speed)

To quantify business value, we can use **Return on Investment** (**ROI**) as a clear metric. The following example shows us how to calculate ROI for a typical project scenario:

$$ROI = (Net\ ROI / Cost\ of\ investment) \times 100$$

This enables organizations to quantify efficiency, validate business cases, and drive sustainable growth.

Here is an example ROI calculation:

- **Investment**: $200K (licenses + implementation)
- **Annual gains**: $450K (revenue + cost savings)
- **ROI**: (450K – 200K) / 200K = 125%

You don't need complex tools to get started. For your BVM activities, leverage what's readily available—Salesforce dashboards and reports, Visio or Lucidchart, Jira, or even Excel/Google Sheets to capture and track value delivered.

Benefits of creating process flows

There are many benefits of creating process flows. Let us list some of the key benefits of a good process flow diagram:

- Users can understand the complete picture if it's represented visually in a logically sequenced step
- Since the steps are connected, we can identify interlinking between cross-functional tasks
- We can identify redundant tasks and eliminate them
- We can identify duplicate steps and fine-tune the process
- It helps us identify gaps and improvement opportunities
- It shows us areas for improvement by identifying bottlenecks in the process
- It serves as a document for new and existing team members to understand the process and their contribution to the process
- It provides artifacts for the technical team so that they can use them for solution design and technical development
- It provides artifacts for the testing team so that they can use them for developing test scripts and creating test scenarios
- These are made available in training manuals so that users get a visual of the end-to-end process
- The process flow can be used to aid requirement traceability

Here, I have listed a few process flow models that I often use and found to be very useful and effective. There are many other models available to capture process flows; it is best to use the one you are most comfortable with:

- **Business Process Model Notation (BPMN)**: This is used to model business processes and is more advanced than flowcharts. BPMN is a flowchart method that allows teams to graphically capture and document business process flows and provide a clear view of a specific process in sequential steps from start to finish. BPMN flows enable us to clarify communication between different project stakeholders and aid in business process improvements.
- **Flowcharts**: This is similar to BPMN but less restrictive in terms of notation. It is useful for less complex flows. A flowchart is a diagram that graphically represents a process in a sequence of steps and decision-making points. Using a flowchart, we can communicate complex processes in a clear, understandable format with our stakeholders, and also improve business processes.
- **Unified Modeling Language (UML) diagram**: This is used to model software systems, but can also be used for process modeling. UML is a general-purpose modeling language that defines a standard way to visualize the designed system. UML is useful for specifying, visualizing, developing, and documenting a software system. It is like a blueprint and is very useful for software developers during the design and development of software systems.

In short, process modeling helps us visualize how the system potentially works and provides a shared language for effective collaboration. With this understanding, let's now explore some practical tips that can help you apply these concepts successfully in real-world scenarios.

Practical tips for success

Let's look at a few practical pointers to strengthen your process flow activities. Drawn from real project experience, these tips can help you save time, reduce rework, and keep stakeholders meaningfully engaged.

- **Start simple, not perfect**: Don't worry about sophisticated tools or the "right" starting point. Begin anywhere—on a whiteboard or flip chart—and build step by step. Once participants see the process taking shape visually, creativity and collaboration naturally increase.
- **Encourage free-flowing ideas**: In the first iteration, invite stakeholders to share everything that comes to mind. Avoid interrupting or challenging initial inputs. There will be ample opportunity to validate, question, and refine in later rounds.

- **Involve the right experts**: While broad participation is useful during requirements elicitation, process mapping benefits most from individuals who perform the work daily. Practical, hands-on knowledge ensures accuracy and depth.
- **Capture the essence first**: Use business language that resonates with all stakeholders. Avoid technical jargon in early drafts. The technical refinement can happen later during design and development.
- **Use the "As-Is" to uncover gaps**: If certain requirements do not align with the current process, that's expected—those represent new capabilities. Conversely, if steps in the process lack corresponding requirements, you may have uncovered missing needs that require clarification.
- **Stop at "good enough"**: Avoid chasing perfection. Time and resources are finite. Once there is agreement on key assumptions, constraints, and major steps, move forward. Refine only when a significant issue emerges.
- **Maintain momentum with quick sharing**: Capture the whiteboard session—via screenshot or photo—and share it immediately. When stakeholders see their input reflected, they remain engaged and invested.
- **Control versioning**: Use a controlled and consistent method for sharing finalized flows to prevent multiple, untraceable versions. Whether you use PDFs or a centralized collaboration tool, ensure everyone reviews and updates the same approved source of truth.
- **Sequence sessions strategically**: Begin and conclude with larger workshops to align on high-level steps and validate outcomes. In between, conduct focused sessions or direct observations to analyze complex or specialized steps in detail.
- **Leverage AI thoughtfully**: Use AI-powered diagramming or process-mining tools to surface bottlenecks or generate initial drafts. Treat these outputs as accelerators—not replacements—for collaborative validation and refinement.

By applying these practical techniques, you not only streamline your process flow activities but also build stronger alignment, clarity, and stakeholder ownership. Let's now summarize the key takeaways from this discussion.

Summary

In this chapter, we started by learning how to develop the current state "as-is" process flow. We took help from key stakeholders and experts in their areas to develop a process flow in which everyone has a common understanding. We analyzed, elicited further, and identified gaps and opportunities. We took the list of prioritized requirements and mapped them to the current flow to derive the future state "to-be" process flow. In doing so, we identified opportunities to enhance the user experience by simplifying and automating processes.

Process flows are static diagrams, and they capture the essence of the business flow for a specific period. The "to-be" process flow we developed will be used as the current or "as-is" process flow for the next phase of the project. With good collaboration and by using the right tools and techniques as a Business Analyst, you will be able to create a great visual flow that helps stakeholders, end users, the technical team, and the testing team understand how the requirements are tied to the business process flows.

If you have never tried out process flows before, give them a try – you and your team will see immense benefits from all facets of the projects. As mentioned earlier, you do not need any fancy tools to get started. All you need is a whiteboard and a few colored markers – or even a few colored pens and paper.

In the next chapter, we will cover the steps and tools to document requirements in a **Business Requirements Document** (**BRD**). Here, we will cover both user and product requirements capturing. We will also outline the details that need to be captured so that the technical team and quality team can understand and use this as the main document for the next phase of solution design, development, and QA testing project activities.

Questions

1. Recollect a few benefits of the current state process flow.
2. Process flows are snapshots of a process for a specific duration. True or false?

Further reading

Essential Business Process Modeling by Michael Havey

Partner Relationship Management: `https://trailhead.salesforce.com/content/learn/modules/partner-relationship-management`

Get this book's PDF version and more

Scan the QR code (or go to `packtpub.com/unlock`). Search for this book by name, confirm the edition, and then follow the steps on the page.

UNLOCK NOW

Note: Keep your invoice handy. Purchases made directly from Packt don't require an invoice.

5

Business Requirements Document, User Stories, and Acceptance Criteria

In the previous chapter, we learned about process flow diagrams. We started by developing the current state process flow and then refined the process by analyzing and identifying gaps and improvement opportunities. By effectively collaborating and using the right techniques, we can develop a process for the desired future state.

This chapter will discuss how to document requirements in a **Business Requirements Document** (**BRD**). We will cover two types of business requirements—user and product. We will discuss functional requirements and non-functional requirements. We will review the level of detail to be captured in the BRD so that a business team, technical team, and quality team can understand the requirements in greater detail with a rationale so that they can address true needs during the solution design phase of a project. We will explore and see how to write effective user stories and corresponding acceptance criteria.

In this chapter, we will cover the following topics:

- Reviewing the need for business requirements documentation
- Understanding user requirements and use cases
- Exploring functional and non-functional requirements
- Learning what level of detail is sufficient
- Explaining a typical BRD and its key attributes
- Learning how to create effective user stories and acceptance criteria
- Practical tips for success

By the end of this chapter, you will understand the importance of documenting a good BRD. Along the way, you will explore different types of requirements, what they mean, and their relevance. You will get to know the key attributes of the requirements matrix and the structure of a BRD document.

Reviewing the need for business requirements documentation

A BRD is a very useful, beneficial, and valuable document for all project stakeholders, irrespective of the project methodology they use. When it comes to larger projects, we use a hybrid approach, where design and testing are done iteratively using the agile approach, whereas the rest of the phases fall under the waterfall model, with some level of iteration to get maximum value. The BRD details various aspects of the requirements so that you get the complete picture. If your project is 100% agile, you can skinny down the document and use only the requirements matrix document (covered in detail in the *Requirements matrix* section), which can serve as your product backlog. The BRD is your most important document for all your subsequent project deliverables. Your effort in documenting the BRD concisely, accurately, and clearly will help reduce issues manifold as the project progresses. For example, one incorrectly understood requirement can generate multiple defects during the testing phase or after post-production.

BRDs are used for recording business requirements relevant to your project implementation in a standardized format so that your business stakeholders and project, testing, training, and cross-functional teams can understand the business requirements very clearly without any ambiguity. The goal of the BRD is to document high-level business processes as they relate to detailed business requirements. First and foremost, the business stakeholder should be able to understand and agree to the requirements, and then we need to make sure of the following:

- The technical team gets enough details for them to start their solution design and technical development
- The QA team understands how to capture all possible scenarios for the test scripts
- The training team understands the documented requirements at a high level so that they can plan training activities
- The BRD can be used as a project artifact to support your project process
- The BRD can be used later in the project to create a requirements traceability matrix
- New stakeholders and project team members can get a complete idea about the functionality and scope of the requirements

I would like to stress that the right level of documentation is essential for future functionality extensions. Let's say you did a few quarterly releases of agile projects and completed your roadmap. The team is disbanded, and team members move to different departments or different companies. Down the line, after 2 years, you plan to enhance the functionality. In Salesforce, for example, you have to enable a new and improved lighting framework and other new features, functions, and enhancements. Documenting details in the BRD will help the new project team members quickly and easily understand the scope of functionality implemented so far, thus saving time and resources.

Now that we know the importance and benefits of documenting business requirements, let's take a look at user requirements and use cases. These two terms are often used in traditional project management methodology.

Understanding user requirements and use cases

A **user requirement** describes the requirements from a user's perspective. For example, what does the user need in simple non-technical terms?

In the past, traditional requirements used to place emphasis on the following:

- Capabilities, such as what a system can do
- Constraints, such as what a system cannot do (limitations)

These traditional requirements have evolved, and analysts started adding the "user" element to traditional requirements. This adds clarity to requirements by describing what a specific user role can do with a software system so that they can achieve their desired goals. For example, a sales analyst shall be able to create prospects or customers from the **Account Management** screen.

Use cases are users interfacing with a software system. These entail sets of steps between the user and the system. In a way, use cases are user requirements, but captured in more detail in the form of steps. Use cases state user needs and ways they can interact with the system to achieve an objective:

- **Who**: The user role (actor)
- **What**: What the user wants to do (action, which includes the steps and sequence to complete a task/process)
- **Why**: Why the user wants the desired goal (benefit)
- **How**: The system reaction (output, such as a success or failure message for the user input)

One effective way to capture a use case is by organizing it in a grid format, as shown in *Figure 5.1*.

Element	Description	Example
Who	*The user role or actor*	*Sales Analyst*
What	*The user's action*	*Submits a quote with additional discount for approval*
Why	*The user's goal or benefit*	*To get a quote discount approved and close the deal*
How	*System reaction or feedback*	*Sends quote to approvers and confirms submission*

Figure 5.1 – Use Case sample in grid format

We will discuss the use case steps before we document user requirements. Almost all the time, I observe stakeholders and project team members referring to user requirements as use cases. In this book, I will use user requirements and use cases interchangeably. In the end, we would like to capture the requirements that are easily understandable and digestible by all our stakeholders and project team members. At the same time, we try not to use technical jargon, systems, or solution details. On average, if your team captures requirements clearly and accurately, for the majority of projects, a Business Analyst should be able to confidently walk through an approved and finalized list at the rate of ~10 requirements per hour with your stakeholders or technical team members.

The next step after understanding use cases and user requirements is to get into more detail about what these user requirements are made of. The user wants to do something, and the system should let the user perform certain steps (actions you can observe) easily and reliably (non-observable). We will discuss this in the next section.

Exploring functional and non-functional requirements

High-level business requirements translate to more detailed user requirements, and these further evolve into system requirements. We can classify these system requirements into two main types, called functional and non-functional. Let's review some of them in detail.

Functional requirements

Functional requirements describe a specific set of capabilities that a system must provide to users. They define a system or capabilities. These are the actions that users would like to perform so that they can achieve the desired and expected business needs. Functional requirements can be stated and captured using various tools and techniques we covered in the previous chapters. With sufficient knowledge of a business area, underlying software, and business analysis skills, and collaboration with knowledgeable stakeholders/SMEs, you should be able to capture these requirements accurately.

Let's look at a small sample of the common functional requirements:

- **Business rules**: These are the main business drivers for your organization. For example, discounts on quotes for customers are based on customer type and the total dollar amount.
- **Authentication**: User authentication is required to access the system. For example, all users accessing Salesforce applications can access them via SSO on the company network or via VPN.
- **Audit tracking**: As per compliance, a company mandate is to track field-level changes, such as who created/changed something and when. For example, the compliance department would like to track changes to opportunity name, amounts, owner, and stage changes.
- **Security**: Who can see what and from where? For example, different users can access a system based on assigned roles, profiles, and whitelisted IP addresses during the 9 AM to 5 PM user time zone.
- **Interfaces with internal and external systems**: No business runs on one system. On average, there is some kind of interfacing with around 6 to 10 systems. For example, in the financial service industry, a Salesforce CRM system can integrate with KYC (Know Your Customer is a verification process used by financial institutions to confirm a client's identity and assess the potential risks) systems, risk rating systems, Splunk, business objects, data warehouses, CPQ systems, SAP systems, and HR systems. Some complex implementations may have way more integrations.
- **Reports and dashboards**: You can add these as default functional requirements to all your implementations. You need tons of them. In the earlier days, we used to gather requirements for reports and dashboards, and the technical team or system analyst used to enable this for users as part of the project release. Now, we empower our users to create their reports. We provide training and guidance as needed. Still, we need to capture this as a requirement, as the technical team needs to make sure that all fields

are available during reports and dashboard creation. For example, in Salesforce, we need to make sure relevant fields are added to custom report classes so that users creating reports have access to those fields. Best practice is to establish a core suite of validated dashboards and reports to serve as the "single source of truth." By verifying these for accuracy, we ensure that both strategic and operational decisions are powered by the same trusted data.

Non-functional requirements

Non-functional requirements describe characteristics or quality attributes. These requirements are not obvious and need experience in the underlying technology to be able to capture them. Collaboration and involving technical team members, such as technical leads, software developers, and solutions architects, can help in identifying and defining these requirements. Understanding functional needs accurately helps the team unearth hidden non-functional needs. Non-functional needs are extremely important for better user adoption and system usability. For example, a simplified **User Experience** (**UX**) does not mean removing some functions but rather keeping more features and automating steps for a user. This means your project team's goal is to hide all the complexities behind the scenes and implement a solution that is intuitive, quick to learn, and easy to use. This can be accomplished only if we can identify possible non-functional requirements. For every requirement, make sure to think through non-functional features associated with each functional requirement.

Let me give you a practical example so you can get a better idea. During one of my first Salesforce CRM releases a very long time ago, the functional requirement stated, "Sales analyst shall be able to create customer record from account screen." It looked pretty straightforward to implement. When our technical team started unit testing, we observed that the account page stretched over four long pages on a regular desktop screen. Added to this, we had multiple validation rules that caused a lot of frustration, as we were unable to save the record unless all those fields were filled accurately. Even after filling in so many fields, the screen used to time out, and all the data had to be rekeyed. Fortunately, our team learned from this and identified a few more functional and non-functional requirements where we could default values, automate processes, and limit fields for users to input. Imagine what could have happened if we had implemented this solution for end users. The lesson we learned was to always think about actions from a user's perspective and see how we can enable simplified technological solutions and help them focus on business, not on how technology works.

Let's look at a small sample of common non-functional requirements:

- **Usability**: Is the functionality easy and intuitive to use from a user's perspective— for example, simplified screen navigation, guided screen flow, and being able to access from any browser/device?

- **Reliability**: The user should be able to trust the reliability of the system. For example, the user should be able to successfully save data and retrieve it later easily without any data loss.
- **Performance**: The user should experience good performance all the time. For example, screen refresh should not take more than a few milliseconds every time. It should be instantaneous, and they should not have to wait.
- **Scalability**: Being able to scale an application—for example, adding more users or data without performance degradation. With a Salesforce CRM cloud application, this is never an issue, as the SaaS provider takes care of this.
- **Availability**: Availability of a system to users other than those scheduled and planned upgrades or maintenance activities.
- **Maintainability**: How easy it is to maintain an application after implementation – for example, can our existing production support team maintain bug fixes, and do they have the necessary training, skills, and access to project artifacts to understand user problems?
- **Data management**: Enable encryption for data at REST and in transit, periodic password recycling, and vaulting of non-human accounts, such as APIs, web service calls, and integration accounts.

We have covered only some of the system requirements to give you a general idea, and you may have many more that may apply to your project implementation. Now, let's explore and see the level of detail that needs to be captured for each of our requirements.

Learning what level of detail is sufficient

Requirements should be captured with sufficient detail in simple language, with business terminology, as much as possible, so that stakeholders, SMEs, and other business users can relate them to their everyday work. As well as its own culture, each organization has its own business language and acronym usage. This is the language you can see everyone using effortlessly, and it is very specific to your organization. Creating a document in its users' terminology will chime with their thinking process and understanding. You can use business terms and elaborate on the requirements a little bit so that others can understand too. Do not make it too detailed and too lengthy; otherwise, no one will read it.

To see what level of detail is sufficient, the first thing you should do is business analysis, and the project team should get conversant with business jargon. Unless you know these terms well, you can never understand a business user, let alone their needs. Make a glossary of all the business terms and socialize with the project team. Business stakeholders assume you are aware of these terms, and they continue to talk in that language whether you understand it or not, so be prepared.

You can capture requirements and details in tools approved by your organization. One of the tools I prefer to use is Jira. In this section, rather than discussing a specialized tool, let's go with Excel spreadsheets. We will document all our prioritized requirements in an Excel spreadsheet. You can call it a requirements matrix, product backlog, or list of approved requirements. It is essentially a list of all your approved prioritized list requirements. I prefer to call this a requirements matrix, and we capture each requirement with the following attributes in an Excel spreadsheet, later attaching this sheet to our BRD. Please make sure that you document the BRD with enough details, even if you use agile methodology. No matter what people say, proper documentation matters, and this BRD is our opportunity to do so. This is the first important document/artifact that other teams and subsequent project phases utilize to bring life to a requirement. This is your business requirements blueprint.

Requirements matrix (prioritized product backlog)

Before we get to the BRD document, let's take a look at individual requirement attributes in a requirements matrix (or prioritized product backlog):

- **BRD ID (unique ID)**: One good approach I have seen people use is grouping requirements by functionality or module. For example, account management starts with Account001, opportunity management with Oppty001, contact management with Contact0001, and so on. This way, team members will immediately know what module a requirement belongs to, as well as how many requirements there are in each module.
- **Purpose**: The objective of a requirement.
- **Summary**: A requirement summary in simple terms.
- **Normal flow**: The most optimistic flow. This is what the user does to achieve their goal when no issues are encountered – a happy path.
- **Alternative flow**: If the user encounters issues, provide steps for them to take a different flow.
- **Exception flow**: In the event of an error, this will be the system response.
- **Business rule**: Capture business rules associated with a requirement. For example, a close date on an opportunity cannot be in the future, or to be able to close a deal successfully, a KYC process has to be approved for a customer account.
- **User actions**: The steps the users perform – for example, logging in to Salesforce, accessing the **Contact management** tab, clicking on **Create new records**, entering all the required fields, and successfully saving the record.

- **System response**: The system displays a human-understandable success, error, or information message – for example, contact "Mr. Srini Munagavalasa" successfully created.
- **Category**: Identify the requirement importance using your method of choice – MoSCoW, priority, or complexity.
- **Phase of project**: Whether a release is in its first phase, the second phase, and so on.
- **Documented date**: The date when a requirement is added to a matrix.
- **In/out scope**: Your prioritized list usually consists of approved in-scope items; in some cases, due to technical limitations or resource constraints, you can defer a few requirements to future releases. Here, you can tag the deferred ones as out of scope.
- **Comments**: Add any comments or details that add clarity to your requirement.

These are some of the key fields; you can add other fields as per your requirements matrix. These documents should be detailed enough but not too detailed. After completing it, read it assuming someone else prepared it, and see how you feel. Get it peer-reviewed and ask for at least a few suggestions to improve the matrix. Reviews provide you with an opportunity to improve the requirement matrix and help you get it as accurate as possible before you publish it to a broader group of users.

If the technical team and training team members often consult you for clarification of the documented requirements from the requirements matrix, it means you did not capture the requirements clearly. Take time to revise and review them. If not, you will waste time clarifying these requirements to different teams again and again.

Explaining a typical business requirement document and its key attributes

In this section, we will look into the main sections of BRDs. I have outlined simplified documents that give an overall picture of the business requirements relevant to your project. If you do not have your project-specific standard templates, feel free to start with the one discussed here, keep adding sections as needed, and create a standard document for your projects.

The typical components of a BRD are as follows. If your organization is mature, you may have your own **Project Management Office** (**PMO**) and **Center of Excellence** (**COE**). This document is highly requested and may be mandated as part of your project documentation and for business requirements approval. Moreover, it has a higher purpose and serves as a starting point for the next phase of project activities, such as your solution design and functional design.

To give you a general idea of what constitutes a BRD, let's look at some of the following sections. Understanding various sections and their purpose will help you document your BRD accurately:

- **Introduction:**

  Project overview: A brief business background for this project.

  Objectives: What is expected from this project/release roadmap.

  Challenges: The current challenges impacting the business. List inefficiencies and major pinpoints.

  Project team members: Everyone who will be directly or indirectly impacted by changes:

  - Stakeholders
  - SMEs
  - Super-users
  - Technical/training/DevOps team members

- **Project scope:**

  In scope: Document core functions at a high level – for example, account management, opportunity management, campaign management, D&B Hoovers AppExchangetool integration, Salesforce DupeBlocker, and so on.

  Out of scope: Highlight items out of scope for a specific release. They can be in scope for a future release. For example, quote/contract management, mobile capabilities, and Data REST encryptions are not in scope.

  Assumptions: Specify your assumptions. For example, all end users are on Windows 10 and use either an Edge or Google Chrome browser.

  Constraints: List limits or restrictions. For example, failing to onboard a solution architect on schedule will directly delay critical system integrations and impact the overall delivery timeline.

  Issues/risks: Things that may adversely impact a project – for example, low stakeholder engagement or requirements changing all the time.

  Project roadmap: Insert your roadmap for the projects. What functions are going in which release?

  Current state analysis: Add your "as-is" process flow. Highlight the pain points and constraints in the current way of doing things.

- **Proposed/desired future state requirements:**

Future state flow: Add your "to-be" process flow. Briefly explain your future state flow so that users get an idea of what they can expect.

List of all requirements (business level): Refer to the requirements matrix. In addition to attaching, add a few lines of each of the following items. Some key high-level stakeholders may not have time to go through your requirements matrix. This provides them with key items that are being addressed as part of your release/project. Do not copy everything from the matrix here; just add a few of the most important items only:

Functional requirements: For example, account management with a 360-degree view of the customer, opportunity management with pipeline reporting and sales forecasting, or campaign management with HubSpot integration.

Non-functional requirements: For example, a user shall be able to see all search results in less than 1 second, or a report refresh should not time out.

Regulatory and compliance requirements: For example, a user should not be able to edit or delete closed-won opportunities.

Reports and dashboards: Document summarized reporting and dashboard requirements – for example, a pipeline report by industry verticals, a matrix report of all opportunities by business unit and stage, or a partner management dynamic dashboard.

Interfaces: Document a one-liner description of the interface in simple terms for business stakeholders to understand – for example, account integration with D&B Hoovers for data enrichment.

- **Data requirements:**

  List data conversions in scope and the respective templates to collect data from legacy systems. (Attach files here – one file per data load with instructions and a few rows of sample data.) The data migration process involves **extracting, transforming, and loading** (**ETL**) legacy data. This is one of the most critical project activities, which can jeopardize your whole project if not done accurately. During the functional design stage, we will capture more details on how to migrate master and transactional data in a usable format.

  Reports and dashboards: A sample mocked-up format of reports. Attach a sample of legacy reports and dashboards so that you have a minimum baseline of what a business needs and try to improve upon it as much as possible. Also, utilize out-of-the-box Salesforce features such as scheduling reports and dashboards for groups of users.

Training requirements: Training widely varies based on the project. If it is a completely new implementation, functionality-wise and software system-wise, then you need to spend extensive time planning, preparing, and facilitating training and creating training artifacts:

Scope of training: The number of users to be trained, time zones, training material requirements, meeting tools (such as Zoom, WebEx, and Teams), recorded training, and so on. We must also incorporate a "Train the Trainer" model to build a core group of internal experts, ensuring the organization can sustain knowledge transfer and support users independently after the project's conclusion.

Knowledge articles: Details about the functionality usage instruction for end users with screenshots.

Cheat sheets: These are also called quick reference one-pagers.

Stakeholder RACI matrix: List a **Responsible, Accountable, Consulted, and Informed** (**RACI**) assignment matrix so that project team members know who needs to be contacted and communicated with.

Service-Level Agreement (**SLA**): An SLA defines how a service shall be provided post going live. If you have a separate production support team, you need to work with them on how SLAs are addressed. Defining and planning for an SLA from the start helps set expectations with end users. Also, make sure you have reporting metrics created to measure an SLA by week/month/quarter.

Glossary of terms: Capture all your company, business, and project team lingo. All acronyms should be captured here, including the most obvious ones.

Appendix: All artifacts related to business requirements are to be captured here. If you are using a document management system, refer to the document via the link from here rather than attaching documents.

Revision history/version management: Like any good document, capture who did what, when, and why here. Versioning helps team members easily identify and understand changes.

We have identified all key sections in a typical BRD, as needed, and tailored it by adding or removing parts of it to suit your initiatives. You may have to spend a good amount of time when you create a BRD for the first time. For subsequent releases on your project roadmap and other related projects, you can reuse most of the content from this BRD. Almost 75% of the content can be reused as is. Investing time now will save time for your project team in the long run.

Now let's take a look at how to simplify business requirements into user stories, making them easy for every team member to understand.

Learning to create effective user stories and acceptance criteria

User stories help teams understand and capture product requirements from the customer's point of view. They explain business needs in simple language that everyone can understand, improving clarity, collaboration, and efficiency. This makes them useful for both Agile and traditional project teams.

Key components of a user story

A great user story follows the **INVEST** principle:

- **Independent**: The story should be self-contained with no dependencies on other stories
- **Negotiable**: The details are open for discussion and not overly rigid
- **Valuable**: The story delivers real, tangible value to the user
- **Estimable**: It's clear enough that the team can estimate its size and effort
- **Small**: The story can be completed within a single sprint
- **Testable**: It has clear criteria for knowing when it's "done"

User story template (the 3 C's framework)

The 3C Framework—comprising the Card, Conversation, and Confirmation—serves as the foundational standard for creating effective User Stories in Agile development. This model shifts the focus from rigid documentation to collaboration by defining the what, the how, and the done of a feature. It begins with a physical Card to capture the "what" (the essence of the user's need), transitions into a continuous Conversation to determine the "how" (the technical details and edge cases), and concludes with Confirmation to establish the "done" (the specific Acceptance Criteria that verify success).

A user story is typically written in a simple sentence format:

"As a [**role**], I want [**feature**] so that [**benefit**]."

Example: *As a Sales Rep, I want to update the Opportunity Stage with reasons for changes so that I can track deal progression.*

Writing strong acceptance criteria

Acceptance criteria define what "done" looks like for a user story. A clear way to write them is using the **Given-When-Then** format:

- **Given** [the context]
- **When** [an action is performed]
- **Then** [a specific outcome occurs]

Example:

- **Given** an Opportunity is open in Salesforce,
- **When** I change the Stage (e.g., from "Proposal" to "Closed Lost"),
- **Then** a required "Loss Reason" picklist field appears, and I must select a value before saving.

This format provides a clear, testable scenario for the development and testing teams.

Let's review a few best practices so that you can be effective in your BRD creation.

Practical tips for success

Listed here are a few tips that are specifically useful during requirements documentation:

- **Collaboration**: You need to work with the technical lead, architects, lead developer, QA lead, and training team members to prepare this document. Their input is very much needed to capture various attributes, such as alternative flow and system response. This collaborative team will help to identify business context-related missed requirements. You need to adopt an iterative approach and need tight collaboration so that the team members are comfortable with what is documented. They are the main consumers of this document. Once the document is finalized and agreed upon by this team, socialize the final version with key stakeholders, walk them through it line by line, and get agreement and approval.
- **Visual artifacts**: Utilize any flow charts and screen mockups created during prior phases while documenting the BRD. This will help to keep the team focused on detailing each requirement. By visualizing requirements early, we confirm with stakeholders that their needs are accurately captured before passing them to the development team, minimizing rework and ensuring alignment.
- **Use simple language**: Use simple and complete sentences that all stakeholders, including the business users, are able to understand. Be generous and use business terms and acronyms as much as possible so that users can relate them to their daily business.

- **Documenting**: Invest time in structuring the document logically and clearly, and ensure it is peer-reviewed by SMEs. You and your team will refer to this artifact many times during your project roadmap. After baselining the document for your release, lock the document to prevent any further edits by team members.
- **User stories**: Write your user stories from the user's perspective, using simple, non-technical language that everyone can understand. Collaborate with developers, testers, and stakeholders to refine these stories, ensuring they capture a complete picture that is clear to every team member, including the end user.

You can make a BRD readable, engaging, and valuable if you can identify and collaborate with the right set of users, use the right visual artifacts, structure document flow logically, and use simple business language.

Summary

In this chapter, we reviewed various elements and components that are important for writing a good BRD. A BRD is a living document, and you learned how to complete the document with stakeholders and project team members iteratively to a point where it is clear and understood by all players. When you reach this stage, you take a baseline and version it. This version shall be your requirement scope for the release. Any changes requested from this point onward need to be compared to the baseline and need approval from the change control board before the BRD can be updated and versioned again. These new updated BRD versions will go through the same process.

You have now gained insight into and tips for what is needed for you to create a BRD that accurately describes the requirements that your stakeholders and project team members can understand.

In the next chapter, we will cover the solution design aspects of system requirements. We will cover aspects where a designed solution is maintainable and scalable. We will also cover data-related requirements – the volume of data, legacy data, and data transformations. We take all these requirements, agree on a solution, and document all the steps with process flow in a functional document.

Questions

1. What are the main requirements that you capture in business requirements documents?
2. Why are transition requirements important? Can you think of a few examples?
3. Can you think of a few good examples where you can derive non-functional requirements with minimal effort?

Further reading

Use case: Wikipedia:

Get this book's PDF version and more

Scan the QR code (or go to `packtpub.com/unlock`). Search for this book by name, confirm the edition, and then follow the steps on the page.

UNLOCK NOW

Note: Keep your invoice handy. Purchases made directly from Packt don't require an invoice.

Part 2

Design, Development, and Testing—Turning Vision into Reality

With a prioritized roadmap in place, this part moves into the solution design, development, and validation phases, where ideas are transformed into working Salesforce solutions through iterative cycles. You will learn how to use prototyping, mock-ups, and wireframes to visualize solution concepts early, allowing stakeholders to engage with the solution from the outset rather than encountering it for the first time at the end of development. AI-assisted insights are introduced as accelerators to help refine designs, surface patterns, and reduce rework across iterations.

This part includes the following chapters:

- *Chapter 6, Solution Design and Functional Documents*
- *Chapter 7, Navigating Declarative versus Programmatic Salesforce Solutions*
- *Chapter 8, Demonstrating Functionality Using Prototypes*
- *Chapter 9, Exploring Conference Room Pilots*
- *Chapter 10, Technical and Quality Testing*
- *Chapter 11, Requirements Traceability Matrix*

6

Solution Design and Functional Documents

This chapter will cover different ways to identify functional and non-functional requirements using process flows during the solution design phase of the project. We will cover aspects where the designed solution is flexible, maintainable, and scalable. We will also cover data-related requirements such as the volume of data, legacy data, and data transformations. We will take all these aspects of the solution and document all the steps within a process flow in the functional document.

In this chapter, we will cover the following topics:

- Understanding solution design
- Identifying functional requirements
- Identifying non-functional requirements
- Reviewing data conversion requirements
- Understanding the functional requirements matrix
- Developing the function document
- Practical tips for success

By the end of this chapter, you will have gained firsthand experience with solution design aspects and in elaborating functional and non-functional requirements. You will also have learned how to effectively analyze and enhance process flows and be able to identify and finish documenting the functional design document.

Additionally, AI-powered analysis can now assist in assessing scalability risks, detecting requirement inconsistencies, and optimizing data structuring, ensuring long-term efficiency.

By complementing traditional methods, AI-driven insights enhance both the precision and adaptability of the solution design.

Understanding solution design

In the previous chapter, we successfully documented the business requirements in our **business requirements document** (**BRD**) using business-understandable and system-agnostic terminology. Solution design enables us to dissect high-level business requirements. In this section, we are going to refine them and deconstruct them into more granular details in the form of functional and non-functional requirements. These detailed requirements are documented in the solution design document, which is also called a **functional design document** (**FDD**) or a **functional specification document** (**FSD**).

The following steps define the hierarchy of the flow of requirements:

1. We start with a prioritized list of business (stakeholder) requirements.
2. We further slice the requirements and add a little bit more clarity and details, and capture the requirements in a BRD. The approved BRD will contain our baseline requirements that have been approved and agreed upon by the stakeholders and project team members.
3. The next step is for us to add more granularity to the requirements to make sure we define requirements that the software system can fulfill. This is done via architectural design to define conceptual feasibility and then solution design to define feasible requirements.
4. Solution design requirements are documented in FD/FDD/FSD in technical terms so that the technical team can use this document to create a usable solution encompassing functional features and other system-related features. This allows the user to reliably and efficiently use the software features and functions.

There are two levels of solution design processes:

- High-level design, also called the solution architecture design process
- Low-level design, also called the component-level design process

The **solution architecture design process** is also known as a high-level solution design and provides potential and alternative solutions. This is when we decide which technology to utilize; for example, what type of middleware do we use for our interfaces? Is it on-premises or in the cloud?

We arrange all the functions in a logical sequence so that we can trace the process from start to finish. This process is iterative, and the decomposition continues until we reach a stage where the solution has been analyzed, understood, defined, and agreed upon. At this point, the system is architecturally defined with all the potential requirements identified, which are verifiable, feasible, and consistent. We do our best within the constraints and project timelines, run this through a few iterations, and freeze the version and baseline. There may be a few open-ended functions that are not on the critical path, which can be added as assumptions and need to be determined soon.

> Note
>
> Always develop multiple conceptual flows; we need at least two alternative paths. This needs to be done at the same time we create the primary flow. We always need to do a *what-if* for every step in the flow. Each path should achieve the desired goal or objective.

The **component-level design process** is also known as **low-level solution design**. The high-level BRD requirements are logically decomposed into the lowest-level functions. Each function is then analyzed for technical feasibility and technical aspects of the requirements, such as availability, performance, and reliability, to achieve an optimal solution. We use a logical decomposition process to improve our understanding of our technical requirements and their dependencies and relationships.

Solution design always starts with the conceptual flow that we created during the requirements gathering phase. We take this conceptual diagram and elaborate on it, along with the BRD requirements. During the initial iteration of solution design, we include and collaborate with the architects – the enterprise and solution domain, business analysts, technical leads, lead developers, and SMEs. We can use many tools to visualize and elaborate the conceptual flows into more granular steps in technical terms. During this phase, we consider the technology that will be used while developing the solution design. An experienced domain expert will be able to identify most of the non-functional requirements and confirm or clarify the feasibility of the functional steps in the flow diagrams. We will discuss this in more depth by covering real-world scenarios. There, we will identify the hidden functional and non-functional requirements.

> Note
>
> There is no such thing as a perfect solution. With constraints on time, resources, and technology, the best we can do is come up with an optimal solution. Based on the complexity and criticality, we can use process flows and prototype techniques to gain more understanding and keep refining the solution design until we reach an optimal solution. This optimal solution approach has to be agreed upon and approved by key stakeholders. During development, design thinking helps us evaluate our development work, fine-tune the solutions, and make them even more optimal and ready for implementation by our technical team. It is critical to recognize that an "optimal

> solution" is a point-in-time decision based on current knowledge. As technology evolves or project requirements shift, what is optimal today may change tomorrow. Consequently, we must document the rationale behind key design decisions. This captures the "why" behind our choices, providing future teams with the necessary context to build upon or rework the solution effectively.

During the solution design phase, we identify functional and non-functional process flow steps. In the next section, I will walk you through a simplified, practical, real-life process flow and discuss how to identify new process steps.

Identifying functional requirements

We reviewed functional requirements at a high level in the previous chapter. We analyze these requirements from a technical perspective during the solution design phase and capture hidden and elusive requirements. These requirements are functional but not obvious to business users, without which we cannot enable the desired functionality effectively—for example, reducing redundant steps by automating certain processes.

Let's take a look at a realistic scenario. I have simplified very complex scenarios for the sake of clarity and understanding.

In terms of the BRD requirements, the following are the key ones; they are interdependent:

- Users shall be able to create customer records and be able to see products entitled by the customer based on the customer attributes, industry, segmentation, and route to market
- Users shall be able to adjust entitled products by adding or removing certain products from the customer record
- Users shall be able to create opportunities and see all entitled products that have been added to the opportunity record from the customer record

The process flow is for opportunity product alignment, but we have to review these three business requirements as they are interdependent. If we don't align the products to the account record accurately, automatically adding products to the opportunity is not possible.

Take a look at the following diagram:

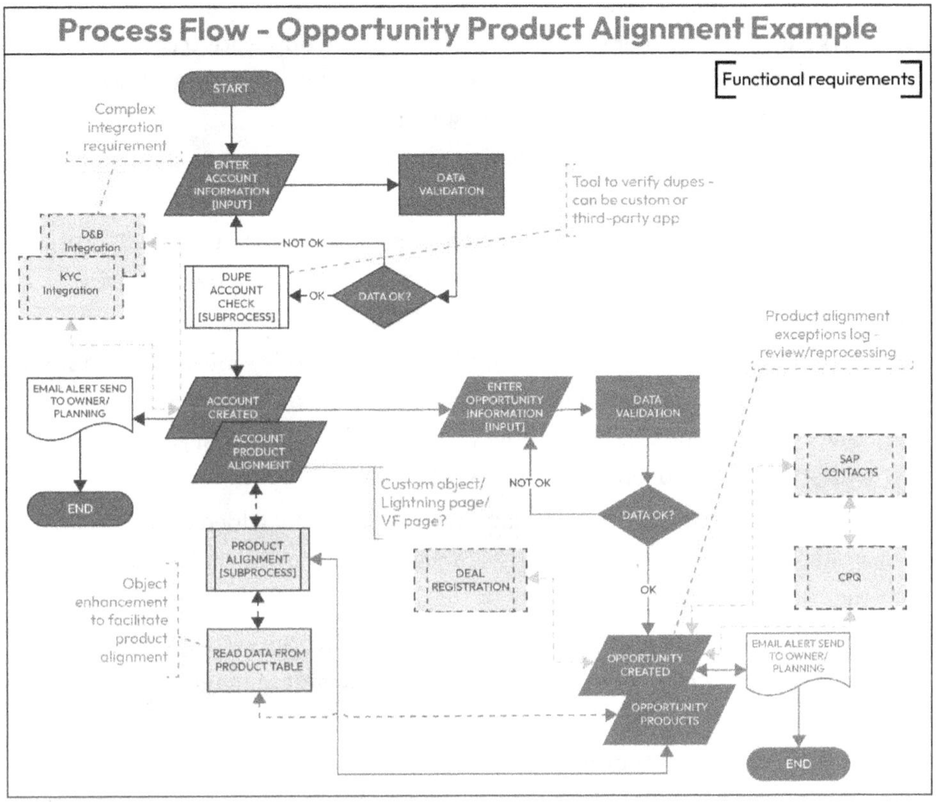

Figure 6.1 – Process flow – opportunity-product alignment example (functional)

The process starts with a user (Sales Manager) creating an account record. We will try to keep the flow charts system-agnostic. Since we already know that our software system is Salesforce, I used Salesforce-specific terminology so that we can identify system-specific requirements.

Let's walk through the process flow from start to finish:

1. The user enters the necessary account information and saves the records. Then, the user inputs all the required fields and other optional fields as needed. A good practice is to input as many fields as possible, since this helps other users have a complete understanding of the record.
2. The system validates the data input values. Here, we verify the business rules using validation rules and prompt users with appropriate user-friendly messages.
3. Any validation errors that occur will prompt the user to correct the data input; for example, the KYC number should be 10 characters for US users and 12 characters for UK users.

4. If the data check is good, the system triggers a dupe blocker check and flags if the record is a duplicate. For example, if the user inputs a duplicate account name, the system lists the duplicate value so that the user can navigate to the existing record and continue with the next step—that is, opportunity creation.
5. After creating the account, the product alignment sub-process kicks in and queries data from the product object. Products are added according to the business logic based on the customer attributes, industry, segmentation, and route to market. The product alignment process is another complex flow on its own, and in our scenario, we assume that we can align the products without any issues.
6. On successful account record creation, a flow email alert is sent to the account owner and the planning team stating that the account record has been successfully created (another business rule). Based on how you configure workflows, you will be able to generate an automated notification with a link to the account record.
7. The user verifies that the products have been successfully added to the Account object. The product alignment object is a custom page or screen and lets the user manage multiple products on a single screen.
8. The next step is to create an opportunity record and let the system auto-create opportunity products. In this case, the user (the Account Manager or the Deal team member) creates an opportunity record.
9. The user inputs the relevant required and optional fields and saves the record. On saving, the system validates it. If no issues are found, it creates the opportunity record.
10. On saving, the system reads the product alignment from the Account object and creates opportunity product line items. There can be one or more opportunity product records based on the product alignment on the Account record.
11. Users shall be able to verify and, as needed, delete or add other products. Note that opportunity products shall be created automatically on new opportunities. Existing opportunities shall not be impacted during updates to the opportunity record.
12. A formatted email alert is sent to the opportunity owner and the planning team with opportunity details and opportunity URL links.
13. The opportunity creation process ends. To simplify this process, I excluded steps such as opportunity edit, delete, and other exception steps on purpose.
14. Other integrations are possible, such as D&B, KYC, CPQ, SAP, and Deal Registration. I added them as dotted boxes to give you a general idea of how complex this can get.

It takes about three iterations to create and agree on this process flow. We refine each iteration based on the feedback. The more the team collaboratively discusses the flow steps in detail, the better we are able to identify the gaps and missed steps.

Imagine what would happen if you had just one session with a key player and you, as a business analyst, presented this and got an agreement without getting any feedback. What if, at each step, the flow breaks after you deploy this to production? Without accurate process flows and the ability to understand every stated and unstated requirement, can this be fixed by the support team after the project team has been disbanded? I will leave this to your imagination.

Now, let's take this through a few more iterations and collaborative workshops/CRPs with our key team members. We must question each step and see where it can go wrong and how we can make it better.

- How do we de-dupe? Can custom code fulfil this requirement? Or, can we use any available third-party tool? Who will be ultimately responsible for the data?
- Where do we capture the product alignment data? Can the user view and manage all the products on a simple screen? Do we need to account for additional development work?
- When products are added as opportunity products based on alignment, what if a record fails? How does the user fix the data? Do they add it manually, or is there a way to capture the data and reprocess it automatically?
- To be able to convert account records from qualifying a lead to converting them into a customer record, customer KYC has to be completed, and a KYC ID needs to be assigned to the KYC system. To enable this, do we need to build an interface or a web service call for the Salesforce system?
- Have alternative flows or options (including manual processes) been defined?

I am sure that if you review the process flow carefully, you will certainly find a few more requirements. Take a look and see if you can find two or three more. We try our best to identify all possible steps within the project's allotted time and available resources.

> Note
>
> Our goal is to identify all technical requirements to fulfill the business needs. How and when we implement them will come during the project roadmap. They can be staggered in releases; all core functions with some level of manual workaround should start within the first release, and we must keep automating as we progress through future releases. We must lay out the end-to-end workflow so that users can get from point A to point B in the best possible way.

Next, let's review the same process flow and see if we can find any gaps regarding non-functional requirements.

Identifying non-functional requirements

Non-functional requirements specify the quality attributes of the underlying system. They are not easy to capture and are not always obvious. Many of the non-functional requirements come to light only during the testing phase, especially during regression, load, or stress testing. The objective of these requirements is to enable the sustained availability, reliability, and performance of the software. They help you ensure a good user experience and ease of system usage.

Take a look at the following diagram:

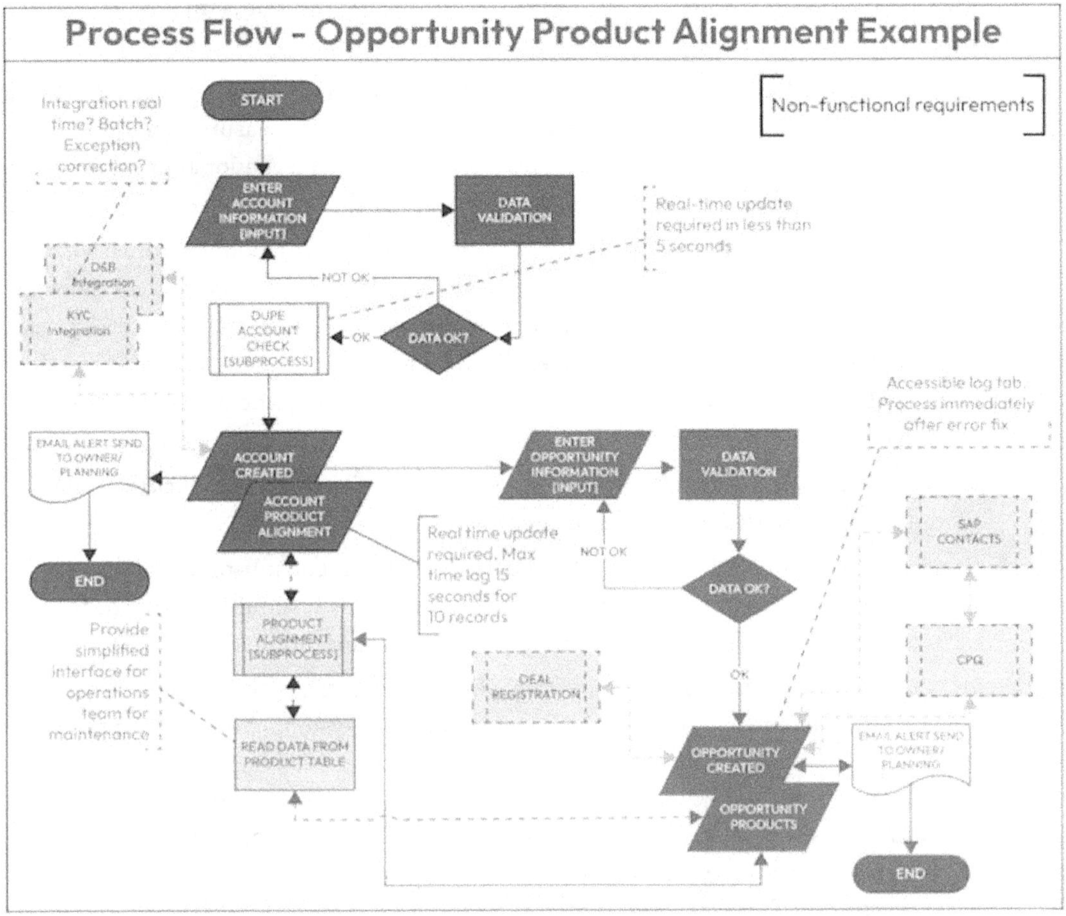

Figure 6.2 – Process flow – opportunity-product alignment example (non-functional)

It gets easier to identify non-functional requirements if you draw out a flow chart and analyze it from start to end. At each step, we must analyze the non-functional aspects of every step in the flow for performance (the response time during peak usage), reliability (whether it's reliable on mobile devices), availability (whether the system is available 99.9% of the time), and so on. Detailed collaborative sessions with multiple iterations will yield a good set of all possible non-functional requirements. Let's list a few here:

- What type of integration do we build with the KYC system (and integration with other systems such as CPQ and SAP)? Do we need it in real time, or can it be a batch job? In this case, it may make more sense to have a batch job as the KYC process takes more time since the customer needs to be vetted and approved by multiple parties. In other instances, such as sending data to SAP contacts or the CPQ system, it makes sense to have a real-time call.

- For the Account dupe check, this should be done in real time, and it needs to happen instantly. Since every requirement needs to have quantifiable measurements, let's say we need the check to be done in 5 seconds. How about using a vendor app? If so, can the vendor app perform the check quicker than in 5 seconds?
- How many product alignment records can be associated with Account records? There will be performance issues if there are too many records and usability issues if there are too many products (the user has to scroll through multiple pages, which may be a bigger issue on mobile devices). We need to capture this requirement and quantify the measure. Let's say that the system shall render 10 product alignment records in 15 seconds.
- We need to capture a way for the operations team to maintain the product table with product alignment attributes from the Account record.
- Upon creating the opportunity, what if the product alignment sub-process fails to create one or more product opportunities? What mechanism should we provide for users to reprocess? The same may be the case with account product alignment.

Hopefully, you can find a few more requirements if you review the flow again. Some of these non-functional requirements may vary based on what software system you implement. Also, some of them may not be obvious from a BRD or process flow perspective. For example, let's say that we are doing a global implementation – do we need translations? Should we enable multi-currency? This will be a significant amount of work as screen fields, reports, flows, and so on need to be translated to the user's locale-specific language.

Here, you can see how easy it is for us to capture these invisible requirements by exposing them on a simple process flow chart. Also, these flows are easy to understand for the team members and help them collaborate better. Start small with a conceptual flow and keep building it iteratively. If you plan and facilitate a few sessions well with the right set of participants, I am sure your team will be able to reflect the business process and create optimized flow charts.

We can summarize both the functional and non-functional requirements in a single flow, as shown in *Figure 6.3*. Some team members like them to be separate, as it is easy for them to understand functional versus non-functional requirements separately. Other team members prefer to add them to a single view. Pick the one that best suits you and your team.

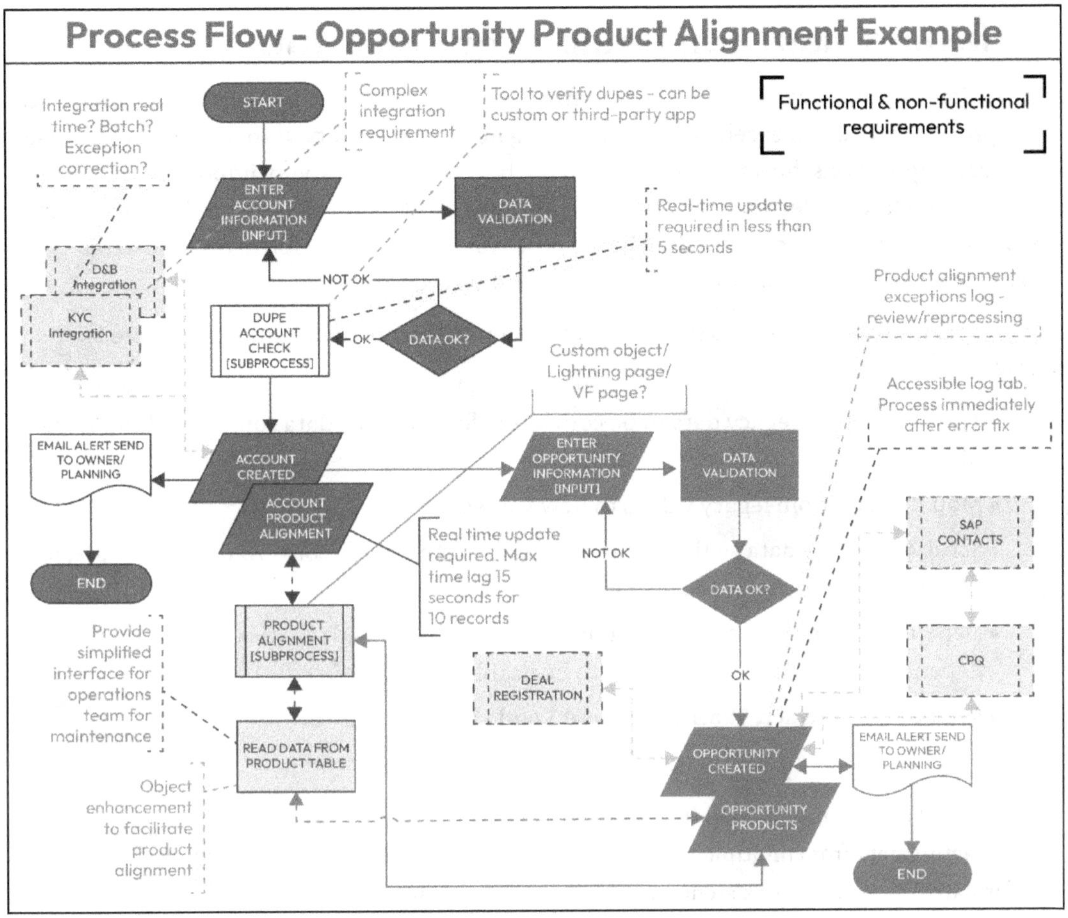

Figure 6.3 – Process flow: opportunity product alignment example (functional and non-functional)

With the aid of process flows, we can capture functional and non-functional process steps. Process-wise, the flow works well when the user creates new transactions (records). Does the functionality work with legacy data without any issues? This is seldom true, and we need to consider migrating existing data from legacy systems. These requirements are not obvious in a process flow, so we need to make sure that we capture these requirements. Let's review them.

Reviewing data conversion requirements

Another important set of overlooked requirements is data conversion requirements. I have seen many projects that do an excellent job of enabling new functionality with a great-looking user interface, automations, flows, reports, and so on, but they miss one very important requirement related to legacy data. Users can only use great features and functions if they can easily access their existing legacy data in the new system in a usable format. These data requirements fall under functional and non-functional requirements.

Some key tasks that you need to think through when capturing data requirements are as follows:

- The scope of the legacy data to be converted; for example, data sources, volumes, and historical data.
- Map the data from legacy values to new values.
- Scrub the legacy data so that it can be extracted before it's converted; for example, for dedupe, completeness, and accuracy purposes.
- Dependencies between different tables/objects. Data needs to stick to the same dependencies in the target system to be usable.
- Define your **Extract, Transform, and Load** (**ETL**) processes.

> Note
>
> Extract, Transform, and Load (ETL) is a data integration process that involves extracting data from multiple sources, transforming it through data mapping and formatting to ensure consistency, and then loading it into a target system.

Now, it's time for us to document what we have identified so far. We will document these newly identified requirements in a functional requirements matrix.

Understanding the functional requirements matrix

The functional requirements matrix captures more granular details and elaborated functional decomposition requirements. For each BRD requirement, we will add more granularity, which may result in multiple functional requirements for each BRD requirement. We take the business requirement matrix and add additional columns to capture the checklist fields for other teams – for example, for the development team to check for requirement completeness, feasibility, and so on, and for the testing team to check for requirement clarity, testability, and so on. One important column that sits next to the BRD summary is the FD summary. It spells out the description in more detail so that the development and testing teams can get more clarity and details about the requirement. Feel free to use technical jargon so that the team developing the functionality is more comfortable. You do not need to make this functional requirement matrix too complex. Reuse the BRD and add a few more fields as appropriate for your project releases. For better clarity, add functional requirements to one tab and non-functional requirements to the next tab. This will add more clarity for developers and testers. If you prefer, you can combine both into one Excel sheet.

> Note
>
> Every requirement in the functional requirement matrix should reference at least one business requirement. Also, every business requirement should map to at least one functional requirement. If not, make sure you identify the redundant (a requirement in FDM but not in BRD) or gaps/missed (a requirement in BRD but not in FDM) functional requirements.

Developing the function document

By collaboratively reviewing and developing the process flow charts, we were able to take each BRD requirement and further subdivide them into one or more functional and non-functional requirements. Each BRD item can be split into multiple functional and non-functional requirements, which the developers can use to build and unit test the subsystem or component. Generative AI tools, such as Copilot, ChatGPT, or Grok, can streamline the creation and review of functional specifications. They can summarize lengthy stakeholder meetings, draft detailed UI field descriptions, and identify potential implementation gaps by cross-referencing requirements with known system constraints. However, human oversight is essential to ensure accuracy and alignment with project-specific needs.

Let's take a look at the functional specification document (or functional design document). A typical functional design document (FDD) includes the following key sections that define the system's functionality, structure, and design approach:

- **Introduction**: Provide a brief introduction of the project: Outline its purpose and core functionality, the business needs and objectives it addresses, the business units or countries impacted, any related or dependent projects, key stakeholders and project team members, and the relevant user roles and profiles.
- **Project approach**: A project management approach defines your team's mindset on how to run the projects. It depends on project characteristics such as size, scope, and team dynamics. Based on the needs of your software project, you may have to pick the right approach. It can be a traditional waterfall (plan-based) approach, incremental (adaptive), or a mix of both.**Methodology**: Project methodologies such as waterfall, agile, hybrid, or any other methodology mandated by your PMO.
- **Conventions and standards**: Project and Center of Excellence standards.
- **Assumptions**: List all assumptions. For example, you can explicitly state the software system you plan to use. As an example, you can have Salesforce as the core CRM system, D&B Hoover for data enrichment, CPQ for pricing and quoting, and so on.
- **Constraints**: What are the constraints that may impact the project? This can include the budget, aggressive timelines, technical resource availability, conflicting projects, and integrations.
- **System landscape**: Briefly describe the new systems and their main features. It will be very helpful if the system's architectural diagram is added here.**System impacted**: What systems are potentially impacted due to this release or project roadmap? Examples include SAP-OTC, CPQ, and KYC.
- **System diagram**: Add the system diagrams that we created earlier, including the current flow, future state flow, and process flows.
- **Business workflow**: List all the workflows that exist, as well as the new ones that have been planned as a part of this release. For example, you could add a workflow that auto-creates products on an account based on product alignment.
- **Schemas/data flow diagram (DFD)/ERD**: Insert the schemas/DFDs that capture how the data flows so that the developer and tester can understand them clearly and plan and execute their development work:
    - Objects
    - Data field attributes
    - Data dictionary

    - Relationships
    - And more
    - Functional and non-functional requirements:
        - Functional requirements matrix (expanded BRD matrix)
        - UI layout
- **Reporting requirements**: List all the reporting requirements, including the ones that need to be migrated from the legacy system (if any). This is to ensure that the specific fields that are created are accessible during reporting.
- **Interface requirements**: List all the interface requirements; for example, whether they are real-time or batch. If a batch process is being used, then what will the frequency be, and what will the data volume be (full volume or only the delta changes)?
- **Standards**: Standards used during the development phase, such as naming conventions, coding formats (including commenting code and code coverage), and reporting formats.
- **Disaster recovery plan**: List the disaster recovery plan and steps to be taken in case a system outage occurs. What will the business continuity plan be in terms of roles, responsibilities, and communication procedures? The plan should include data loss scenarios; if data loss occurs, then what is the plan to recover the data?
- **Appendix**: Add any relevant documents that help the technical team, such as your BRD, any conceptual flows, business presentations with key stakeholders, business plan, and so on. Add them as links or attachments.
- **Acronyms and abbreviations**: Company and technology-specific acronyms that are used in this document.

This is a comprehensive list of key sections in functional documents. As needed, add other relevant sections that you think add value to your implementation. Similar to BRD, you review this with technical and testing leads and SMEs, get agreement and approval from all, and lock this document. You should share this document with business SMEs and stakeholders so that they can review and provide input. However, their approval may be optional. This baseline version is your starting document for subsequent releases on your roadmap. AI-driven requirement traceability tools maintain reliable links between BRD and FDD artifacts by automatically identifying unmapped requirements, suggesting matches, and generating traceability reports. This reduces manual tracking effort and enhances auditability.

Leverage AI assistance with solution design and functional documents.

AI can assist with solution design and functional documents in several ways. With many tools available in the market—and more emerging constantly—here are some key ways you can benefit from using them:

- **Automating documentation drafts**: AI can generate initial drafts of FDDs or solution design documents based on requirements, use cases, or system specifications, saving time and ensuring consistency. Tools such as ChatGPT, Copilot for Word, and Writer.com are particularly helpful.
- **Requirement traceability**: AI can link business requirements to functional specifications, flag gaps, and suggest mappings to ensure nothing is missed. Tools such as Jama Connect, Helix RM, and ReqView provide significant value in this area.
- **Process flow and diagram generation**: AI tools can transform textual descriptions into flowcharts, wireframes, or UML diagrams, offering clear visual representations of system processes. Lucidchart AI and Miro AI are especially useful here.
- **Validation and consistency checks**: AI can review documents for missing details, inconsistent terminology, or conflicts across requirements and design artifacts, helping maintain accuracy and completeness. Grammarly is my preferred tool for this.
- **Collaboration and review assistance**: AI can summarize changes, highlight key points, and provide recommendations to improve readability and stakeholder review efficiency. Notion AI is a powerful option in this space.

Overall, leveraging AI in these areas reduces manual effort, streamlines documentation, improves accuracy, and accelerates the handoff from design to development.

Practical tips for success

The following are a few tips that are specifically useful during solution design and functional documentation:

- Document the complete business process from end to end by function. For example, let's say you have three functions – account management, campaign management, and quote management. Here, you should use three end-to-end process flows.
- Capture all the steps, manual or automated. Remember, process flows are system agnostic, and not all steps can be automated in one release. A manual process in one release can be an automated process in a future release.

- Create process flows with input from key team members. Incorporate feedback, finalize the flow, and get agreement from this core team. All members should be on board with the overall solution design before actual development work is started.
- The functional document is the main point-of-reference document for the technical and testing teams. Make sure enough details are captured, if possible, in technical terms.
- The functional document should address the **user interface** (**UI**) and usability of the application for better user adoption. As needed, it will be beneficial to mock up the screen's navigation, look, and feel.
- Address scalability requirements. If the data volumes are going to grow exponentially, the technical team needs to consider this during technical development. Also discuss legacy data migrations, volumes, and retention policies.
- Another important aspect to consider is the performance of custom code or complex components on the page layout. For example, the product alignment page displays all the products on one page on the account record.
- It's important to assess how effectively a system handles and logs exceptions or errors. This includes whether errors are captured accurately, meaningful messages are provided to users or administrators, and detailed logs are maintained for troubleshooting and auditing purposes. Proper exception handling ensures system reliability, transparency, and easier issue resolution.
- Plan the security aspects from the start. This includes a user's access based on location, time zone, IP restrictions, MFA, encryption, and so on.

Doing functional document peer reviews before getting it signed off helps make it a complete document. Experts with knowledge in that area can provide valuable feedback, help iron out any open issues, and provide more clarity on how to document the requirements.

Explore AI-based design assistance tools that can transform wireframes or conceptual diagrams into prototype mock-ups, offering a visual and interactive preview for stakeholders before development begins. Tools such as Figma, Adobe XD, and Uizard use AI-assisted features to convert wireframes or diagrams into interactive prototypes, enabling stakeholders to visualize and provide feedback early in the design process. This promotes early feedback and reduces rework later in the cycle.

Now that we've covered some practical tips for success, let's summarize this chapter.

Summary

As projects grow in size and complexity, we need to make sure that we plan and allocate time and budget for the solution architecture and solution design aspects during the design phase of the project. We can identify all the solution components and subcomponents by decomposing high-level functional requirements.

In this chapter, we learned about solution design tasks, where we perform architectural design to identify all the steps in the process conceptually. Then, we learned about the functional and non-functional requirements with the help of process flows. Using this new knowledge of process flows, we captured the requirements in the functional requirement matrix. In the end, we reviewed a typical functional document and reviewed various important sections of the design document so that technical and testing teams can understand and use this as a baseline document for the next stage of the project.

Throughout the solution design process, the strategic use of AI tools—be it for requirement gathering, data mapping, testing simulation, or documentation support—can dramatically reduce oversight and improve quality. These tools act not as replacements for human judgment, but as accelerators for insight, iteration, and clarity.

In the next chapter, we will cover how to mock up quick, semi-working solutions that we can demonstrate to stakeholders and team members and get early feedback on. We will also discuss the benefits of prototyping, conducting, and capturing the prototype by collaborating with the right stakeholders and team members.

Questions

1. State a few benefits of the functional document for your technical and testing teams.
2. What are the three main artifacts you might find useful during the solution design phase of your project?
3. List three key participants whose input you need to involve during the solution design phase.

Further reading

- *Salesforce Architect's Handbook: A Comprehensive End-to-End Solutions Guide*, by Dipanker Jyoti and James A. Hutcherson
- *Becoming a Salesforce Certified Technical Architect: Prepare for the review board by practicing example-led architectural strategies and best practices*, by Tameem Bahri

Get this book's PDF version and more

Scan the QR code (or go to `packtpub.com/unlock`). Search for this book by name, confirm the edition, and then follow the steps on the page.

UNLOCK NOW

Note: Keep your invoice handy. Purchases made directly from Packt don't require an invoice.

7

Navigating Declarative versus Programmatic Salesforce Solutions

In the previous chapter, we explored solution design, requirements analysis, and process flows, including how AI can streamline documentation and improve accuracy.

This chapter covers fundamental building blocks essential for Salesforce project teams. Salesforce development has undergone significant shifts in recent years, transitioning from code-first practices to predominantly low-code and no-code approaches. Today, over 70% of Salesforce solutions are built using declarative tools, reflecting a growing emphasis on speed, accessibility, and collaboration. This shift empowers Business Analysts, administrators, and super users to handle most development tasks, but requires understanding the full implications of these tools.

Salesforce's power lies in its dual nature: robust declarative tools alongside comprehensive programmatic capabilities. This flexibility enables solutions from simple automation to complex custom applications. Understanding when to use each approach is crucial for development speed, maintenance costs, scalability, and project success. With AI accelerating configuration and code generation, knowing when to use clicks versus code is more vital than ever.

This chapter explores declarative versus programmatic solutions, guiding you on when to leverage each approach effectively.

We will cover the following topics:

- Understanding declarative Salesforce development

- Exploring programmatic Salesforce development
- When to choose declarative versus programmatic solutions
- Scenarios and examples
- The power of hybrid solutions
- Practical tips for success

Let's dive into each of these topics at some level of granularity so that you get the gist of it to make an informed decision on what development route best adds value for your projects.

Understanding declarative Salesforce development

Declarative development in Salesforce refers to building functionality *using clicks, not code.* It's often described as "no-code" or "low-code" because it allows users—typically Salesforce administrators or Business Analysts—to configure and customize the platform without writing a single line of programming. This approach leverages Salesforce's built-in tools, making it accessible to a broader range of users and enabling rapid development.

What is declarative development?

At its heart, **declarative development** means configuring Salesforce to meet business needs using its intuitive **graphical user interfaces** (**GUIs**). Instead of writing instructions for the computer, you tell Salesforce what you want it to do by selecting options, dragging and dropping elements, and filling out forms. This abstraction from the underlying code is a significant advantage, particularly for common business processes.

Benefits of declarative development

Some of the key benefits are listed here:

- **Speed and agility**: Declarative tools enable incredibly fast solution delivery. Simple automations or UI changes can be implemented in minutes or hours, allowing for quick iterations and rapid prototyping.
- **Lower cost**: Since this approach doesn't require specialized programming skills, it often translates to lower development and maintenance costs.
- **Reduced technical debt**: Solutions built declaratively are generally more resilient to Salesforce platform updates, as Salesforce manages the underlying code.
- **Accessibility**: Declarative tools empower a wider range of users, including business users with strong logical skills but no coding background, to contribute to customization. This fosters greater collaboration between IT and business departments.

- **Easier maintenance**: Declarative configurations are typically easier to understand, troubleshoot, and modify for anyone familiar with the Salesforce admin interface.
- **Built-in best practices**: Salesforce's declarative tools often guide users toward best practices, ensuring that solutions are scalable and performant within the platform's architecture.

Building on these advantages, the following section highlights the core tools that drive declarative development today.

Key declarative tools in Salesforce

Salesforce provides a rich ecosystem of declarative tools, each serving a specific purpose. You may already be using them and aware of them. Let's quickly recap them:

- **Custom objects and fields**: These form the foundation of any Salesforce implementation. You can declaratively create custom objects to store unique business data and define the fields that capture essential information.
- **Page Layouts and Lightning Record pages**: These control the user interface for records. Page Layouts determine the fields, related lists, and buttons visible on a record's detail page. For greater flexibility, Lightning Record Pages, built with the Lightning App Builder, allow you to drag and drop components to create dynamic and personalized user experiences.
- **Validation rules**: These enforce data quality by preventing users from saving records that don't meet specific criteria. For instance, a validation rule can ensure an *Opportunity Close Date* is always in the future or that a *Discount Percentage* does not exceed 25%.
- **Salesforce Flow**: This is the most powerful and versatile declarative automation tool. Flow enables administrators to build complex business processes, including the following:
    - **Screen Flows**: For guided user interaction
    - **Record-triggered Flows**: For automation when records are created, updated, or deleted
    - **Scheduled Flows**: For processes that run on a set schedule
    - **Platform event-triggered Flows**: For responding to events in the platform

  Flow handles complex logic, loops, and integrations, blurring the line between declarative and programmatic capabilities.
- **Approval processes**: These automate the approval of records, such as quote discount requests. You can define a clear series of approval steps, assign approvers, and specify

actions to take upon approval or rejection. (Check out new flow approval processes, an enhanced alternative to classic approval processes.) At the time of writing this book, there is no Trailhead module, but you can find step-by-step instructions on the Salesforce help site at `https://help.salesforce.com/s/articleView?id=platform.automate_automated_approvals.htm&type=5`.

- **Lightning App Builder**: This is a drag-and-drop interface used to create custom Lightning pages (Home pages, Record pages, and App pages) by arranging standard and custom Lightning components.
- **Reports and dashboards**: These are powerful tools for analyzing and visualizing Salesforce data. Users can declaratively build custom reports (tabular, summary, matrix, and joined) and create interactive dashboards to monitor **key performance indicators (KPIs)** without writing any SQL queries.

Modern declarative tools, especially when combined with AI assistants or Flow Builder enhancements, empower non-coders to build powerful workflows that used to require development teams. Let's look at some examples.

Examples of declarative use cases

Here are some common business challenges that declarative tools can solve:

- **Automating quote assignment**: Use a Flow to automatically assign new quotes to sales representatives based on criteria such as industry, region, or lead source. Lead and case assignments rules can be handled directly through out-of-the-box Salesforce functionality, offering a fully declarative, configuration-driven approach.
- **Enforcing data consistency**: Implement a validation rule to ensure that a shipping address is always provided if the delivery method is *Physical Shipment*.
- **Streamlining opportunity stages**: Create a Flow that guides sales reps through the required fields and actions as an opportunity progresses through different stages.
- **Sending automated notifications**: Use Flow to send an email alert to a manager when a high-value opportunity is created or updated.

Declarative development is the recommended starting point for most Salesforce customizations. It offers a fast, cost-effective, and maintainable way to meet a significant portion of business requirements. However, not everything can be done with clicks alone. There are limits to what can be achieved with declarative tools, which is where programmatic solutions come in.

While declarative tools provide the foundation, programmatic development unlocks a deeper level of customization. Let's explore those solutions in the next section.

Exploring programmatic Salesforce development

Programmatic development in Salesforce involves writing code to extend the platform's capabilities beyond what's possible with declarative tools. This approach provides maximum flexibility and power, allowing developers to build highly customized solutions, integrate with external systems, and optimize performance for complex scenarios.

What is programmatic development?

Programmatic development means coding (writing instructions in a programming language that Salesforce understands). The primary language is Apex, a strongly typed, object-oriented programming language such as Java. Other key programmatic elements include the following:

- **Visualforce**: For custom UI (legacy). Still being used and going to stay for a while
- **Lightning Web Components (LWC) and Aura Components**: For modern UI development
- **SOQL/SOSL**: For database queries
- **Various APIs**: For integration with external systems

Benefits of programmatic development

You can meet virtually any business requirement with code—though it comes with higher complexity and cost. Some of the key benefits are listed next:

- **Maximum flexibility and customization**: Code allows for virtually limitless customization. If a business requirement cannot be met declaratively, programmatic development is the answer, handling complex business logic, custom algorithms, and specific data manipulations.
- **Complex integrations**: While some basic integrations can be done declaratively, robust and real-time integrations with external systems (ERPs, marketing platforms, and custom databases) almost always require programmatic solutions using Salesforce APIs.
- **Performance optimization**: For very large data volumes or highly concurrent operations, programmatic solutions can be fine-tuned for performance in a way that declarative tools cannot.
- **Advanced user interface (UI) development**: When standard Salesforce UI elements are insufficient, programmatic UI frameworks such as LWC enable the creation of pixel-perfect, highly interactive, and responsive interfaces.

- **Advanced error handling and logging**: Programmatic solutions provide granular control over error handling, custom logging, and robust exception management, which is critical for complex applications.
- **Reusability and modularity**: Developers can write reusable code components and libraries, promote modularity, and make it easier to maintain and extend functionality across different parts of an application.
- **Version control and testing**: Code can be managed in version control systems (such as Git), allowing for collaborative development, change tracking, and easier deployment. Programmatic solutions also require comprehensive unit testing, which ensures code quality and reliability.

With AI becoming more and more relevant and reliable, AI-based coding assistants such as GitHub Copilot or Einstein for Developers are also reducing the learning curve and speeding up programmatic development.

Let's check out programmatic tools for Salesforce development.

Key programmatic tools and languages in Salesforce

Let's quickly review some of the tools that you can use for coding:

- **Apex**: Salesforce's proprietary, strongly typed, object-oriented programming language. Executed on the Salesforce platform, Apex is used for the following:
    - **Triggers**: Code that executes before or after records are inserted, updated, or deleted. Triggers are essential for enforcing complex business rules, updating related records, or integrating with external systems based on data changes.
    - **Apex classes**: Reusable blocks of code containing methods, variables, and logic. Classes are used to build custom business logic, web services, email services, and more.
    - **Batch Apex**: Designed for processing large numbers of records (e.g., millions) that would exceed normal governor limits.
    - **Scheduled Apex**: Used for running Apex classes at specific times or intervals.
    - **Queueable Apex**: Facilitates asynchronous processing, allowing long-running operations to be executed in the background.
    - **Future methods**: A method for executing long-running operations asynchronously, typically for callouts to external web services.
- **LWC**: Salesforce's modern, lightweight, and high-performance UI framework, built with standard web technologies (HTML, CSS, and JavaScript). LWC is the preferred way to build custom user interfaces, components, and applications in Lightning Experience.

- **Salesforce Object Query Language** (**SOQL**): A SQL-like language used to query Salesforce data. Developers use SOQL to retrieve specific records and fields from the Salesforce database.
- **Salesforce Object Search Language** (**SOSL**): A text-based search language for performing searches across multiple objects and fields in Salesforce.
- **Salesforce APIs**: A suite of powerful interfaces that allows external applications to interact with Salesforce data and functionality. Common APIs include the following:
    - **REST API**: For simple, lightweight integrations using standard HTTP methods
    - **SOAP API**: For more complex, enterprise-level integrations that require strict message formats
    - **Bulk API**: For asynchronously loading or deleting large sets of data
    - **Streaming API**: For receiving real-time notifications of changes in Salesforce data

Examples of programmatic use cases

Programmatic development is essential for handling business needs that go beyond declarative capabilities. Here are a few examples:

- **Complex business logic**: Use Apex to calculate complex commissions based on multiple factors or to implement a custom pricing engine that considers various product configurations and customer tiers.
- **Real-time integrations**: Synchronize customer data between Salesforce and an external ERP system in real time when a record is updated.
- **Custom UI for data entry**: Build a highly customized data entry screen using LWC for a specific business process. This can include dynamic field visibility, complex calculations, and multi-step workflows that are not achievable with standard page layouts.
- **Mass data manipulation**: Automatically correct data inconsistencies across millions of records using Batch Apex (data cleaning and data hygiene).
- **Custom web services**: Expose Salesforce data or functionality to an external application via a custom REST or SOAP web service.
- **Trigger-based automation**: Use an Apex trigger to automatically create a service request in a separate system whenever a case in Salesforce reaches a specific status.

Programmatic development offers unparalleled power and flexibility, but it comes at a higher cost and requires specialized skills. It also demands rigorous testing and maintenance. The key is knowing when this power is truly necessary and when declarative tools are sufficient.

We cannot go all declarative or programmatic. It is somewhere between these two extremes. You always need some level of programmatic development, unless you work on small implementations. For medium to large implementations, due to massive data volumes, the ratio of programmatic to declarative is relatively on the higher side.

Choosing between declarative and programmatic solutions

Now that you understand the concepts of declarative vis-à-vis programmatic solutions, let's see how each can add value for your implementations. Let's discuss with examples.

The decision between declarative and programmatic solutions is one of the most critical choices in Salesforce development. The guiding principle is to prioritize *clicks, not code*, which means you should always explore declarative options first. This is crucial for faster delivery, but it's not an absolute rule. Even with declarative options, it's wise to consult your technical team, as non-functional requirements can often cause unexpected trouble.

Understanding the nuances is essential for building efficient, scalable, and maintainable solutions.

The clicks, not code principle

The *clicks, not code principle* states that if a requirement can be met using Salesforce's standard declarative tools (e.g., Flow, validation rules, Lightning App Builder, etc.), you should always choose that approach over custom code. This is truer if your work on smaller implementations (say 500 or so users and data volumes are easily manageable).

Following this principle provides several key advantages:

- **Faster development**: Less time spent coding means quicker delivery and faster time to market
- **Easier maintenance**: Configuration is generally easier to understand and update than code, reducing reliance on specialized developers
- **Lower cost**: It reduces the need for expensive developer resources
- **Platform resilience**: Declarative solutions are less likely to break with Salesforce platform updates, as the platform manages the underlying code

Exploring some real-world scenarios

Let's look at some practical scenarios to see this principle in action.

The following are some scenarios and examples, starting from simple to complex implementations.

- **Scenario 1: Auto-assigning cases—A declarative approach is the best fit**:
  - **Requirement**: When a new case is created, automatically update its status to *New* and send an email notification to the case owner.
  - **Choice**: Declarative (Flow). This is a straightforward, record-triggered automation. Flow can easily handle this with minimal configuration.
  - **Why not code?** Writing an Apex trigger for this would be overkill, take longer, and be harder for an administrator to maintain.
- **Scenario 2: Lead scoring—A hybrid fit**:
  - **Requirement**: Implement a lead scoring system that calculates a *Lead Score* based on a weighted average of multiple fields (website visits, email opens, and job title), then updates the lead's `Rating` field (`Hot`, `Warm`, or `Cold`) based on the score. The weights may change frequently.
  - **Choice**: Hybrid (declarative + programmatic):
    - **Declarative (Flow)**: Can be used to trigger the calculation when a lead record is created or updated, and to update the `Rating` field based on the score.
    - **Programmatic (Apex class)**: The complex weighted average calculation, especially if it involves dynamic weights or querying related objects, is best handled by an Apex class. The Flow can then call this class.
  - **Why hybrid?** Flows alone might struggle with dynamic weighting and complex mathematical operations. Apex provides the necessary computational power and flexibility, while Flow handles the orchestration.
- **Scenario 3: Custom order interface—Go programmatic**:
  - **Requirement**: Build a custom order entry screen that allows sales reps to select products, apply complex pricing rules, calculate taxes in real time by integrating with an external service, and generate a PDF quote—all within a single, intuitive interface.
  - **Choice**: Programmatic (LWC + Apex + APIs):
    - **LWC**: Essential for building rich, interactive, and responsive UI with dynamic product selection and real-time totals

        - **Apex**: Handles the complex pricing logic, interacts with the external tax service via API callouts, and manages record creation and PDF generation
        - **APIs**: Used for the integration with the external tax service
    - **Why not declarative?** Standard Salesforce order entry is too rigid. Flow's screen capabilities are insufficient for this level of dynamic interaction, real-time calculation, and external service integration.

After seeing the preceding scenarios, it is not always black and white. There is always a middle ground that only your team can decide on the best approach.

Middle ground: the power of hybrid solutions

Declarative and programmatic solutions are not mutually exclusive. In fact, many of the most robust and efficient solutions today are hybrid, combining the strengths of both approaches, as in these examples:

- A Flow can trigger an Apex class to perform complex calculations or call an external API, then continue with declarative actions based on the Apex result.
- A Lightning Web Component (programmatic UI) can interact with standard Salesforce objects (declarative data model) and trigger Flows for specific automations.
- Validation rules (declarative) can enforce basic data integrity, while Apex triggers (programmatic) handle more complex, cross-object validation or custom error messages.

This hybrid approach allows organizations to maximize development speed and maintainability by using declarative tools wherever possible while still having the power and flexibility of code for requirements that truly demand it.

By understanding the concepts and tools discussed in this chapter, you have gained the valuable skills necessary to make informed development decisions. You now have a solid grasp of the following:

- **The capabilities of declarative tools**: The benefits and use cases of no-code and low-code solutions
- **The power of programmatic options**: The advantages and applications of Apex and other programmatic tools
- **Strategic tool selection**: The ability to identify scenarios that call for the most efficient and effective development approach

> **Note**
>
> The perceived ease of declarative configuration can be a double-edged sword in large-scale organizations where "simple" changes often trigger significant downstream effects. It is critical to maintain strict governance, ensuring that admins and Business Analysts treat configuration with the same level of discipline as code. By mandating that all declarative work follows a formal path through sandboxes, we eliminate the risk of direct production edits and ensure platform stability.

Let's wrap up this chapter with a few practical tips.

Practical tips for success

While the *clicks, not code* principle is a solid starting point, it's not always the complete solution. Making the right choice between declarative and programmatic development is key to successful Salesforce implementation.

Use the following decision framework to make an informed choice that balances speed, cost, and long-term maintainability.

Factor	Choose declarative (clicks)	Choose programmatic (code)
Complexity	Simple, straightforward business logic; standard automation; basic data validation	Highly complex business logic; custom algorithms; multi-step, conditional processes with intricate branching
UI	Standard Salesforce UI; minor customizations to page layouts; drag-and-drop components	Pixel-perfect custom UI; highly interactive components; non-standard layouts; complex data visualization
Data volume	Small to moderate data volumes; operations on single records or small batches	Large data volumes (millions of records); bulk processing; performance-critical operations

Factor	Choose declarative (clicks)	Choose programmatic (code)
Integrations	Basic integrations with prebuilt connectors; simple data synchronization with external systems (e.g., AppExchange apps)	Real-time, complex integrations with external systems; custom APIs; handling various data formats (XML, JSON)
Performance	Standard performance adequate; no extreme speed requirements	High performance required for critical operations; need for optimized queries and execution
Error handling	Basic error messages provided by the platform and limited custom error handling	Granular, custom error handling; robust exception management; detailed logging
Reusability	Reusing standard components or flows in different contexts	Creating reusable code libraries, Apex classes, or LWCs for widespread application
Testing	Built-in platform validation; manual testing	Requires comprehensive unit tests (Apex test classes); automated testing frameworks
Resources	Limited development resources; reliance on administrators or Business Analysts	Access to experienced Salesforce developers; budget for developer salaries
Maintainability	Easy for administrators to understand and modify; less prone to breaking changes	Requires developer expertise for maintenance; more susceptible to breaking changes with platform updates if not carefully managed

Factor	Choose declarative (clicks)	Choose programmatic (code)
Security	Leverages standard Salesforce security model (profiles, permission sets, sharing rules)	Requires careful consideration of security in custom code (e.g., with sharing/without sharing)
AI/automation assistance	Supported with native Einstein capabilities	Supported with code-generation tools or AI dev assistants

Table 7.1: The Declarative vs. Programmatic Strategic Matrix

This matrix must have given you a good idea to make an informed choice.

Let's now summarize the most essential takeaways to ensure your long-term success.

AI is set to significantly reduce time for both declarative configuration (for Business Analysts/admins) and programmatic development (for developers). By employing effective prompt engineering and AI tools, Business Analysts and admins can more confidently select and deliver declarative solutions in compressed timeframes. The rise of AI-assisted development also introduces new governance challenges, particularly regarding the quality and validity of generated code. Moving forward, organizations must balance speed with scrutiny, implementing oversight mechanisms to review AI outputs for technical debt and security risks. While the governance landscape is still maturing, maintaining a *human-in-the-loop* approach is essential for long-term platform health.

Summary

This chapter explored Salesforce's dual-path development, combining the speed of declarative tools with the precision of code. As AI continues to enhance both approaches, your ability to choose wisely between clicks and code will determine the success of your solutions. Adopt a hybrid mindset and always ask, *What delivers the most value for the business today, and scales for tomorrow?*

The *clicks, not code* philosophy remains a guiding principle, encouraging us to first leverage declarative tools for speed and maintainability. However, when facing complex logic, deep integrations, or custom user experiences, programmatic tools such as Apex and LWC become essential.

The most effective solutions often blend both approaches, ensuring scalability and robustness. By understanding these options, you can make informed decisions, selecting the right tool for the right job to build applications that truly empower your organization. Let AI tools support your build and decision-making.

In the next chapter, we'll explore prototyping best practices, including how to collaborate effectively and capture requirements through rapid iteration.

Get this book's PDF version and more

Scan the QR code (or go to `packtpub.com/unlock`). Search for this book by name, confirm the edition, and then follow the steps on the page.

UNLOCK NOW

Note: Keep your invoice handy. Purchases made directly from Packt don't require an invoice.

8

Demonstrating Functionality Using Prototypes

In the previous chapter, we explored the strategic balance between declarative tools and programmatic development, establishing a hybrid mindset for building scalable solutions. Now, we move from architectural theory to practical execution, using prototypes to bridge the gap between business requirements and technical reality.

In this chapter, we will cover the following: demonstrating functionality aspects of how to translate the functional specification into a visual working model. We will cover how to mock up quick static or semi-working solutions that we can demonstrate to stakeholders and team members. During this phase, team members will be able to see a visual of the requirements and get an opportunity to ideate, collaborate, discuss challenges and workarounds, and continuously provide feedback. Furthermore, we will explore the wealth of declarative (no-code, low-code) solutions available, guiding you on when to leverage these before considering programmatic development.

We will be covering the following topics in detail:

- The need for prototyping and its categories
- Prototype stages
- What and how do you prototype?
- Tools to document prototyping
- The benefits of prototyping
- Focus on declarative vs programmatic solutions
- Practical tips for success

By the end of the chapter, you will have gained knowledge and understood the importance of prototyping activities. You will also learn how you can plan and develop a good prototype that will avoid surprises at a later phase and get a consensus on the solution design aspect of the requirements.

The need for prototyping and its categories

A prototype is a mock-up, or a model, of an idea based on the business needs that team members can develop, interact with, and provide feedback on. A prototype can be just a static model or can be a limited functionality model and provide a way to visualize the proposed design solution beforehand. This idea is developed iteratively and organically with input and feedback from key team members, and helps us move in the right direction. Building and socializing prototypes helps us see abstract ideas in a solid form where users can visualize them, concur, and confirm or reject them. We basically get all the associated team members on the same page, and a greater understanding of the idea can be put into action. In some cases, the user who defined the business need or requirement may not really want the prototype solution at all or may want it to be different. Prototyping as an activity responds to actual user needs by helping the users understand and see their own needs firsthand.

Categories of prototypes

We can use prototypes to test both functional and non-functional solution aspects, such as usability, scalability, and performance, to a certain extent. I mostly focus on business requirement prototypes and UI and usability prototypes. Cloud application performance and capabilities are taken care of by the SaaS providers, and I will let this be run by the QA team doing regression and stress testing:

- **Requirements**: Handled during elicitation to understand and demonstrate business processes.
- **User interaction and usability**: Handled during the design phase to define and demonstrate its look and feel, interface design, usability, and navigation.
- **Performance**: Handled during the end of the design phase and the start of the build phase to predict system performance with concurrent users. This prototype is mostly aimed at technical teams to prove the non-functional requirements and design the technical aspects accordingly to mitigate any constraints.
- **Capability**: Handled during the design phase to make sure that the underlying software can handle the proposed design.

Let's look at a simplified example: users would like to manage customer business plans where they can capture customer information, key contact information, product information, quarterly business plans, and opportunity forecasts. This form is filled out collaboratively by the sales team and customer team members.

So, where do you start? Currently, business users use Word document templates to capture customer business plans and collaborate on these documents via email.

What do we do? We have multiple options, and for simplicity, we will explore two scenarios:

- **Scenario 1**: Take the Word document template and mirror it field by field in the target system, running over multiple pages. In this scenario, the user experience is somewhat inefficient and ineffective, but at least the business plan has a home.
- **Scenario 2**: How about redesigning the complete user experience and the UI and making it more fun and enjoyable for your business users and customers? We do not know whether our users like this design yet and we do not have the time, money, or resources to create this experience in the system. This is when prototyping comes in handy. We do a quick mockup of the UI and the experience on paper (or any tool of your choice), mapping all the user needs and thinking it through in their shoes. Your team will have to create multiple variants of the prototype, socialize with key team members, and iteratively enhance it until it is agreeable and acceptable to your business users.

The outcome of the second scenario is displayed in *Figure 8.1*.

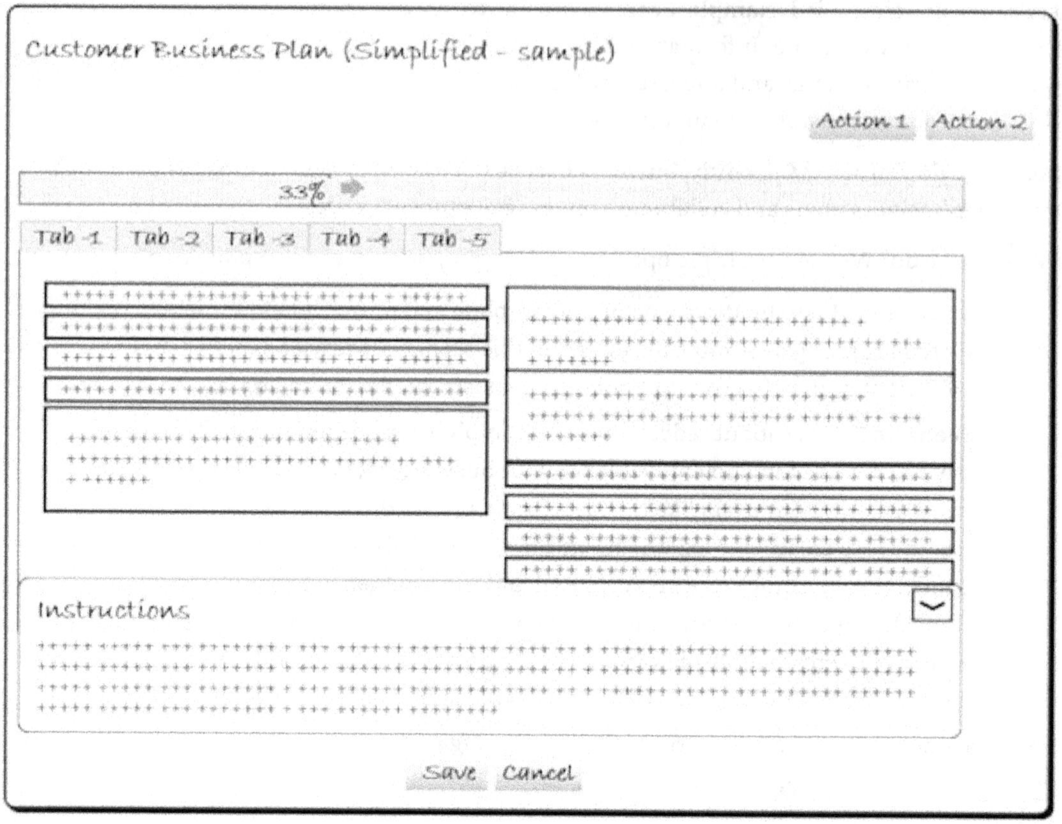

Figure 8.1 – A simplified sample wireframe

Let us explore each element on the screen:

- We added tabs to capture the data for each of the functional elements. Users can navigate to each specific functional element by just clicking on the respective tab, rather than scrolling a few pages down:
    - Customer information
    - Key contact information
    - Product information
    - Quarterly business plans
    - Opportunity forecasts
- We added boxes for screen elements—fields such as text, date, amount, and picklists. Do not make them too detailed in this initial phase.

- We added a few action buttons where users can save, edit, print, or clear the data on the screen.
- We added a progress bar indicator above the tabs so that the user gets an idea of what percentage of the form is complete.

Note

We need to strike a balance between too little and too much prototyping. Too little effort means business users may not care, and too much is risky. It should be enough to add just a little bit more to create some excitement. As in our example, we added action buttons and a status bar.

When to do prototyping

So, at what phase of the project or when is the best time to do prototyping? Typically, I would say you make a prototype during the solution design phase. You start with a rough draft prototype and progressively elaborate on it and finalize it by the time you conclude the design phase of the project.

There may have been instances where I made a few prototypes based on very high-level business plans and during elicitation. You can make a prototype this early to validate whether the idea is viable and technically feasible within the constraints of the project.

Let us look at one example from one of my early projects. The requirement was to develop a partner locator in which customers would be able to locate distributors, integrators, and technology partners by location and product type. When we implemented this as part of Salesforce **partner relationship management** (**PRM**), we did not have many AppExchange tools or other third-party tools, and we were one of the early implementors of PRM. After doing some serious research and analysis, we came up with multiple options and zoomed in on one of them where we took an unmanaged package and redeveloped it to fit our needs. We quickly enabled this in one of our sandboxes and tested this with a small set of partner users. This is a true working model, and we enabled this for five users and worked with them, incorporating their suggestions and feedback.

This prototype is functional in the simplest possible way, without exception handling, automation, or integrations. After we got the go-ahead from these pilot users, we conducted another random usability test with a different set of users before turning it into a full-fledged working solution with all the functions, automation, and integrations for our global audience, incrementally, during three releases. This is a case where you develop a working model prototype, then use this for **proof of concept**, and eventually the working model. We used evolutionary prototyping techniques to enable the functionality by starting simple and adding more incrementally by getting feedback from key team members and business users.

> **Note**
>
> When integrating a complex, unknown function, always implement it incrementally in a few releases. This approach helps you gauge whether the sponsor(s) would like to move forward and invest resources into the next release. You do not need to implement and deploy 100% functionality in the first release. Implement the core functions with some level of automation and let the real user use them. Gather usability metrics and any pain points, such as too much search result data or a page rendering too slowly, and solicit feedback from users of the tool. If the usability reports show too low usage, maybe you need to rethink your next steps. Assuming the usage looks encouraging, incorporate your findings and add more automated functions and features in your next release.

Prototype stages

Let us look at the three stages of software prototypes:

- **Low-fidelity**: Low-fidelity prototypes are used to elicit initial feedback or to check whether the idea makes sense at all. These are draft or scratch prototypes where your team quickly creates relatively less functional and more flexible prototypes. Based on the feedback, they can be changed quickly.
- **High-fidelity**: High-fidelity prototypes are more functional and less flexible. We start with low-fidelity ones, refine the idea based on the feedback, and enhance the prototype with more features and functions, thus making it more sophisticated and closely reflecting the proposed functional solution. High-fidelity prototypes are working models and can eventually be used to build the final solution.
- **Medium-fidelity**: A medium-fidelity prototype, as the name suggests, is between the low- and high-fidelity prototypes. I listed this one last for a reason since I usually do my prototypes at this level. My rationale for this is to have enough confidence in my prototype that key stakeholders and end users are comforted by seeing some level of functionality. High-fidelity prototypes are exponentially expensive and time-consuming, and not a popular option, as there is a risk that you may ditch the relevant approach or functionality. Medium fidelity offers just enough features and functions with a good level of flexibility to adjust. Again, "medium" is a broad spectrum, so adjust it based on the functionality your team wishes to prototype.

Prototypes help us improve requirement gathering, solution design, collaboration, technical development, quality testing, and training artifact creation. They enhance understanding between stakeholders, SMEs, end users, and project team members. This also aids us in improving the UI and user experience.

Prototypes are made at every stage of the project to gain a better understanding and allow all key team members involved during the planning, designing, development, testing, and training phases of the project to collaborate. Prototype activity can be simple or become very complex. Based on your project, you can decide on the level of prototyping you need to do.

There are two main types of prototypes:

- **Temporary or transient prototypes**: These are also called throwaway prototypes. Examples of this type include simple wireframing or mockups of screens. As with other project activities, prototyping is also iterative. Key stakeholders and project team members are involved as part of the workshop or conference room pilot and the team will work on developing and designing the prototype collaboratively.
- **Evolutionary prototypes**: These are working models that simulate real-life functions. They are incrementally improved based on feedback from key identified team members and users. We keep adding functions and features and ultimately evolve this into a working solution. Remember – this will not be fully functioning as per the business requirements. For prototyping, we enable functions and features, but most of the steps are not yet automated or tuned. You can take this prototype as a model and build the complete solution during the technical development phase, where all features and functions are automated and integrated, and the UI is designed and enhanced.

Note

The key steps involved in an evolutionary prototype are concept (idea), developing an initial prototype, socializing it, refining it until it is acceptable, and locking it down in technical development.

Prototyping can be horizontal, vertical, or both:

- The horizontal prototype helps with understanding and demonstrating the overall scope of the functionality at a high level, where we create the breadth of the solution developed before getting into granularity. It provides a broader view of the complete system in scope for the project. Utilized to capture high-level requirements.
- A vertical prototype evolves as we keep building functionality on one specific function. Each feature is added incrementally until the proposed solution is developed. This

prototype elaborates specific functions of a system and helps capture detailed requirements. The vertical prototype handles backend functions such as sizing, security, and performance.

What do you prototype, and how?

Prototyping does not come free, and some project implementations do not like the idea of prototyping, as they think it is a sunk cost. The reason for this is that getting the right SMEs and knowledgeable team members is not always easy. Also, business stakeholders do not like to sign off on the design approach.

I encourage you to do prototyping for any new feature and function that is specific to your project. You do not need to use fancy tools to do prototyping. All you need is a pen and a sheet of paper (a whiteboard or a flip chart, or a stylus pen and a pad).

Consider the following aspects when doing prototyping:

- **What is the scope?**: Keep it very narrow, only including the core and critical functionality for a pilot business unit with backend simulations (no or minimal automation or integrations).
- **Low, medium, or high fidelity?**: Start with low and refine it to medium. High fidelity is needed only if you plan to incorporate this logic in your final solution. Get the buy-in from key stakeholders at various stages and not at the end.
- **How much functionality to prototype?**: Start small and incrementally add more. Start with the absolute core functions, making some level of incremental addition based on feedback. Make sure you don't demonstrate a bare skeleton to business users. They may reject it outright on this basis.

Let's review the steps so that you get an idea. As with all project activities, proper planning and communication are very critical.

1. Select the requirements that you plan to prototype from a prioritized and approved list of requirements from the business requirements document. Pick the ones that are complex and that team members find difficult to visualize or grasp proposed solutions for.
2. For the requirements that you plan to prototype, create business scenarios for each of the functions or sets of functions. Scenarios should include one happy path where everything works perfectly, and a few alternative paths where you may run into issues. You can refer to process flows to get the sequence of the flow. These scenarios can be a simple set of step-by-step instructions of functionality from start to end.

3. We add more details to the prototype to show how the proposed functionality works on the system. We can add page layouts designed in a logical sequence, enable fields based on the previous fields' attributes, and help users navigate them seamlessly. We can also prototype the same pages on mobile devices and verify navigation there too. Note that mobile navigation will be completely different from desktop browser navigation for Salesforce.
4. The prototype model is shared among team members and refined based on feedback. This process is iterative, and the core team needs to work in an agile mode so that we can do the demo, get the feedback, incorporate the feedback, and redo the iterative process.
5. We continue to revise and enhance in an iterative loop to create a comprehensive, well-rounded prototype. The core team members should be very critical and willing to provide open and honest feedback.
6. This final prototype, after its approval, can be utilized for the next steps in the project in the development of a functional solution. Although we invested a good amount of time into prototype activities, we are paid back when the prototype is accepted. This will cut down the development time, and the risk of businesses rejecting the solution is rather slim.

Let us look at a practical example.

Here's the business requirement (or use case): a user (a sales analyst or sales manager) wants to be able to create and manage account records. Based on the account attributes, relevant products are added to the account screen (refer to *Figures 8.1* and *8.2* in the previous chapter).

We start with a quick and easy low-fidelity prototype of this functionality by wireframing the screen layout. This can be done rather quickly in a few hours by collaborating with the right set of key stakeholders and technical team members. By the end of the session, we should be able to wireframe screen layout design for the account and product alignment, as shown in *Figures 8.2* and *8.3*. At this point, let us not worry about how it can be technically enabled. We need to find out exactly the best and most simplified way for the business to utilize the functionality. Try to get to the optimal design solution that the team can approve and agree on.

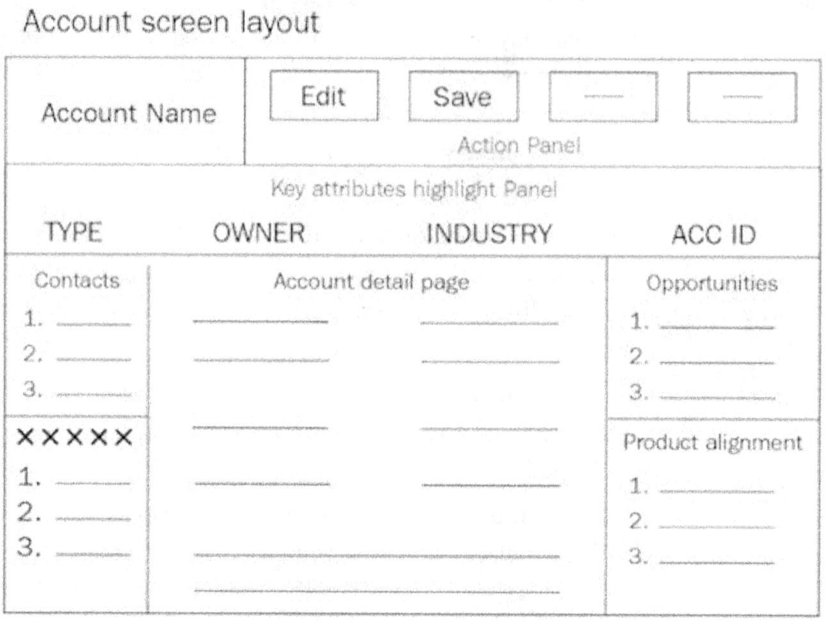

Figure 8.2 – The account screen layout wireframe

Here is a representation of the product alignment:

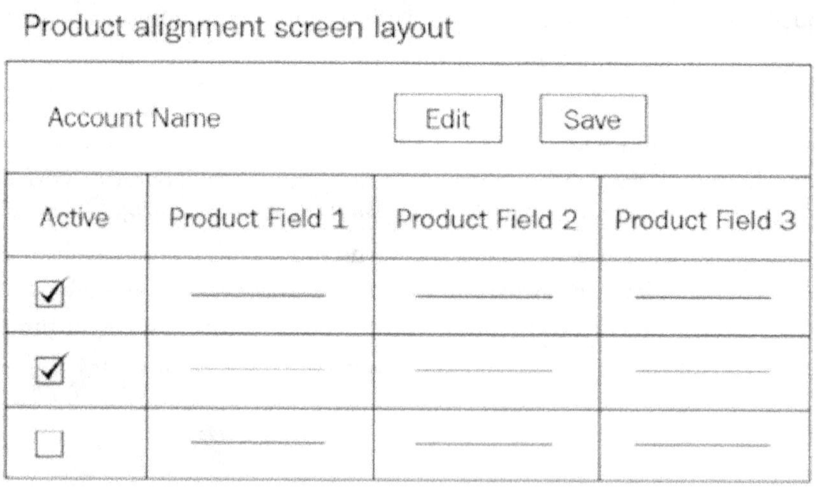

Figure 8.3 – Product alignment in the screen layout wireframe

The preceding wireframe clearly shows us the account screen layout and product alignment layout:

- A highlight panel displaying the key attributes of the account.
- Action buttons at the top (your business users may need them at the bottom too).
- Three-column 360-degree console view displaying the account details and related object details such as contacts, opportunities, and product alignment.
- From the account screen, the user can navigate to the product alignment screen (as we can see, the action button or link to navigate to product alignment is missing in *Figure 8.2* – make sure to capture the action button in your next iteration so that the user has a way to navigate to the product alignment screen).
- The product alignment screen lists all the products that are aligned to our account and the user can activate or deactivate products (again, we missed the action button for the user to be able to add new products, so make sure to incorporate this in the next iteration).

You can see how easy it is for us to get real-time feedback by visually depicting the business requirements in the form of a wireframe. This process helps us create designs in a short span of time with a common understanding across the entire project team.

Now that we have the okay from key business stakeholders in terms of the high-level UI design, let us add more details to this prototype. In this next level of prototyping, you need to involve your architecture, technical, and testing team members. Key business users and business SMEs need not be involved, as it involves more of a technical discussion that may include system capabilities, performance, and capacity-related non-functional requirements. We typically share this with key business users during the last iteration to get feedback on adding, removing, or rearranging fields or action buttons on the screen layout.

This is a good example of a horizontal prototype and provides a UI and user interaction rather than system functionality. Look at the following three figures (*Figure 8.4*, *Figure 8.5*, and *Figure 8.6*) and see if you can find opportunities to improve them in your next iteration.

A sample account screen layout view for the sales team is shown in *Figure 8.4*.

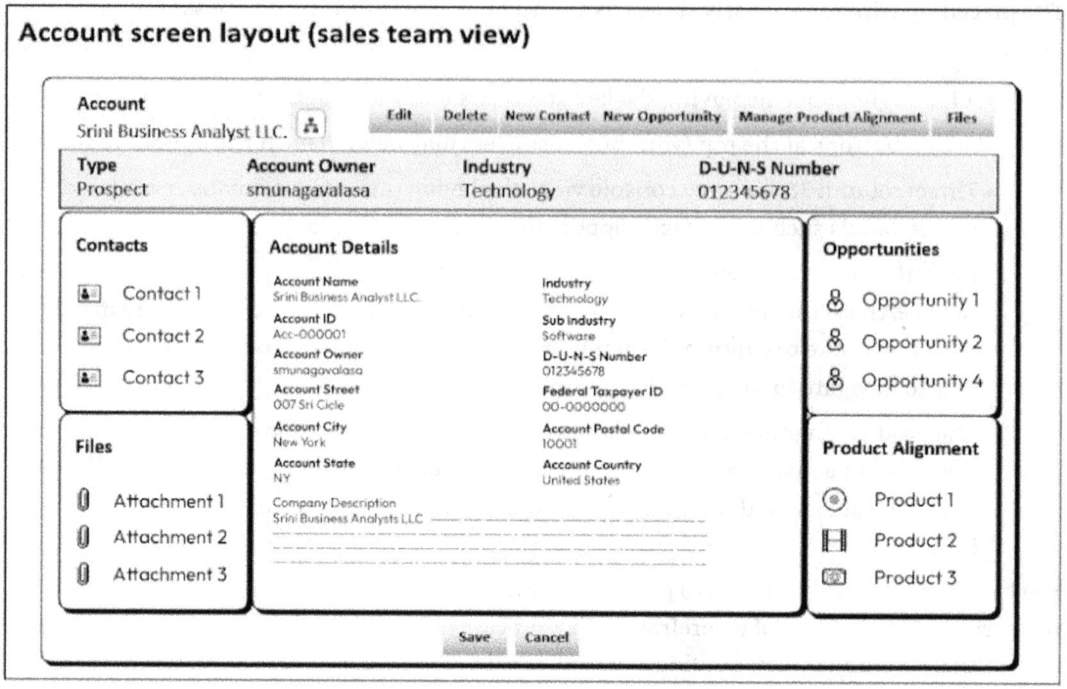

Figure 8.4 – A prototype of the account screen layout

A sample product alignment screen layout is shown in *Figure 8.5*.

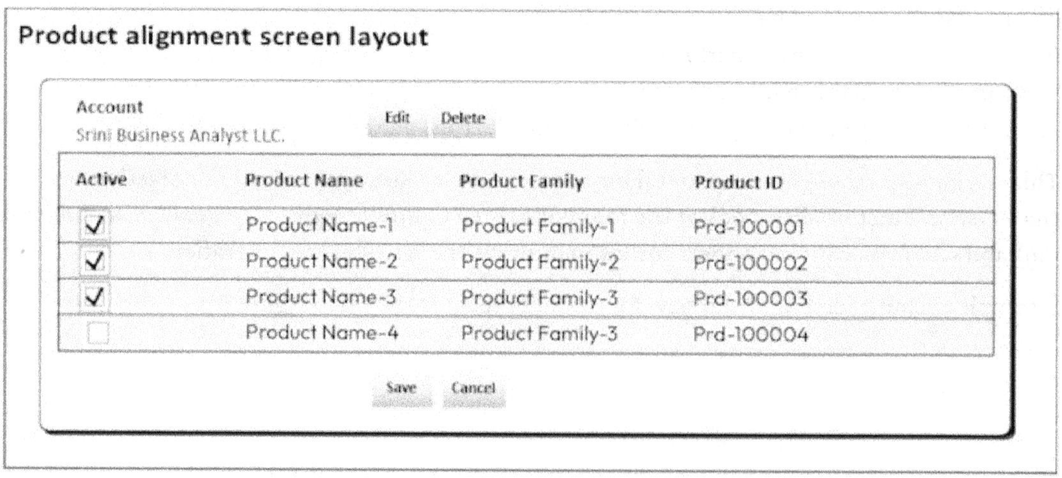

Figure 8.5 – A prototype of the product alignment screen layout

The following screen layout is a variant of the account screen layout. In this case, our service team needs completely different data attributes on the account screen. By rearranging fields and actions, we can create a completely different user experience for our service team. This will help us achieve high levels of user adoption.

Figure 8.6 – A prototype of the account screen layout (service team view)

As you can see for yourself, there's considerable value you can create by prototyping and sharing this with the core team and getting their feedback to iteratively and progressively enhance the quality of the prototype and, hence, the understanding of the proposed design solution.

Let us take a look at some of the tools that help us create these prototypes.

Tools to document prototyping

There are many excellent tools available on the market, and you can pick the one you are most comfortable with. I prefer to use a whiteboard and Visio to start my prototyping activities and then move into one of the sandbox software systems. I have listed a few of the ones I observed, tried, and used during my prototype activities and found very useful. I have heard there are other great tools too, so feel free to browse the web and try out a few trial versions:

- **Whiteboard/Flip chart/Visio**: This is the best and easiest when you are creating collaboratively with the team.

- **Balsamiq**: An easy-to-use and very effective tool. Best for wireframing and provides your team with the bigger picture.
- **Freehand**: A product from InVision. An efficient tool best for prototyping apps.
- **Adobe XD**: A feature-rich tool that requires some learning to use. An excellent tool for a **user experience prototype** (**UXP**) or **user interface prototype** (**UIP**).
- **The software system itself**: When we try to prove the feature or function, we can develop the feature in the Salesforce system itself. Remember, this is only a prototype, so we do not need to prove 100% functionality.

The benefits of prototyping

Here are some key use cases to justify prototyping:

- Helps with the elicitation and clarification of business needs
- Identifies the missed steps or gaps in process tasks
- Identifies and refines redundant and duplicate tasks
- Aids in discovering design problems
- Involves end users from the start
- Allows us to identify complex functionality
- Gives stakeholders and SMEs a preview of the proposed solution
- Allows us to receive feedback from stakeholders and key end users
- Allows us to test and assess the feasibility and fitness of the solution
- Allows us to confirm and agree on a final design

Focus on declarative vs. programmatic solutions

Declarative solutions focus on defining the desired outcome rather than prescribing every step needed to achieve it. You specify what you want the system to do, not how it should be done. These solutions are typically visual, configuration-driven, and user-friendly, making them ideal for rapid prototyping and iterative improvements.

Salesforce Flow is a prime example of a declarative tool. Using Flow, you can design complex business processes—such as multi-step approvals or automated email notifications—by dragging and dropping elements onto a canvas and configuring their properties. There's no need to write lines of code for logic, conditions, or data updates. Instead, you declare the intended behavior through a visual sequence of actions. This approach not only accelerates development but also makes the logic transparent, enabling stakeholders without a technical background to easily follow the flow and provide meaningful feedback.

Using Salesforce's declarative tool, Flow Builder, you can quickly create a functional prototype that can be refined iteratively with minimal effort. *Figure 8.6* displays a visual Prototype. Here, we apply opportunity discounts based on the Account support level and the opportunity amount

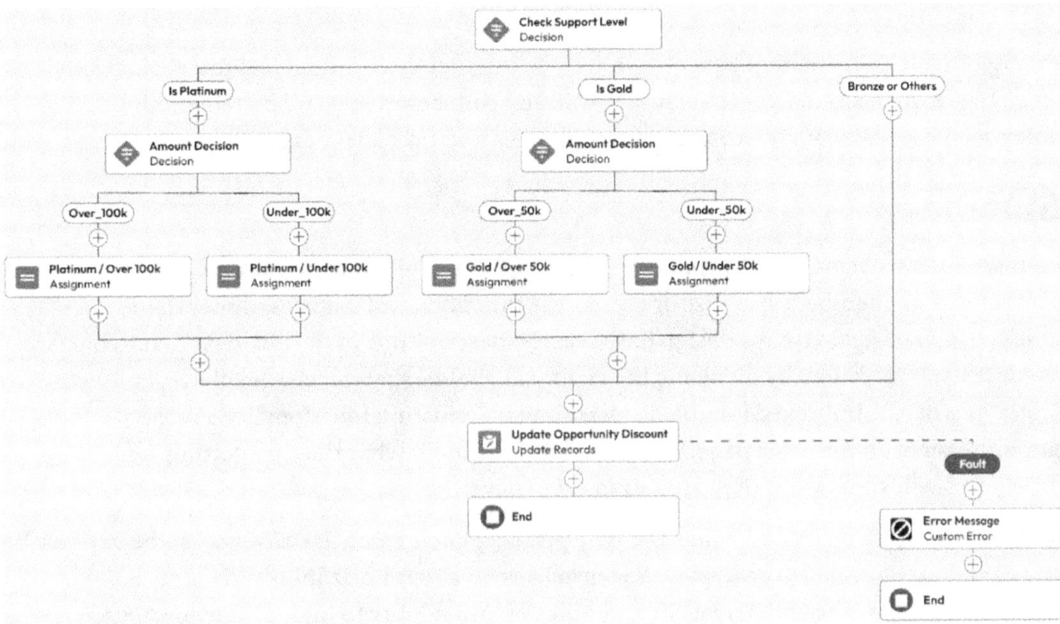

Figure 8.7 – A prototype example using the declarative tool Flow Builder

Practical tips for success

Listed here are a few tips useful during the prototype phase:

- You need no specialized tool to start a prototype activity. This should not be a reason for you not to do prototypes. Simply use a whiteboard with markers.
- Prototype what is essential and not everything or anything. Time is limited, so choose functions and the level of functionality wisely.
- Consider user groups and how they interact with the software system. This brings in the most benefit to users – for example, sales analysts and service analysts can see a screen with different elements on it.
- Start with an inside-out approach where we prioritize the information and elements that are important to end users.
- Identify key participants during prototyping discussions and demos. Everyone needs to bring input to the table and strive to make it productive and useful.

- Make sure the technical team is involved and on board with the prototype design. They are the ones who will use them to build the final solution.
- Document the final version and share it with the team, along with other project artifacts. These versions will be very useful when the team enhances the functionality at a future date.

Prototyping helps team members see what direction they are heading in. Prototyping activities guide the team to see the potential future solution collaboratively and incrementally, and in doing so, help them course-correct any deficiencies and take advantage of any efficiencies.

Summary

Prototyping is extremely useful and helpful during software implementations. Prototypes help users and team members visualize or try out the functions and features, rather than interpreting and evaluating a design based on the descriptions in the business requirement documents. In addition, by involving the right stakeholders, we receive feedback, and prototypes can be improved iteratively by adding or adjusting functionality. Prototypes keep the entire team on the same page. The end users will know what they are getting, and developers will know what they are supposed to develop.

In this chapter, we discussed when and why prototyping is essential, along with the various stages and categories of prototyping. You also learned about horizontal and vertical prototyping, as well as ample real-life examples of low-fidelity to high-fidelity prototyping. We concluded the chapter by covering the benefits of prototyping and a few practical tips that you can use for your project's success.

In the next chapter, we will cover the key aspects of conference room pilots, where the product is demoed to a wider audience. You will learn how to facilitate a conference room pilot (**CRP**) effectively, who to invite to these sessions, and how to keep the team focused on the agreed business requirements. You will also learn the key success factors and best practices that can help you during your own CRP sessions.

Questions

1. How is piloting different from prototyping?
2. When do you need horizontal prototyping and vertical prototyping?
3. Recall some of the prototyping techniques that we can use during prototyping.

Further reading

- *Agile Project and Service Management* (*Chapter 6, DSDM*) by O'Reilly

Get this book's PDF version and more

Scan the QR code (or go to `packtpub.com/unlock`). Search for this book by name, confirm the edition, and then follow the steps on the page.

UNLOCK NOW

Note: Keep your invoice handy. Purchases made directly from Packt don't require an invoice.

9

Exploring Conference Room Pilots

In the previous chapter, we discussed prototype activities and their benefits and came up with a solid design solution. You gained an in-depth understanding of various prototype stages and categories with practical examples. In addition to prototyping skills, you learned about the benefits of good prototypes and practical tips that can make you successful at creating prototypes.

In this chapter, you will learn how to showcase prototypes to a wider audience. We will see how **Conference Room Pilots** (**CRPs**) help us progress from individual requirements to proposed design solutions in the right direction without any surprises. We will also see how the testing team and the UAT team can benefit from the demos by helping them understand requirements, as well as how they shape up into a functional working solution. This helps them come up with possible holistic scenarios and validate the solution.

No project goes entirely smoothly. You will encounter surprises, and that's what makes it more challenging and exciting. The earlier you encounter surprises, the better it will be for the team. This gives your team an opportunity to quickly reassess and understand the business needs better and align the project back in the right direction. This is where CRPs come to our rescue.

We will cover the following topics in this chapter:

- Understanding what CRPs are
- Exploring the timing and participants of CRPs
- Facilitating CRPs
- Managing scope creep during CRPs

- Reviewing the benefits of CRPs
- Practical tips for success

By the end of the chapter, you will have gained knowledge and understanding of the importance of CRPs. You will understand how CRPs can help identify and fine-tune functionality and usability, and address any gaps in the requirements through a series of CRPs at critical junctures of the project. Concurrently, you will learn about the benefits that the testing team can derive from this activity.

Understanding what CRPs are

CRPs are workshops where key stakeholders, along with project team members, collaborate at various stages of projects to understand the business needs and transform them into proposed business solutions. CRPs help stakeholders collaborate and see how their needs progress through each phase of the project, as well as provide feedback. This helps users see what they are getting and keeps the process transparent. Also, these CRP sessions help the technical team and testing team understand the needs better, so they are able to deliver what the business truly wants.

Based on the complexity of the business requirements, the project team can decide when to do CRP and how often to do the CRP sessions. As a rule of thumb, from my personal experience, I prefer to go with three CRP stages for a project with medium to high complexity, and maybe a fourth one if the project is highly visible and critical or highly critical.

The four stages when we conduct the CRPs are as follows:

- **Scope CRP**: In this stage, we elaborate on the business needs and requirements. This is done during the plan and analyze phase of the project.
- **Design CRP**: In this stage, we connect various functional steps and integration points to understand the needs from a design perspective. This is done during the solution design phase of the project.
- **Build/development CRP**: In this phase, we show the users the actual functionality of the system. This is done during the technical development phase of the project.
- **Test CRP**: This is optional and recommended only for highly visible and very complex functionality. In this phase, we do a complete demo of the functionality, including any changes requested. This is to get all the stakeholders on the same page. Any suggestions or requests for changes are tabled and scoped for a future release.

Based on the availability of time and resources, your project team can decide how many CRPs they would like to do.

The CRPs we discuss in this chapter are critical project activities where the project team plans to do the following:

- Implement functionality on a new system, such as moving from old legacy systems into a totally new system. As an example, during our PRM implementation, we migrated partner data and functions from legacy systems and manual Excel sheets. Users do not know how to articulate their business needs. All they want is a system that they can use effectively.
- The project team implements totally brand-new functionality with a redesigned user interface and user experience. This functionality is very uncommon, and your team may be one of the early adopters, such as implementing a partner locator.
- Your business users' needs are critical and highly visible. This is when you cannot go wrong at any cost, and you have dedicated business resources available for your project.

After understanding the various stages of CRPs, it is time for us to explore at what point in the project and how often to facilitate the session. We will discuss which participants need to be invited to these sessions to make them valuable and productive.

Exploring the timing and participants of CRPs

For each of the CRP phases, plan to do two sessions. The first session is done mid-way through the project phase so that users get a chance to see how things are progressing. The second one is done at the end of the phase to get agreement and approvals. The first session will usually be longer and can consist of 1 to 3 full-day sessions. The second session will usually be shorter. You do not need to plan exactly the same duration for all phases, as it depends on your business needs. For example, if the requirements are vague, then the scoping CRPs can run for longer. Similarly, if the design is complex, then the design CRP needs to run for longer. In my case, when we did a PRM release, which is a high-priority company initiative, our first sessions lasted a week, where we invited key stakeholders from various regions to collocate in a full-day conference session. The second session we did was a hybrid model, as it was too much for users to travel for in-person sessions.

Participant invitations will vary based on CRP phases. Since this session is time-consuming, invite only stakeholders and project team members who can add value and are directly responsible for specific functions or capabilities.

A sample simplified schedule of the CRP is displayed in *Figure 9.1*. In the following timeline, the project phases have a duration of about 6 weeks. Above the timeline, the CRPs are planned approximately 10 days after the start of each phase, and the second one just before ending the phase.

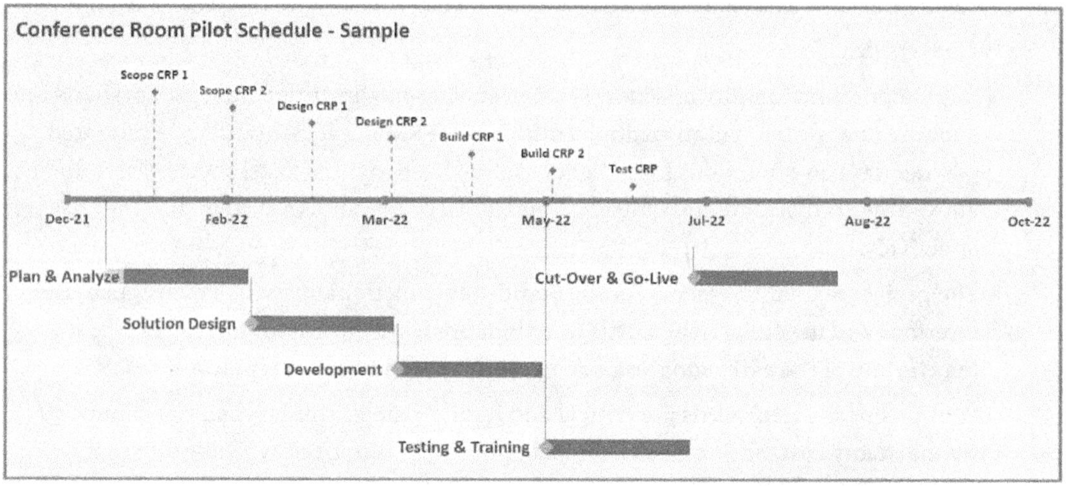

Figure 9.1 – CRP schedule (sample)

Let's discuss each CRP stage in detail in the following sections.

Scope CRP

During the scope CRP, we start with a whiteboard and progressively develop it into a simplified process flow where the team has the opportunity to identify gaps and missing requirements. This is the phase where we develop the as-is and to-be process flows collaboratively with input from business users and SMEs. By the end of the scope CRP, our team comes up with a simplified process flow for one specific functionality in our project scope, as shown in *Figure 9.2*:

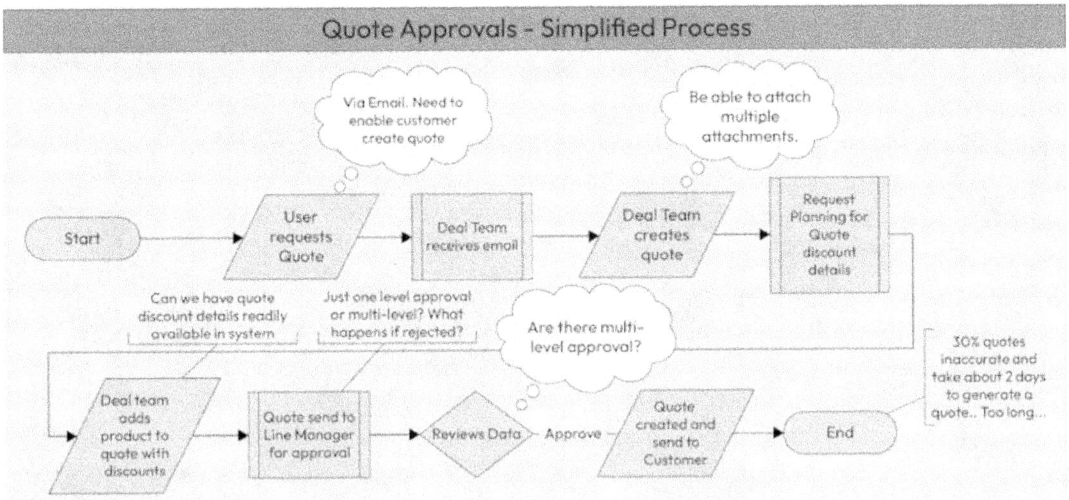

Figure 9.2 – Quote approvals: simplified process flow

We used this process flow as the starting point for our next CRP.

During the scope CRP, invite key stakeholders, SMEs, and only the core project team leads. Developer, QA, and training team members are not required at this stage.

Design CRP

During our design CRP, we refine the flow and create a more detailed process flow and screen mockups. For the user interface design aspect, we can mock up the screen with fields and design the pages and navigation. In our simplified example for one of the functionalities, we came up with a flow from start to finish for a quote approval process, with each role performing specific tasks, as shown in *Figure 9.3*:

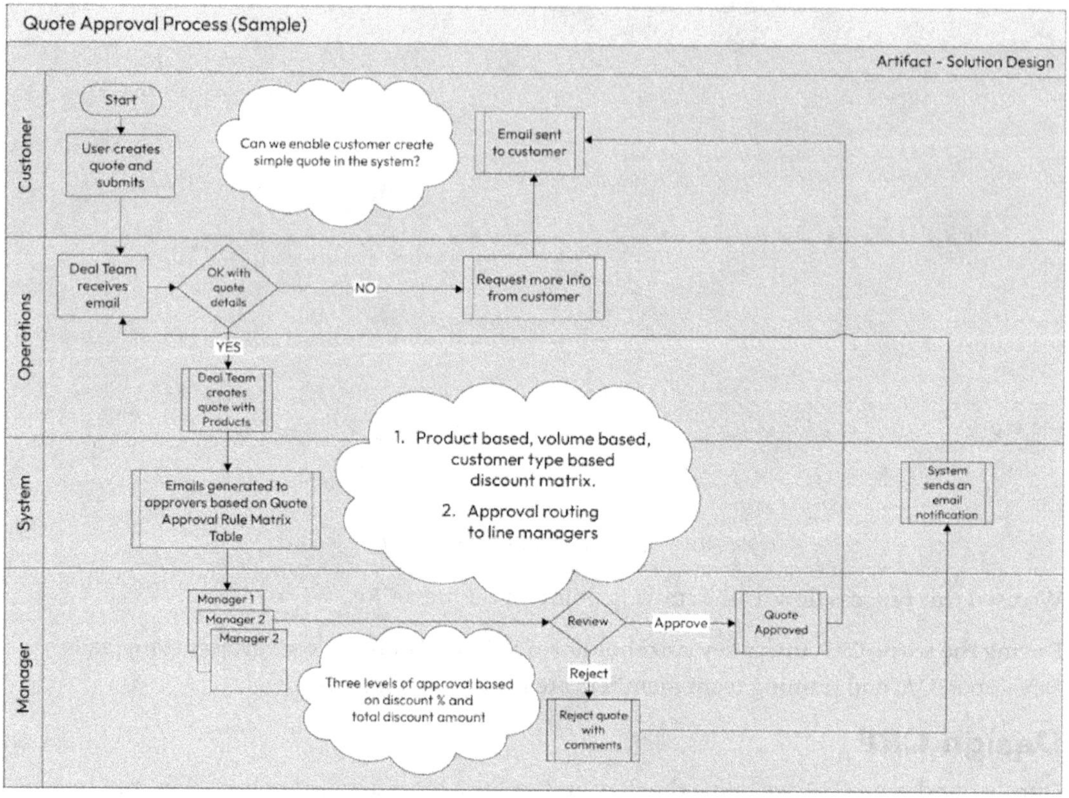

Figure 9.3: Quote approval process

This process helps the stakeholders and the project team, especially our technical team, understand the process visually and come up with all appropriate non-functional requirements.

During the design CRP, invite key stakeholders, SMEs, solution architects, technical architects, tech leads, and core project team members.

Build CRP

During the build CRP, our technical team starts developing the functionality of the system. The demo done during the first build CRP will be more focused on the user interface and the happy path (or happy flow). After socializing and incorporating the input from participants, the technical team goes ahead and completes the fully functioning solution with all possible exceptions and error handling conditions. This fully baked product is demoed during the second build CRP. This is where the stakeholders and business users can view and get a feel for the proposed functionality of the system. The business users, at this point, usually tend to ask for more enhancements, and it is up to the business analyst and project manager, along with the project sponsor, to manage and see what can be implemented now and what can be implemented later, in a future release. A sample simplified solution for quote approval is shown in *Figure 9.4*. The figure displays the fully functional quote layout screen with action buttons such as **Create PDF**, **Submit for Approval**, and **Email Quote**.

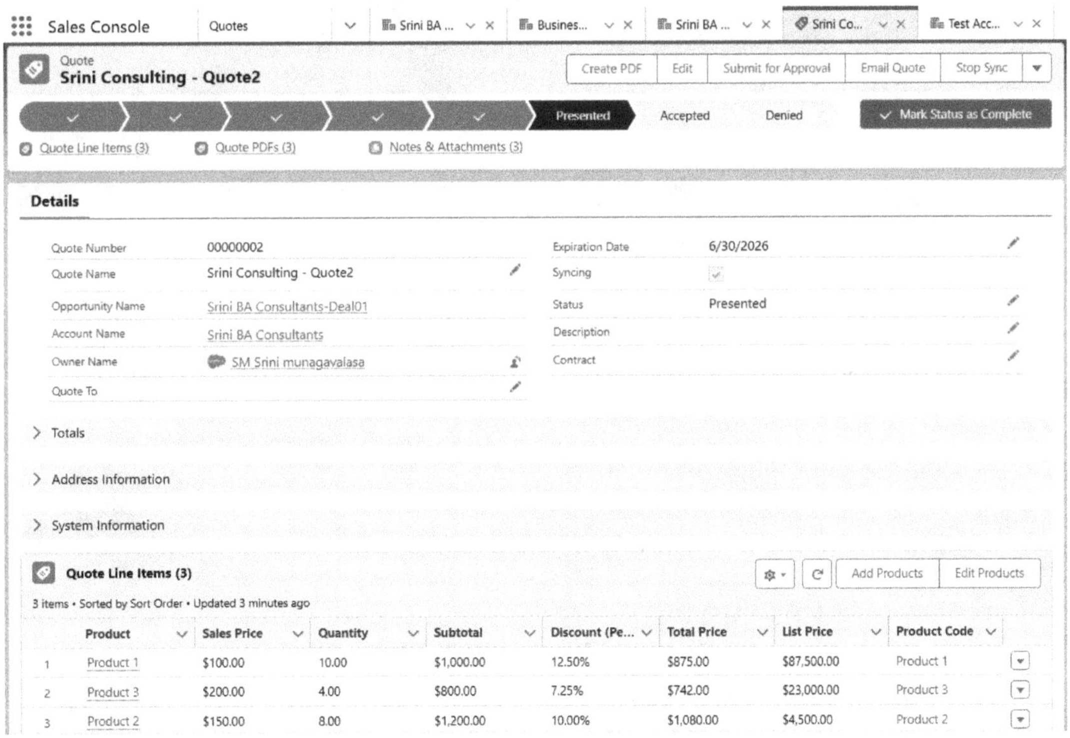

Figure 9.4 – Sample quote screen with fully functioning actions and buttons

During the build CRP, invite key stakeholders, SMEs, solution architects, technical architects, tech leads, development team members, QA leads, and core project team members.

Test CRP

The last CRP is just before starting testing. We prep and load test data so that the user can use this data to test various scenarios. This one is optional, as you can include this in the design CRP. Since this can be done via remote methods, I prefer to have this so that the business users doing UAT will have an opportunity to understand and see the functionality from end to end. This will result in fewer queries and less waiting during the actual UAT phase. A sample screenshot with the output of the quote in PDF format is displayed in *Figure 9.5*:

Company Address	US	Created Date	1/23/2026
		Expiration Date	6/30/2026
		Quote Number	00000002

Prepared By	SM Srini munagavalasa
Phone	(631) 942-5609
Email	srini.munagavalasa@gmail.com

Bill To Name	Srini BA Consultants	Ship To Name	Srini BA Consultants
Bill To	1251 NY - 312 Constitution Place Austin, TX 78767 USA Austin, TX	Ship To	1251NY-312 Constitution Place Austin, TX 78767 USA

Product	List Price	Sales Price	Quantity	Discount (Percentage)	Total Price
Product 1	$87,500.00	$100.00	10.00	12.50%	$875.00
Product 2	$4,500.00	$150.00	8.00	10.00%	$1,080.00
Product 3	$23,000.00	$200.00	4.00	7.25%	$742.00

Subtotal	$3,000.00
Discount	10.10%
Total Price	$2,697.00
Grand Total	$2,697.00

Quote Acceptance Information

Signature ______________________

Name

Figure 9.5 – Sample quote PDF page

During the test CRP, invite all team members as required. This can be just one session (about 2 to 4 hours) done in a hybrid format (on-site and/or remote).

Spacing the sessions logically and planning them well in advance helps the team members get value out of the sessions. Their active participation and involvement keep everyone on the same page and leave no room for misunderstanding related to requirements, the designed solution, and finally, the build.

> **Note**
>
> Try to keep the session participants to approximately 20 team members. More than this will be excessive and may not be productive. Also, you do not need the same team members in all CRPs. Pick the ones who have the required knowledge and can add business value.

Facilitating CRPs

CRPs must be planned well in advance to provide an opportunity for the participants to make arrangements to attend these sessions. This means some participants may have to make travel arrangements and free up their calendars to be able to dedicate their attention and time to CRP sessions. To make this a rewarding experience for your participants, you need to ensure that the session is planned and executed efficiently and effectively.

Let us look at some of the important tasks that we can perform to make CRP facilitation successful:

- Plan and create a CRP road map.
- Identify key participants of these CRP sessions: key stakeholders, SMEs, architects, and key project team members. Communicate with the participants after finalizing adding or removing team members, before making a final list. Always keep a primary and secondary team member.
- Prepare a detailed agenda approximately 2 to 4 weeks in advance and communicate this to the participants. This will help the users know which meetings to attend and come prepared for the sessions.
- To optimize usage of time effectively, schedule main sessions for 90 minutes with 15-minute breaks. Breakout sessions with smaller groups of participants can be 60-minute sessions.

> **Note**
>
> Breakout sessions are useful for teams to discuss in smaller groups and come to a consensus when there is a divergent understanding or misunderstanding of requirements or functionality.

- Assign a junior team member to take care of meeting logistics, such as conference room booking and arranging the resources required during the meeting, including flip charts, markers, sticky notes, a projector, and microphones.
- Identify a scribe for these meetings to take meeting notes and record any open questions. This person should be knowledgeable and able to take notes effectively. Team members, when actively discussing or debating, will not stop or pause for the note-taker to take notes. The scribe should be able to take notes, elaborate on them in detail, and document them for the team. Assigning a junior team member will be very ineffective.

When on-site attendance is not feasible due to budget or travel constraints, a high-impact remote CRP can be achieved by leveraging collaborative digital whiteboards and video conferencing tools that mirror the "in-room" experience. To maximize engagement, sessions should be shorter and more frequent to combat virtual fatigue, utilizing "digital breakout rooms" for the deep-dive discussions previously held in physical corners.

Success in a remote environment relies heavily on pre-session preparation; providing participants with "pre-read" materials and interactive prototypes ahead of time ensures that the live call is dedicated to active decision-making rather than passive information sharing. By using tools such as diagrams.net or Balsamiq in real time during the call, the scribe can visualize consensus instantly, ensuring that remote participants remain as aligned and invested as those on site.

Let's take a look at a sample CRP.

Agenda: Opportunity management and discounting

Objective: To validate the automated discount logic and user interface for the new business sales process.

Time	Topic	Lead	Format
00:00 - 00:10	Welcome and context: Review the session goals and parking lot rules.	Project Lead	Presentation

Time	Topic	Lead	Format
00:10 - 00:40	Scenario walk-through: Live demonstration of the Opportunity Discount Flow (as seen in *Figure 8.7*).	Architect/Business Analyst	Live Demo
00:40 - 01:10	Hands-on validation: SMEs test the prototype with real-world edge cases.	SMEs/users	Interactive
01:10 - 01:25	Feedback capture: Discussion of gaps, UX friction, or missing logic.	Scribe	Open forum
01:25 - 01:30	Next steps: Confirm action items and the date for the next iteration.	Project lead	Closing

Table 9.1: A sample agenda

This sample agenda is designed to keep a 90-minute CRP focused and productive, providing the necessary structure to manage stakeholder expectations from start to finish.

In this section, we learned how prior planning of a few simple but important tasks can help us effectively facilitate our CRPs. Now, let us take a look at how these CRP sessions can introduce a few pain points and how we can manage them.

Managing scope creep during CRPs

Planning and conducting many CRPs has its own pros and cons.

- The pros are that we keep everyone informed and on the same page. By collaborating as a group during the CRP session, participants get an opportunity to progressively see the product (functionality) develop. This helps with having open and honest conversations and helps the team steer in the right direction.

- The cons are that there is a lot of room for scope creep. Business stakeholders may realize they failed to identify or inform other business needs. This is a good thing as far as the scope of the CRM phase is concerned, as the main goal here is to identify gaps and improvements.

Let us see the impacts of these pros and cons during each stage of CRPs and how we can manage them to our advantage.

During the scope CRP phase, we certainly should expect many requests, and the majority of them are usually valid. What is in scope and what is not in scope needs to be carefully managed by you as a business analyst and the project manager.

In the design phase, the scope needs to be controlled more aggressively. Anything new cropping up should be evaluated and parked for a later release or provided with an alternative simplified solution, and this can be a manual process too. The most important outcome of this design CRP should be identifying usability aspects and non-functional and integration-related requirements.

The build phase should be focused on changes, if any, related to the user interface and user experience. If the design CRP is done productively, we should not see any functional gaps. The tech team may find some non-functional related gaps or technical constraints, and this CRP can help identify them, and the technical team can utilize CRP sessions to inform the business stakeholders.

> Note
>
> For every constraint that is not feasible, the team needs to come up with a workaround. Without a workaround, the business may not have a way to operate, and you cannot simply say there is a constraint and no workaround.

The testing CRP should be more of a demo to all the project team members, and this will help the operations team, training team, and production support teams understand the functions and features. This will help prepare the team for go-live and post-go-live support.

Any changes—big or small—need to go through the change control team. This team, comprising project sponsors and key project team members, should determine whether the change can be absorbed in the release or pushed to the next release. There may be cases where, based on how critical the requirement is, the project date is extended. Make sure the project team documents all additional requests (which could be gaps, usability, or enhancement requests) and captures who raised them and when, a brief description, the importance, who they were reviewed by, who accepted them, or if they were kept on hold.

> Note
>
> Do not be too rigid in change control. Any low-hanging fruits that are easy to implement should be added to the scope after being socialized and agreed on by the team during these CRPs. This is a great motivating factor for CRP participants; you will see better engagement, and it will be a win-win scenario for the project team and business team.
>
> The change control team should be participants in these CRP sessions, and any new requirements that come up should be added during the breakout session. I would say each day, in the CRP schedule, the change control meeting should take place an hour before the session closes. This session should not take more than 15 to 30 minutes, and a decision on go/no-go for additional requirements should be communicated by the close of the session. This saves an enormous amount of time for the whole team.

Reviewing the benefits of CRPs

A well-oiled CRP, planned and managed efficiently and effectively, will provide many benefits. Let us list some of them here:

- Provides transparency and a common understanding of business needs, the designed solution, the product being built, and the final product.
- It is a platform for effective collaboration and idea generation. Effective CRPs, facilitated efficiently, let the team interact naturally, allow them to contribute, and create the most productive outcome.
- Multiple dedicated in-person sessions away from regular work will help create bonds with different team members and enable team members to learn from others. For example, the opportunity/quote management team can learn how the contract team operates and will have an opportunity to understand their business processes and procedures. Similarly, the contract team can learn from the quote team. This helps them empathize with others' work by understanding the intricacies (procedures and policies) and helps bring out the best in people.
- It is an opportunity for stakeholders, SMEs, and project team members to socialize and share experiences. Bonding and creating friendships makes future interactions between team members much easier.

- Getting approvals and resolving disagreements will be much faster as all the key team members are in the same sessions. This saves a lot of time for the team members and the project.
- CRPs allow users to see the mockup solution/prototype firsthand. This helps build confidence not only within the participants but also within the rest of the team, as the session attendees can take the prototype back to their team and communicate to them how their needs are shaping along with the project.
- CRP attendees can help by encouraging and answering queries from their team members. This helps increase user adoption. Your team can identify a few trailblazers from these sessions and recommend them as SPOCs/champions from their group. These experts can help you bridge the connection between the project and the end user.
- The technical team will benefit immensely as they understand exactly what is needed by the business. Iterative feedback and listening to discussions during CRPs help them deliver a great final product with proposed features and functions.
- The QA (testing) team will benefit by understanding the progression of the needs to the final solution. The testing team will be able to design and test the right test scripts and scenarios, and be able to know what to test from a business user perspective. This helps in reducing user acceptance testing defects/queries.
- The training team will be able to prepare and curate the training materials and deliver them productively.
- It is a good place for idea generation. Team members are encouraged to be innovative and free to express their ideas, and this provides your team with an excellent opportunity to capture and document them. Many of them may be off the chart, but are excellent ideas that can be implemented in future releases or other projects in your organization.
- It is a good source for project team members to understand the evolution of business needs into a workable solution. This can immensely help the team with the documentation and creation of various project artifacts, such as flow charts, process flows, FDDs, DDDs, and training material.

Now that we've seen how CRPs create a strong foundation for your project, the real value comes down to how you run them. Let's jump into some practical tips to help you facilitate these sessions effectively and keep everyone on track.

Practical tips for success

A few practical tips that can be beneficial during your CRP sessions are as follows:

- **Use templates**: Standardize and use the same format for all your CRPs – for example, an agenda, a PowerPoint deck, or an issues/enhancement tracker. This helps participants get comfortable with processes and procedures.
- **Communication with stakeholders and project team members**: Send status reports periodically with action items and due dates to all participants and possibly include their managers and other project team members who are not at the meeting. Make all artifacts available (a read-only version) on a central document management system that team members can access, like a SharePoint/Teams site or a document management tool of your choice.
- **Engage leads**: Always make it a point to engage leads so that resources assigned to the project are completely motivated for the entire duration of the session. Also, provide feedback, especially when positive, to the respective leads. These types of small things make a huge difference to the project.
- **Checkpoints**: Add checkpoints throughout the session, both during and at the end, to get a pulse on how things are progressing. I usually prefer to break the leads and key stakeholders into smaller groups to get a pulse during breaks, and these can be informal check-ins. The whole group can be included in a 15-minute session before ending the session for the day.
- **Lessons learned**: At the end of each session, make it a ritual to note the lessons learned. You'll get valuable insight and feedback that can be incorporated into the next session. Ask each member simple questions, such as the following:
    - What went well?
    - What did not go well? How could it have been improved?
    - Any concerns?
    - Suggestions for improvement
- **Next steps**: Just before you end the session, make sure you communicate the next steps with concrete dates, and, if possible, include an agenda for the next session.
- **Facilities**: Ensure you have organized the facilities, such as the availability of a meeting room for the entire duration, including all meeting room equipment, such as a projector, whiteboard, flip charts, and telephone system.

- **One note-taker/communicator**: Designate an SME-level person who can understand and take notes. This designated person should be able to distill and refine the notes and prepare minutes for communication to all team members.
- **Centrally located documentation for effective collaboration**: Make sure team members have access to all project-related documents, including any flow charts, process flows, project artifacts, and all meeting minutes. These artifacts should be easily accessible from multiple devices.
- **Give ample time for a Q&A before ending the CRP session**: Stakeholders always love to ask for the next steps and committed dates, so plan and prepare well in advance.
- **Plan to send MoM**: Send meeting minutes on the same day after ending the session to all participants and their leads while the topic is still fresh in their heads.

CRPs are effective methods for team members to experience and see the progression of business needs into a fully functioning business solution. A well-planned and well-spaced CRP during various stages of the project helps identify and resolve issues effectively. These sessions also create opportunities to improve user adoption.

Summary

CRPs help bring stakeholders, SMEs, architects, and QA, training, and project team members together. Holding these sessions at different stages of the project helps team members collaborate effectively to gain a common understanding of business needs and the proposed solution. Well-managed CRPs help teams steer in the right direction, add business value, and avoid any pitfalls along the way, while progressively shaping the final product.

In this chapter, we discussed possible phases where you can plan your prototyping activities. You learned how to effectively facilitate CRP sessions with the right participants and the right timing while keeping an eye on how to manage scope creep. We also saw the benefits of CRP sessions, and finally, you learned a few practical tips that will possibly benefit and prepare you to be successful at facilitating and managing CRP sessions productively.

In the next chapter, we will cover technical and quality testing approaches and the role of a business analyst in making testing efforts effective and fruitful. We will review how to identify the skills we need our testers to have, help them understand the intricacies of the system and business concepts, and aid them in identifying scenarios and the right set of usable test data.

Questions

1. List a few benefits of CRPs.

2. What is change control, and why is it important?
3. Given resource constraints, give one example of how you could optimize a CRP session.

Get this book's PDF version and more

Scan the QR code (or go to `packtpub.com/unlock`). Search for this book by name, confirm the edition, and then follow the steps on the page.

UNLOCK NOW

Note: Keep your invoice handy. Purchases made directly from Packt don't require an invoice.

10

Technical and Quality Testing

In the previous chapter, we discussed possible phases in which you can effectively plan your prototyping activities. You learned how to effectively facilitate CRP, how to manage scope creep, and some practical tips that will possibly benefit you during your CRP sessions.

Testing is exploring the system's functionality and its usability in a systematic manner to find issues and report them as defects. After getting fixed, these defects will be retested.

In this chapter, we will cover technical and quality testing approaches and the role of the Business Analyst in making testing efforts effective and fruitful. We will review how to identify the skills needed by our testers, help them understand the intricacies of the system and business concepts, and aid them in identifying scenarios and the right set of usable test data.

We will cover the following topics in this chapter:

- Planning testing activities
- Testing strategy
- Testing approach
- Testing phases
- Types of testing
- Sample test script/case fields
- Benefits of testing
- Practical tips for success
- Role of AI in testing efforts

Testing cannot be 100% effective, and finding zero defects is not realistic. Start testing as early as possible to uncover any design deficiencies, also called shift-left testing. This will give you room to fix design issues and reduce defects down the line.

Planning testing activities

Software testing should be planned well in advance, and the testing team should be involved from the start of the project. On any type of project, we cannot do exhaustive testing and test everything in all possible combinations, as it is practically not feasible. Planning helps us make educated choices and make the testing sensible and meaningful. The testing plan is a progressive document and gets refined during the entire course of the project, starting from the requirements phase and getting more granular and refined as we progress.

Let us look at what tests need to be planned during various project phases:

- **User Acceptance Testing** (**UAT**) planning is done during the requirements specification phase. This test plan outlines what the business users may possibly be testing during the acceptance phase of testing. This UAT plan incrementally gets updated as it helps us with the finalized UAT plan with relevant scope and scenarios.
- **System Integration Testing** (**SIT**) planning starts during the functional specification phase. SIT involves the overall testing of a software system, including integrations with and to other systems. By the time we have the functional requirements document, we should have a good understanding of the scope of system testing and results in the SIT plan.
- The **integration testing plan** is initiated in the technical specification (HLD) during the architectural design phase. The architect and the technical team will be able to identify and plan for integration testing scenarios to test the integration between various dependent and independent software components.
- The **unit testing plan** should start as soon as technical development is started and during module/technical development (LLD). This is where the technical team will do detailed testing of each of the units or a combination of a few small units.

Note

Regression testing, which is rerunning tests to confirm that software features that have already been developed and tested continue to operate as expected when a change is introduced, needs to be planned to include it at every stage of testing. Small modifications can occasionally cause havoc with your implementations when they are implemented without a regression test.

In this chapter, software testing includes a hybrid methodology. We combine traditional waterfall development models for certain phases and agile development models or a combination for other phases of the project. *Figure 10.1* is a high-level testing plan sample for a medium- to high-complexity project. This is a simplified sample, and your testing strategy may be more complex and may look very different.

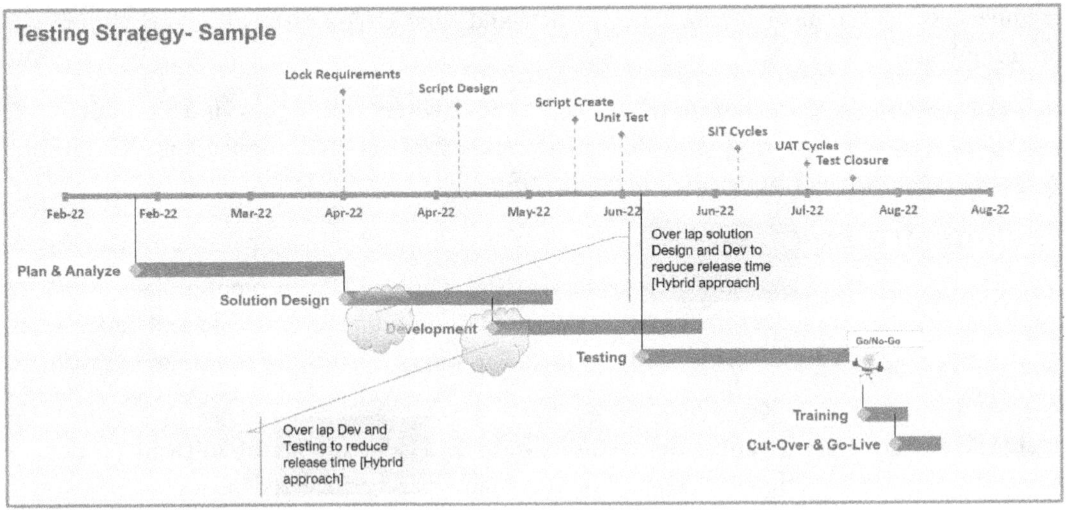

Figure 10.1 – Testing plan

Let's quickly review the stages:

- **Plan and analyze**: By the end of the analysis phase of the project, all the requirements are prioritized, agreed upon, and approved by stakeholders and are baselined for the release. No more changes without CCB approval are entertained, and essentially all requirements for this release are locked. During this phase, we follow the traditional project management methodology.
- **Solution design and development build**: The design and build are staggered and done iteratively using agile methodology to get instant testing feedback. Unit testing and integration testing are part of the build activity, and good planning and execution will help us with minimizing defects in the later phases.
- **Testing (system testing and acceptance testing)**: System testing is started after completing unit and integration testing cycles. This is done in traditional waterfall methodology and performed in multiple cycles. Regression testing should be integral to each of the test cycles every time any changes are promoted to avoid breaking any existing critical functionality.

No testing will be planned or performed during the training and go-live phases. These are the last two major project activities, where you start training only after successful test completion and a Go-live decision is made. After go-live, the technical team will verify code and data migrations, and Business Analysts, along with key business SMEs, will validate the functionality before opening the system for production usage.

Creating a testing strategy for your project with a timeline and duration will help team members get the complete picture of how, when, and what kind of testing is in scope for the project release.

In the next section, I will walk you through different activities, techniques, and methods associated with a good testing strategy. A good testing strategy needs meticulous planning and keeps testing processes disciplined and predictable.

Testing strategy

A testing strategy helps you define testing levels to be conducted during your project implementation. It provides direction to make sure test objectives are covered and understood by all team members associated with the project. For minor projects, we can collapse testing to fewer levels.

Technical and quality software testing helps us verify and validate that the software product meets the proposed solution with respect to documented and prioritized business requirements:

- **Verify**: Make sure that the output is accurate, true, and justified to ensure the solution follows standards and meets the agreed upon and documented requirements. This verifies that we deliver the solution in the right way.
- **Validate**: Check the accuracy of the output, which helps us to ensure the right solutions are implemented that meet the business needs and are usable by the users of the system. This validates that we are implementing the right solution.

Testing levels

Our main goal of testing is to find defects and issues as early in the project as possible. Proper planning and testing ensure that the identified defects are related to specific requirements. Plan to do exhaustive testing as much as possible with available resource constraints and adhere to the agreed exit criteria.

For a typical project release, we have four levels of testing, as listed here. For each of the testing levels, we define the testing methods that will be used:

- **Unit testing**: Verify the smallest possible unit (entity) independently of other units (entities). This is done during development to make sure each developed unit works before moving on to the next unit development.

- **Integration testing**: Test plans are developed during the high-level solution design phase to make sure the individual units, when combined, can work together seamlessly. This is done at the module level, or with a few modules grouped together.
- **System testing**: This is done for the entire functionality in scope, as well as anything connected to these functions, including integrations. This testing should include functional and non-functional testing.
- **UAT**: This is developed during the requirements phase and should be tested by the end users. The test system should represent a true production system, and the business users should test their end-to-end scenarios (a day in the life of a user).
- **Regression testing**: Verify the end-to-end functionality of the entire system to ensure that new changes or bug fixes have not negatively impacted existing features. This is performed periodically via automation throughout the build to catch issues early, followed by a final, complete regression at the end of the project to confirm total system stability before production.

Testing methods

There are two testing methods, which can be used either independently or in combination. These two methods are manual or automated. Based on organizational project requirements, you can use company-approved tools such as **HPE Micro Focus** and **Selenium**.

Testing schedule

Based on the complexity of the project, SIT is usually performed in about three cycles, with one regression test as the fourth cycle. For SIT and regression testing, the assumption is that we use a testing tool. Create four folders for each cycle. If not, doing four rounds of testing will take a significant amount of time and we may have to reduce the cycles.

Let's look at a sample testing schedule for a typical global CRM project depicting different cycles of testing done by the QA team and UAT team:

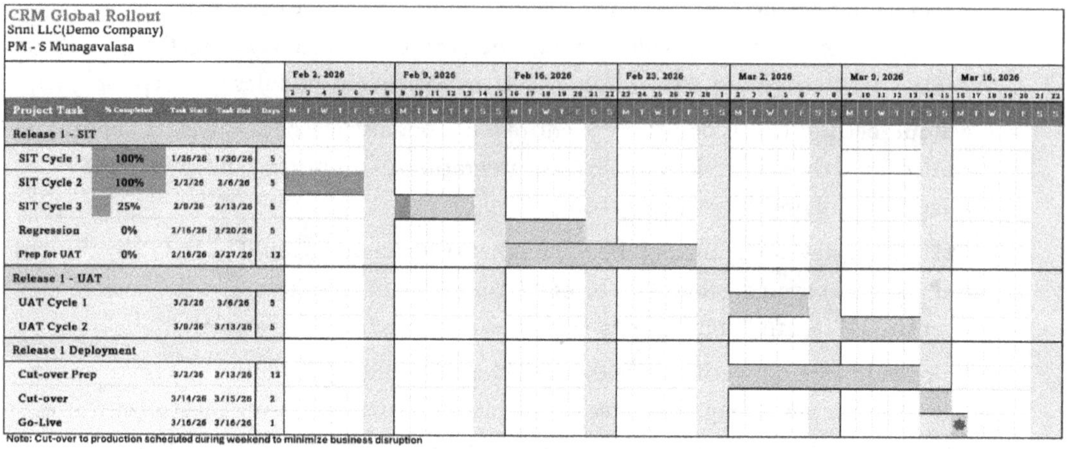

Figure 10.2 – Testing schedule (for a sample CRM global release)

We'll review each cycle in detail:

- **First cycle**: Test a full round of all test cases/scripts. Defects are created for failed test cases and communicated to Business Analysts to review and send them to the development team for fixing. After these issues are fixed, Business Analysts will do validation to approve it for retesting in the next cycle. You will find a good number of defects during this cycle. Prepare a summary report for cycle 1.
- **Second cycle**: Review test cases/scripts and adjust them as needed. Rerun failed test cases and make sure the test cases run successfully. Do your second round of testing for all the test cases/scripts and create defects for failed test cases. These defects are reviewed, fixed, validated, and approved for retesting in the next cycle. The defect count should drastically reduce, and some enhancements (missed functions or missed scripts) will surface. Prepare a summary report for cycle 2.
- **Third cycle**: Review test cases/scripts and adjust and retest failed cases until they are successfully tested without issues. Do the final round of testing to make sure you have very few or no failed test cases. We should see a handful of failed cases that need to be reviewed and either approved or parked based on Business Analyst analysis. Prepare a summary report for cycle 3.
- **Regression cycle (cycle 4)**: This cycle will test end-to-end scenario scripts, including integrations with backend systems and any third-party apps of the whole system. This is to ensure we do not accidentally break the existing functionality. Basically, we are testing out the functionality the way we do in production. This environment will have a clone of the production data. This means we load any legacy data and use it to test the

functionality and integrations. Minimal defects are expected and fixed or parked accordingly. As needed, fixed defects should be retested before approving them for UAT (covered in more detail in *Chapter 12, User Acceptance Testing*). It should be noted that the regression cycle described here is the final, comprehensive validation of the end-to-end system. To avoid the risk of late-stage rework—where a bug discovered now could invalidate weeks of prior testing—you should adopt a "shift-left" approach by running automated regression scripts nightly during earlier cycles. This ensures that by the time you reach this final cycle, the process is a formal verification of a stable system rather than a discovery phase for critical defects.

> Note
>
> If you see significant failed test cases during cycle 2, take a pause and review the test cases/scripts and development work. It is worth reviewing, as this will cause major issues down the line. If it happens during cycle 3, you need to reconsider revisiting the design and test strategy. Moving forward in this situation will be a disaster and will lead to project remediation efforts after implementation.
>
> If you are migrating large volumes of legacy data from existing legacy systems, you should consider setting up conversion mock cycles. It takes a few cycles to get the data right, as it depends on the complexity of your existing metadata. Each cycle helps refine the process, capture the time it takes to perform the tasks, and prepare the deployment team in advance. These data load runs are done after SIT and before regression testing.

Let's take a look at different testing approaches that can help us with testing. Adopt a combination of techniques and methods for each of your testing levels that meets your project needs. Picking the right approach will help you verify and validate that your software functions efficiently.

Testing approach

There are multiple testing approaches that we can utilize during various stages of the project, and they fall under one or more of these techniques/methods/processes:

- **Static testing technique**: Static testing, as the name implies, is a verification process and is done without executing any software functionality. Done by an SME, this technique helps us proactively prevent defects early in the project. Examples are code walk-throughs, technical reviews, inspections, and so on, to project documents such as requirements documents, test scripts, and source code.

- **Dynamic testing technique**: Dynamic testing, as the name suggests, is actual testing conducted on specific functionality and it does the validation of the executed functionality. This is when we uncover many issues. The sooner we unearth them, the better it is for the project. Examples are unit testing, integration testing, system testing, and so on.
- **Passive testing technique**: Passive testing is done from the output of dynamic testing. Team members who are testers will not interact with the functionality in the system but rather analyze the system logs, debug logs, and system traces to look for similar patterns from past projects. This is more like forensic analysis, where samples (that is, logs) are collected and sent to remote labs for analysis.
- **Exploratory testing technique**: Exploratory testing is used on agile projects and testing activities are continuously done iteratively, which encompasses concurrent learning, test designing, test execution, and test result interpretation. This yields excellent testing quality when done by knowledgeable team members. This testing will be helpful when testing completely new functionality for the first time to get rapid feedback.
- **Blackbox testing method**: Blackbox testing aims to test the functionality of the application based on functional specifications, with no need to understand how it is implemented internally. This is like when we drive a car—our goal is to go from point A to point B comfortably and safely and we do not need to know how the car engine works or how the A/C unit performs. This testing can be done at any testing level, such as unit, system, integration, and UAT. Business users use this technique while performing acceptance testing.
- **Whitebox testing technique**: Whitebox testing is also called open box testing, where users examine the program code logic. This technique helps the technical team look at and improve the code, making it robust and clean. It is helpful when the functionality is complex and technical team members with in-depth knowledge will be able to unearth errors hidden in the code and remove any redundant code. This technique is very useful during unit testing and integration testing.
- **Graybox testing technique**: Graybox testing, as the name suggests, is a mix of the blackbox and whitebox techniques. It is very useful to test functionality related to web-based applications or specific complex domain testing.

There are other approaches that can be used, such as the scenario testing technique, the load testing technique, and so on. Based on the methodology and project implementation cadence of your organization, you can use a combination of these approaches that best fits your project needs. In the next section, we will review different testing phases of our testing life cycle.

Testing phases

Software testing, for the most part, follows the following six phases. Based on your project, you can merge or skip some phases. Before testing can be started, we need to establish test entry/exit criteria. These testing phases are important to SIT and are performed by an independent testing team, also called the **QA** team.

Let's list the entry/exit criteria for typical software testing:

- Requirements are prioritized and finalized
- Acceptance criteria for testing have been agreed
- Testing phases and methods are established

Let's quickly review each of these phases:

- **Requirements analysis**: During this phase, testing team members understand the requirements in detail from a testing perspective, so that they can plan and estimate the testing scope and efforts.
- **Planning**: During this phase, the QA test lead determines the overall test strategy, including the specific test environments required for each phase of the project. They also define the testing effort, resource requirements, and the specific tools needed to ensure a stable and representative staging area for validation.
- **Test case/script design and development**: The testing team identifies and prepares scripts/scenarios and each requirement is mapped to one or more of the test cases/scripts. Test data requirements are identified, created, and reviewed for tester usage.
- **Environment setup**: During this phase, the proper testing environment is identified and set up. Setting up includes moving all the configuration metadata and actual test data, along with access to user records. This phase also makes sure the environment is ready for use and is stable by doing a smoke test.
- **Execution**: During this phase, the actual execution of test cases based on the test plan is performed by the testers. The tester will execute test scripts and report issues by creating defects. During this phase, all fixed defects will be retested in all test cases, executed with a status of pass or fail. Also, every test case is mapped to requirements, and a **requirements traceability matrix** (**RTM**) is created to ensure that every test case can be traced to requirements and marked with an execution status.
- **Closure**: During this phase, test coverage reports, defect reports, issue dashboards, and test closure reports are generated. After SIT, the testing team will perform smoke and sanity tests in a production environment to make sure the system is ready and stable for UAT.

Note the following:

- Smoke testing (system stability) is a software testing method to confirm that the build solution is stable, important features work as expected, and there are no showstoppers in the build that is under testing
- Sanity testing (system rationality) is a quick and basic test to determine whether a particular software functionality is behaving correctly at a basic level before subjecting it to the next stage of rigorous testing

In the next section, we will learn about different types of testing that are available for us to perform testing on functional and non-functional aspects of our software functionality.

Types of testing

Let us review some important testing types in the context of SaaS CRM implementations.

We will focus on testing related to the SaaS model software. With SaaS providers such as Salesforce, HubSpot, or NetSuite, we do not need to worry much about performance, scalability, and security issues if we follow the software provider's guidelines and best practices.

There are two main types of testing that we are interested in in this chapter:

- **Functional testing**: This is a software testing technique to test the features and functionality of the developed solution. Functional testing includes positive, negative, and boundary scenarios. Let us look at some common functional testing techniques:
    - **Unit testing** (also called development unit testing): Unit testing is done by the technical team member on individual units/modules to determine whether there are any bugs in the code. Following the unit test life cycle, a unit test helps with identifying issues early and enables us to reduce the cost of testing.
    - **Integration testing**: This involves individual units being combined and tested to ensure individual modules work together seamlessly without any issues as one single entity.
    - **System testing**: All components of the system are tested to evaluate system compliance against specified business/functional requirements.
    - **Interface testing**: System components are tested to confirm that data and controls are exchanged as planned. In the event of failure to exchange, exceptions are handled accordingly.
    - **Regression**: This involves re-executing a specific set of test cases that may be impacted due to code changes. This is to confirm the stability of the product due

to changing requirements. The main aim of regression testing is to uncover issues in previously working software that have been introduced unintentionally because of the change.

- **UAT**: This is testing performed to confirm the correctness and completeness of the business requirements specification. This is the final stage of testing before the specification can be promoted to production.

- **Non-functional testing**: This is a software testing technique that examines a system's non-functional attributes, such as performance, usability, reliability, scalability, security, and so on. It is designed to test the preparedness and readiness of a system. Let's look at a few techniques:
    - **Documentation testing**: This involves testing documented artifacts such as the functional requirements document, test plan, test cases, and static code analysis. Salesforce provides the Apex testing framework for Apex test classes to define and generate code coverage. This is to ensure correctness, completeness, and clarity.
    - **Installation testing**: This testing is to make sure the installed components or software are working as expected. For example, installing a plugin such as the D&B Hoovers managed AppExchange package in Salesforce.
    - **Performance testing**: This is performed to confirm system responsiveness, availability, reliability, stability, scalability, and so on, and to measure the following quality attributes of the system:
        - Load testing
        - Stress testing
        - Endurance (or soak) testing
        - Spike testing
    - **Security testing**: This testing is used to determine that the system protects data, authorizes and authenticates the right users, and renders intended functionality.

During SIT and UAT phases of testing, the majority of these functional and non-functional test scripts are executed as per the test plan. Issues identified during testing are reported as defects and retested after the defects are addressed by your development team.

Defects identified during testing will impact test execution. Test defects are classified as critical, high, medium, and low. A critical defect can require a simple fix, but if it impacts multiple test scripts, it is the one with the highest priority for our testing. A medium defect can involve complex changes, but may impact only one or two test cases, and so it can wait until others are fixed. This severity value gives us insight into which defects need to be prioritized.

> **Note**
>
> Test severity is not the same as business priority. When we say the test severity is critical, that means the tester cannot move forward with testing for that module unless this defect is addressed.

Let us look at a sample test script/test case template. These are typical fields that we would see while creating a test scenario. This can be used for manual testing or can be used to upload our business specification into a testing tool.

Sample test script/case fields

Test scenarios are high-level actions that provide an overview of what needs to be tested. They help in the testing of end-to-end functionality. Test cases are low-level activities and help with thorough testing of the application. They enable us to test small parts of functionality in detail. Each test script can have multiple test cases.

The following are some of the important fields that can be used to create test scripts/cases:

- **Test Script ID**: TS-Account Management-001
- **Test Script Name**: The user will be able to create and edit accounts in Salesforce
- **Test Script Description**: The user will be able to create and edit account records in Salesforce after entering the required fields and will be able to save successfully
- **Pre-conditions**: The user will have appropriate access and be able to log into the Salesforce system via a browser and/or mobile apps
- **Test System Name**: SIT
- **BRD ID: BRD**-R1-1.001
- **Complexity**: Medium
- **Variations**: 6 (Sales Analyst, Sales Manager, Service Analyst, Service Manager, Planning, and Legal)
- **Database Table/Object name**: Account
- **Test Case ID**: TC-Account Management-001-Create-01
- **Cycle**: 1
- **Planned Execution Date**: MM/DD/YYYY

- **Test Case Description**: The user will be able to create a prospect and be able to input all required and optional fields, and be able to save the record
- **Variation Description**: The user (sales analyst) will not be able to delete the prospect record
- **Test Case Result**: Output from the testing (example – user able to successfully create a prospect)
- **Responsible Tester**: XXXXXXXX
- **Evidence**: Links to screenshots.
- **Results**: Final result, which can be Pass/Fail/Not in scope

Creating test scripts/cases simplifies your review and approval process, as Excel documents can be shared via a central shared site. After approval, they can be loaded onto a testing tool of your choice.

Figure 10.3 shows a sample SIT test script:

SIT Test Scripts			System Integration Testing - Cycle 1 (2 weeks starting MM/DD/YYYY)													
Test Script ID	Test Script Name	Test Script Description	Pre Conditions	Test System Name	BRD ID	Complexity	Variations	Database Table/ Object	Test Case ID	Cycle	Planned Execution Date	Test Case Description	Test Case Result	Responsible Tester	Results
TS ID 1	TS Name 1	xxx xxxxxx xxxxxxxx xxxx	1. xxxxx 2. xxxxx	Salesforce	BRD x.xx.xx	M	Sales Analysts Sales Manager Planning	Account	TC-001	1		xxx xxxxxx xxxxxxxx xxxx	xxx xxxxxx xxxxxxxx xxxx	xxxxxx	Paaa/Fail
															Paaa/Fail
															Paaa/Fail
															Paaa/Fail
															Paaa/Fail
TS ID 1	TS Name 1	xxx xxxxxx xxxxxxxx xxxx	1. xxxxx 2. xxxxx	Salesforce	BRD x.xx.xx	M	Service Analyst Service Manager Planning	Account	TC-002	1	MM/DD/YYY	xxxxxxxx xxxxxxxx xxxxxxxx	xxx xxxxxx xxxxxxxx xxxx	xxxxxx	Paaa/Fail
															Paaa/Fail
															Paaa/Fail
															Paaa/Fail
															Paaa/Fail
															Paaa/Fail
TS ID 1	TS Name 1	xxx xxxxxx xxxxxxxx xxxx	1. xxxxx 2. xxxxx	Salesforce	BRD x.xx.xx	M	Compliance Legal	Account	TC-003	1	MM/DD/YYY	xxxxxxxx xxxxxxxx xxxxxxxx	xxx xxxxxx xxxxxxxx xxxx	xxxxxx	Paaa/Fail
															Paaa/Fail
															Paaa/Fail
															Paaa/Fail
															Paaa/Fail
															Paaa/Fail
TS ID 2	TS Name 2	xxx xxxxxx xxxxxxxx xxxx	1. xxxxx 2. xxxxx	Salesforce	BRD x.xx.xx	M	Sales Analysts Sales Manager Planning	Account	TC-004	1	MM/DD/YYY	xxxxxxxx xxxxxxxx xxxxxxxx	xxx xxxxxx xxxxxxxx xxxx	xxxxxx	Paaa/Fail
															Paaa/Fail
															Paaa/Fail
															Paaa/Fail
															Paaa/Fail

Figure 10.3 – SIT test script

Sample templates can be utilized for UAT too. Feel free to add/remove fields as fits your project testing.

Benefits of testing

Proper software testing, when planned and executed well, will yield many benefits. Project success or failure and user adoption greatly depend on how well the system responds and makes sure that the end users do not run into post-production deployment issues.

Some of the benefits that can be realized are the following:

- The risk of failure of the product after deployment into production can be greatly minimized.
- Integrations with other systems work seamlessly, and in the case of failure due to any reason, there is a restart mechanism or a documented way to handle the issue.
- By delivering quality software products, end users do not face issues and are able to perform their business without needing to worry about software issues.
- An issue-free software functionality or system will build trust and drive business user adoption. We will have satisfied business users/customers.
- It's a great opportunity to verify and validate the security features of the software functionality and provide software free from any vulnerabilities. Vulnerabilities in test systems can be controlled and fixed with minimal risk. The same thing happening with end users in production systems can be a major risk.
- Finally, good testing results in cost-effectiveness. Spending a little bit more during testing pays off manyfold in the long run, in addition to many other benefits.

Practical tips for success

A few practical tips that can benefit you during your testing activities are the following:

- Do not skip the test strategy. Make a checklist for the test strategy.
- Where possible, use automated tools, especially for SIT and regression tests. Regression tests must be run multiple times whenever an issue is fixed.
- UAT should be done by business users who are SMEs in their area. Following prior documented test scripts is very ineffective. In addition to test scripts, business users should run through ad hoc real-life scenarios. If there are any issues, this is our last opportunity to find and fix them.
- The QA team or SIT team should be made up of independent team members with good system knowledge, with some level of business domain knowledge. The technical team members who developed the application should be the last people to do SIT.
- Team members should take static testing seriously. A review of the static artifacts by SMEs and leads helps clarify and keep the documents clean and unambiguous. The identification of issues with static testing does not require code fixing and retesting. All that is needed is a few hours of dedicated time from experts.

- Perform code reviews and functionality demos within the project team, and especially the technical team, where the leads and experts can provide immediate feedback.
- The project's test lead and Business Analyst should spend time triaging defects. Try to group similar defects by what is called defect clustering. We often find 70%-80% of defects in 20-30% of the functionality.
- At the end of each cycle, revise and update test cases. Periodic reviews keep the test cases current and relevant.
- Software applications are accessed by users on various devices and browsers. Make sure to do regression tests on all browsers and devices.
- It is okay if a few defects cannot be resolved, and I have never seen a defect-free implementation. If the defect is not business-critical, or if it is critical but there is a workaround agreed by business stakeholders, then this defect can be parked for future release prioritization.
- Create and test reports and dashboards. This test system should have a good set of data for SIT and should mirror the production instance for UAT.
- Always include sufficient test cases to test functionality with loaded legacy data. The data converted from a legacy system should work as well as new records created in the system.
- Facilitate and capture feedback from team members, especially around testing activities. These lessons learned from documents will be valuable artifacts for your future releases.
- Do not forget to acknowledge and recognize individuals and teams who went above and beyond and helped with testing activities.

Role of AI in testing efforts

As we all know, AI is shaping how we work with software, not just through technical advancements but also in testing and quality assurance. AI is not a magic wand but an advanced analytical tool that relies heavily on quality data. The Business Analyst (BA) role is crucial in ensuring that the data fed into these AI tools, such as the quality of requirements as inputs, is accurate so that AI can help us identify the right test scenarios and scripts, especially edge cases. It can be immensely useful in prioritizing where to focus efforts in testing. Let's see a few examples so that you get a flavour of what AI tools can do.

- **Test scenario generation**: **Generative AI** (**GenAI**) can analyse documentation, user stories, and existing code bases to fill test coverage gaps more efficiently than manual efforts alone.
    - Test case amplification can take a high-level user story and automatically generate dozens of low-level, detailed test cases, covering positive paths, negative tests, and error conditions.
    - **Edge case prediction**: AI models analyse system behavior and data constraints to dynamically create edge cases—inputs at the boundaries or in unexpected formats.
- **Risk-based testing prioritization**: One of the valuable outputs of AI in testing is its ability to quantify and prioritize risk. **Machine learning** (**ML**) models can analyse complex data points to tell the testing team where to test, not just what to test.
    - AI analyses the code base, correlating high defect rates with technical factors such as complexity and developer activity. It then flags these modules as high-risk for the upcoming release, allowing the BA to focus testing on those specific features.
    - **Change impact analysis on code changes**: AI can trace the dependencies across the application to predict which existing tests are most likely to fail or which features may be impacted. This allows for highly targeted regression test selection, reducing execution time significantly.
- **Creation of regression test scripts**: To scale quality assurance, one can utilize AI to bridge the gap between requirements and execution. By feeding partially AI-generated test cases into Copilot, a team can rapidly produce high-quality Playwright scripts, allowing for an increase in the depth and breadth of regression testing without a proportional increase in development time.

Using AI tools shifts quality assurance from a manual task to an intelligent, data-driven, and predictive process. The BA's success depends on adopting these new tools and ensuring the core requirements and data are organized to maximize the capabilities of ML.

That brings us to the end of this chapter.

Summary

Software testing is an extremely important activity on any project. Testing is not just a phase that can be done at the end of development, but rather a continuous process that requires the QA/testing team's involvement in all phases of the project. The testing process starts with team members understanding the business requirements and being able to plan and come up with a solid test strategy. The testing team should be able to understand the scope, tools, and methods they can use to make the testing process effective and productive.

In this chapter, we discussed the importance of a good testing strategy and how it can benefit our project team with testing activities. You learned about various testing approaches, phases, and types. Finally, we concluded the chapter with how and why testing can benefit your projects and some good practical tips from my experience. These practical tips will help you avoid a lot of pain points and save you time during your test cycles. We have seen how using AI tools can shift testing from a manual task to an intelligent, data-driven, and predictive process. As a BA, your success depends on adopting these new tools and ensuring the core requirements and data are structured and organized to maximize the capabilities of AI tools.

In the next chapter, we will cover dependencies between test cases and requirements, and how to trace them and establish 100% test case coverage. You will learn the importance of the RTM and what to capture in the matrix. We will also discuss the advantages of good requirements traceability and a sample RTM template.

Questions

1. List some testing tools that help with automated testing.
2. Is regression testing the same as retesting?
3. Think of a few examples of blackbox testing.

Further reading

- *Secrets to Successful Data Conversions* (`https://sapinsider.org/secrets-to-successful-data-conversions/`)

- *The different types of testing in software* (`https://www.atlassian.com/continuous-delivery/software-testing/types-of-software-testing`)
- *Software Testing: Principles and Practices* (`https://a.co/d/6Eu7zEp`)

Get this book's PDF version and more

Scan the QR code (or go to `packtpub.com/unlock`). Search for this book by name, confirm the edition, and then follow the steps on the page.

UNLOCK NOW

Note: Keep your invoice handy. Purchases made directly from Packt don't require an invoice

11

Requirements Traceability Matrix

In the previous chapter, we discussed the importance of a good testing strategy and how it can help us to identify issues early in the project so that we can deliver usable functionality that meets our stakeholders' needs and, at the same time, reduce costs by addressing issues as soon as possible.

In this chapter, we will understand the importance of the relationship between requirements and various project artifacts and how they help us establish traceability. Requirements traceability guides us to ensure that the projects proceed on the right track and address issues along the way. It helps us in identifying and bridging gaps to make sure each of the business requirements provides the intended functionality and fulfills business needs. We will see how to link requirements to project deliverables and make sure we have 100% coverage. We will also see how to identify inconsistencies with testing artifacts and the overall testing execution status—and, hence, the progress of the project.

We will cover the following topics:

- Understanding the importance of a **Requirements Traceability Matrix** (**RTM**)
- Learning what to capture in an RTM
- Exploring types of traceability
- Reviewing an RTM template sample
- Benefits of an RTM
- Practical tips for success

An RTM is a worksheet that comprises all your prioritized requirements for the project release, along with corresponding test scripts and test cases. It also includes their status, as well as references to other project artifacts. This helps the project team to understand the level of testing activities performed or yet to be performed for each functionality and ensure that no requirement is left uncovered.

Let's look at the importance of an RTM in the next section.

Understanding the importance of an RTM

Most often, an RTM is created during the test planning phase of the project. It will be very useful if you start preparing this document right from the requirements phase and keep adding details as you progress through each phase of the project. This will make it easier to capture details accurately without missing out on any important items. Collaborating on and reviewing this document, along with other artifacts, during each stage of the project enables us to maintain an active and up-to-date version of the requirements traceability. Even in Agile or hybrid delivery models, where requirements evolve frequently, an RTM anchors the team by providing continuity, visibility, and alignment across sprints. Think of requirements traceability as the way we track the progress of the movement of goods from one point to another. Let's assume a customer purchased a car. If there is a problem with some part, the car company can trace back and check where the part originated from. Similarly, if there is a defect identified with a specific part (say, a seatbelt), the company can identify the customers and send a recall notice (to fix or replace the seatbelt at their nearest dealer) to them. Requirements traceability does the same thing for software requirements. Any defects along the way can be traced bidirectionally and addressed efficiently so that they are accurately solved, and business user requirements are delivered as originally proposed.

Issues are unavoidable, no matter what they might be. How soon we identify them and how fast we address them makes all the difference. Identifying and fixing issues or bugs needs to be made as seamless as possible for the end users. The majority of the time, users should not even realize that these issues exist. A good example is regular updates to your laptop's software and patches. These are fixes for bugs or improvements, and the majority of users do not even realize or experience the issues before they are patched.

I have listed here some of the reasons for having a well-documented RTM. This document is more valuable if your projects are relatively complex to highly complex. It does not take much time to create an RTM, but the value it adds can be manyfold. Let us look at a few of the reasons for having an RTM. An RTM aids the project team in the following ways:

- Helping us ensure that each of the prioritized BRD requirements is tested adequately and there is complete coverage
- Establishing transparency of processes and the ability to track changes
- Ensuring that the delivered solution fulfills all requirements and helping prevent failures by identifying gaps
- Finding defects, issues, and enhancements during project implementation at every stage of the project, and helping us quickly identify the root cause, thus saving time

- Providing context to the development team so that they can refer to the business requirement or trace forward to test coverage
- Streamlining the development life cycle by connecting project artifacts
- Defining expectations for the testing team
- Ensuring the right product is built the right way

Here, we looked at a few good reasons for the use of an RTM. In the next section, let us see what elements to capture in the RTM, as well as how to make it useful and helpful to understand and, at the same time, get a complete view at a glance.

Learning what to capture in an RTM

A well-designed RTM should have enough fields for project team members to get a 360-degree view of the linkage from the business requirement to the test case status. Too many fields lead to confusion, and too few fields make it incomplete. I have captured a few important fields in this section for reference so that users, at first glance, will be able to trace the artifact bidirectionally. You can add more fields if it makes sense for your project implementation, and you can always hide a few fields and unhide them when needed.

You can utilize prior artifacts such as business requirements documents, functional documents, solution design documents, wireframes, process flows, test scripts, and test cases, and link key fields to establish and capture traceability. You can create either a long document with all possible fields from these artifacts or a simplified version with a few key unique fields. Based on these key unique fields, you can refer to the respective documents to get granular details to understand the cause of test failure or scope creep.

The following are the fields that I prefer to include in the RTM. It is your choice whether to pick your own set of fields, as long as you can establish effective traceability:

- **BRD requirement ID**: Requirement ID from our business requirement document
- **BRD requirement description**
- **Conceptual diagram name**
- **Process flow name**
- **FDD ID**: Functional requirement ID
- **Solution design document name**
- **Functional area**: For example, account management, opportunity management, and so on
- **DDD name**: Design document ID
- **Test script ID**: Script ID

- **Test case ID**: Case ID
- **Test script variants**: For example, sales analysts from different business units may see different field and picklist values
- **User type**: Role of the user being tested. For example, sales agent, sales manager, sales operations, marketing user, and so on
- **Test case description**: Brief description of what is tested
- **Status**: Pass, fail, or invalid

We have defined a list of RTM fields, but before we can capture details under these fields, let us see the types of traceability and how this set of fields helps us with different traceability types.

Exploring types of traceability

There are three types of traceability. We move from left to right, right to left, or either way. They are as follows:

- **Forward traceability**: We start with a prioritized requirement and trace it each way to see the design, development, and testing progress in the right direction toward our proposed and intended functionality. Essentially, it helps us to make sure that we captured the requirement correctly, we have all the information related to the requirement, and that this is the right requirement.

  > Note
  >
  > Link requirements → design → test cases
  >
  > Ensures all requirements are implemented and tested

- **Backward traceability**: We start tracing backward from a specific phase of the project. It can be from test script to development to design to business requirement, or it can be from solution design to functional design to business requirement. This is to make sure we are doing the right thing and staying on the right track. This type of traceability ensures that we can trace each individual functionality developed in the system back to the prioritized business requirement. Essentially, it helps us to make sure we deliver the right solution, that the requirement is valid, and that the solution adds business value.

> **Note**
>
> Link test cases → design → requirements
>
> Ensures each test or deliverable maps back to the valid requirements

- **Bidirectional traceability**: Bidirectional traceability ensures we can trace each requirement forward to its test cases and deliverables and trace each defect or test result backward to its originating requirement—both ways, depending on the given scenario. If we see a failed test case, we can trace it back and get to the root cause. If we had additional requirements, such as scope changes, we could help with analyzing the impacts of changes to requirements.

> **Note**
>
> Bidirectional traceability:
>
> Combines both forward and backward traceability, offering a complete audit trail

In addition to tracing business requirements to the end solution and vice versa, we need to consider mapping them to the following entities to make it complete:

- **Business units**: This helps us ensure that we do not miss any operational steps performed by specific business roles (sales analyst, service analyst, planning, and so on) and aligns with the business process flow steps. Any missed and redundant activities or tasks can be identified and fixed.
- **User role**: This helps us identify and fix all steps that the user performs while using the system. For example, the service analyst's role is to create and manage cases, and this may be their primary function, whereas the sales analyst's role is to capture and qualify leads and close more deals.
- **Database object**: Tracing to and from database objects helps us with security requirements in confirming availability. For example, service agents do not need access to campaign management. Another example is CRUD permission to the object to determine who can and cannot create, read, update, and delete the record.

We have learned about the types of traceability and three distinct mapping entities. Now, let's look at a sample RTM template and see for ourselves how it can help us see the traceability and various data points and artifacts in the traced path.

Reviewing an RTM template sample

Let us look at sample RTM data. You can use various RTM tools available on the market based on the nature and complexity of your project release. In our case, I am using a simple Excel spreadsheet, as shown here. This matrix is a simplified version of a more complex RTM. An RTM for a complex project will span multiple columns and rows and would not fit into a single screenshot. You can add more columns and capture details related to BRD, FDD, and so on, and keep the columns hidden. When you see a failed test case, you can unhide the columns to get details from a single document.

Requirements Traceability Matrix													
BRD Requirement Id	BRD Requirement Description	Conceptual Diagram Name	Process Flow Name	Solution Design Document Name	Functional Area	FDD Id	DDD Name	Test Script Id	Test Case Id	Test Script Variants	User Type	Test Case Description	Status
RQ_ID001	Account Management	None	Account Flow	Release1_Track01	Accounts	FDD_001	DDD_001	Script-101	TST_001/TST_002	2	3	TC Description_001	Pass
						FDD_002	DDD_002	Script-102	TST_003/TST_005	2	3	TC Description_002	Pass
						FDD_003	DDD_003	Script-103	TST_006/TST_008	1	3	TC Description_003	Pass
RQ_ID002	Contact management	None	None	Release1_Track01	Contacts	FDD_004	DDD_004	Script-104	TST_00x/TST_00y	2	2	TC Description_004	Pass
						FDD_005	DDD_005	Script-105	TST_00x/TST_00y	1	2	TC Description_005	Fail
						FDD_006	DDD_006	Script-106	TST_00x/TST_00y	1	2	TC Description_006	Pass
RQ_ID003	Case management	None	Case Flow	Release1_Track01	Cases	FDD_007	DDD_007	Script-107	TST_00x/TST_00y	5	3	TC Description_007	Fail
						FDD_008	DDD_008	Script-108	TST_00x/TST_00y	4	3	TC Description_008	Pass
RQ_ID004	Opportunity Management	Opportunity diagram	Opportunity Flow	Release1_Track02	Opportunities	FDD_009	DDD_009	Script-109	TST_00x/TST_00y	2	3	TC Description_009	Pass
						FDD_010	DDD_010	Script-110	TST_00x/TST_00y	2	3	TC Description_010	Pass
						FDD_011	DDD_011	Script-111	TST_00x/TST_00y	2	3	TC Description_011	Pass
RQ_ID005	Quote Management	None	Quote/Quote Approval flow	Release1_Track02	Quotes	FDD_012	DDD_012	Script-112	TST_00x/TST_00y	3	1	TC Description_012	Pass
						FDD_013	DDD_013	Script-113	TST_00x/TST_00y	3	1	TC Description_013	Pass
RQ_ID006	Quote Approval Rule Matrix	None	Quote/Quote Approval flow	Release1_Track02	Quotes	FDD_014	DDD_014	Script-114	TST_00x/TST_00y	2	2	TC Description_014	Pass
						FDD_015	DDD_015	Script-115	TST_00x/TST_00y	1	2	TC Description_015	Pass
						FDD_016	DDD_016	Script-116	TST_00x/TST_00y	1	1	TC Description_016	Pass
RQ_ID007	Product Alignment	Product Alignment diagram	None	Release1_Track03	Products	FDD_017	DDD_017	Script-117	TST_00x/TST_00y	3	2	TC Description_017	In Progress
						FDD_018	DDD_018	Script-118	TST_00x/TST_00y	3	2	TC Description_018	No Run
RQ_ID008	Campaign Management	None	None	Release1_Track03	Campaign	FDD_019	DDD_019	Script-119	TST_00x/TST_00y	5	3	TC Description_019	No Run

Figure 11.1 – Requirements traceability matrix

Based on this data and using test case artifacts, we can create a sample traceability chart, as shown next. There are many tools available that can help you with creating complex and more sophisticated traceability matrices:

Requirements Traceability Chart													
Test Script Coverage				Test Coverage		Business Requirement ID							
Test Script ID	Complexity	Variants	User Types	Required	Actual	RQ_ID001	RQ_ID002	RQ_ID003	RQ_ID004	RQ_ID005	RQ_ID006	RQ_ID007	RQ_ID008
Script-101	H	5	3	15	15								
Script-102	H	6	2	12	10								
Script-103	M	9	3	27	21								
Script-104	M	6	3	18	18								
Script-105	H	6	1	6	6								
Script-106	L	4	3	12	12								
Script-107	M	6	2	12	12								

Figure 11.2 – Requirements traceability chart

Let's review each script. There are three good scenarios here. Let us take a look at each one of them in detail:

- **Scenario 1: Script-101** is a highly complex script with five variants and three user types. So, the test coverage required to be covered at a minimum will be 5x3=15. We can have more, but at a minimum, we need to test 15 scripts. In reality, our tester tested all

15, and this fulfills business requirements **RQ_ID001** and **RQ_ID002**. This is what we want, and all is good so far. This is the same with **Script-106** and **Script-107**.

- **Scenario 2**: In coverage of **Script-102** and **Script-103**, we have a gap in required versus actual. In the matrix, we do not see any testing done for **RQ_ID005** and **RQ_ID006**. So, from this simplified matrix, we are able to quickly identify that the testing either failed or was not yet executed for these two scripts. Based on the test script ID and business requirement ID, we can refer to the requirement traceability matrix and identify the corresponding project artifacts, such as FDD, DDD, and process flows, which can tremendously help the project team to quickly find the source so that further analysis can be done to address the failed test script.
- **Scenario 3**: For **Script-105**, we see that all six test scripts were executed, and none of them are aligned or belong to any of our test scripts. There are a few options here: test scripts may be redundant, they may have missed out on being assigned to prioritized requirements, or we may have tested requirements not in scope for our release. From this simple chart, we can identify them quickly and fix the chart by either removing the test scripts from our testing scope or tagging the correct business requirement in the RTM.

I could go on with many more examples, but these three scenarios should have provided you with a good idea of how you can use an RTM to trace in either direction.

Let's briefly discuss the role of AI here. The key is to start small, experiment with these tools, understand their capabilities, and gradually build your confidence and skills. As you progress, you'll be better equipped to harness this powerhouse effectively and integrate AI seamlessly into your daily workflows.

As mentioned in earlier chapters, AI is rapidly evolving, and in the very near future, it will handle most of these routine traceability tasks for you, freeing you to focus on more creative and innovative work.

When it comes to the RTM, now you can delegate the requirements of traceability management in Jira and Confluence to AI-driven automation. Instead of relying on manual mapping, AI can automatically link user stories, design documents, and test cases by analyzing contextual similarities and metadata. For example, when a new requirement is created or an existing one is modified, tools such as Atlassian Intelligence, ChatGPT for Jira, and GitHub Copilot for Docs can suggest related artifacts, ensuring complete coverage while reducing manual effort and oversight.

AI also enhances documentation quality and alignment. With tools such as Writer.com, Confluence AI Assistant, and Notion AI, requirements can be automatically summarized, categorized by type (functional, non-functional, or regulatory), and linked to corresponding user stories or design artifacts. These intelligent assistants help maintain real-time synchronization across Jira and Confluence, giving Business Analysts, developers, and testers a unified, accurate view of project requirements.

Now, let's see a few benefits of an RTM in the next section.

Benefits of an RTM

Some of the benefits of an effective, well-designed, and well-managed traceability matrix include helping us identify missed test coverage and, hence, potential issues that can be addressed prior to releasing the solution to the end user. Here's a detailed list:

- Traceability to the best possible extent ensures all important requirements are not missed after production deployment.
- Traceability helps the team with auditing from requirements to the final solution and ensures transparency.
- An RTM is a very helpful artifact to meet compliance needs, especially with financial, healthcare, and other industries.
- It establishes trust with stakeholders, SMEs, and other team members, as we will be able to prove our traceability, that the project work progressed as planned, and that the correct products were delivered.
- In case of change requests that crop up during various phases in projects, this helps the project team and CAB approvers evaluate the impact of potential changes and helps with related impact analysis.
- Scope changes can be easily managed, as any deviations in scope can be traced to missing design elements and test scripts.
- One very important benefit that I found extremely helpful is that it allows us to identify dependencies between requirements. We can uncover missing dependencies.
- It saves time and adds efficiency as any team member will be able to identify and trace back from failed test cases to requirements and vice versa.
- It helps with better collaboration and transparency. Anyone on the project can know the exact status of the testing scripts.

Traceability is not just about tracing requirements but ensuring each one is linked to its source, design component, test case, and deployment artifact; it also establishes accountability, supports impact analysis, and validates that all business needs are met by the delivered system. Given that there are so many benefits that can be achieved with requirements traceability, it is worth putting effort into an RTM.

Practical tips for success

Listed here are a few practical tips that have added value to my own RTMs:

- RTMs can get very complex. No matter what tool you use, try to keep it simple. Extract an Excel or PDF version (at least one daily snapshot) and make it available to all project team members.
- Certain business rules cannot be traced, and you should not waste project time and effort writing test scripts for those unless they are critical for your organization. For example, a user will use only company domain-specific emails and not personal emails, or users should be on the company network/VPN to access an application.
- Keep your RTM current. Anytime there are changes to any project artifacts, such as BRD, FDD, DDD, and test scripts, make sure the RTM is reviewed and updated.
- Include defect linkage. Extend traceability to defects found during testing to ensure every issue ties back to a requirement or design element.
- The RTM responsibility should be given to only a few team members so that only they are authorized to make additions or updates to the matrix. Always keep track of the version, even if you manage the RTM on a simple Excel sheet.
- Traceability should be reviewed, verified, validated, and agreed on by key project team members. This is especially critical for non-functional system architectural requirements that improve the quality and usability of the system.
- Business Analysts facilitating a one- to two-hour session and walk-through of the RTM with a technical team and testing team will aid everyone with effective knowledge transition compared to just sharing the documents.
- With modern AI-enabled tools, maintaining an RTM makes it easier, as the automated nature of AI tools can highlight gaps, suggest missing links, and keep traceability current across changing requirements.

Integrating these practical tips helps maintain the RTM as an effective tool for ensuring full requirement coverage. This brings us to the end of the chapter, where we will summarize the key elements of a structured testing strategy.

Summary

In this chapter, we discussed various aspects of traceability and how it can help the team identify and fix variances between the actual business requirements and the final functional solution. We got a chance to discuss the importance of a good RTM, different types of traceability, advantages of an RTM, and a sample scenario. We concluded the chapter with RTM benefits that you may be able to realize in your projects and some good practical tips, which will help guide you to create a productive RTM. We also touched on how AI-driven tools are beginning to automate traceability, offering real-time insights, suggesting links, and helping teams maintain alignment with minimal manual effort—making RTMs more intelligent and dynamic.

In the next chapter, we will explore why user acceptance is crucial for a successful go-live and how we can improve user adoption and gain trust by working with business stakeholders and helping them test real-life business end-to-end scenarios. We will explore how to focus on getting feedback on usability when the user does end-to-end scenario testing.

Questions

1. How does forward traceability help us?
2. What does backward traceability do?
3. Forward traceability is a verification process. True or false?
4. Backward traceability is a validation process. True or false?

Further reading

- The links in *Chapter 29*, *Software Requirements*, of *Software Requirements 3, 3e (Developer Best Practices)*, by Karl Wiegers and Joy Beatty, Microsoft Press US

Get this book's PDF version and more

Scan the QR code (or go to `packtpub.com/unlock`). Search for this book by name, confirm the edition, and then follow the steps on the page.

UNLOCK NOW

Note: Keep your invoice handy. Purchases made directly from Packt don't require an invoice.

Part 3

Empowering the End User—Adoption, Enablement, and Career Growth

The final part of this playbook focuses on where true success is measured: sustained end-user adoption. A technically sound solution delivers little value if users are not confident, engaged, and supported in their daily work. This part equips you with structured strategies to ensure that Salesforce becomes embedded in business operations, not merely deployed.

This part includes the following chapters:

- *Chapter 12, User Acceptance Testing*
- *Chapter 13, Communication and Knowledge Management*
- *Chapter 14, End-User Training*
- *Chapter 15, Post-Production Support and Super Care*
- *Chapter 16, The Salesforce Productivity Tool Kit*
- *Chapter 17, Salesforce Business Analyst Certification*
- *Chapter 18, Career Opportunities and Related BA Roles*

12

User Acceptance Testing

In the previous chapter, we discussed various aspects of traceability and how it can help the team identify and fix variance between the actual business requirements and the final functional solution. We had the chance to discuss which key elements to capture, the types of requirements for a good traceability matrix, and the advantages we can derive from being able to trace requirements effectively and address any gaps in coverage.

In this chapter, we will explore why user acceptance is crucial for a successful go-live. We will look at how we can improve user adoption and gain trust by working with business testers. We will see how we can work with business users and help them test real-life business end-to-end scenarios. We will explore and see the ways to focus on getting feedback on usability by encouraging testers to follow through with end-to-end scenarios and exploratory testing.

The primary goal of **user acceptance testing** (**UAT**) is to ensure that the new functionality does exactly what it is intended to do and meets the business requirements. UAT is a formal type of testing; it needs to be planned and executed in a structured way and provide objective evidence that the system is performing as intended and in line with the agreed acceptance criteria. UAT needs to include scenarios that involve end-to-end testing and cover all business processes that are directly and indirectly impacted by these changes.

In this chapter, we will discuss the following topics around UAT:

- Identifying the right set of UAT users
- Learning how to help UAT users test effectively
- Getting feedback on usability
- Exploring the need for UAT
- Leveraging Agile techniques

- Reviewing the benefits of UAT
- Practical tips for success

Identifying the right set of UAT users

Finding the right testing team members with the right skills, business knowledge, and the right attitude plays a very important role during UAT. For UAT to be effective, there are multiple dimensions. The most important dimension in testing is the tester who is performing UAT.

UAT testers should be involved right from the start of the project, and they are usually your key stakeholders who help define, refine, prioritize, and approve your project requirements. These users are involved in every phase and are intimately aware of various project artifacts at every stage of the project. They should be aware of how things have taken shape along the course of the project phases. They are the recipients of the final software solution, and they have the commitment and attitude to make the project successful. UAT gives these experts an opportunity to test-drive production in terms of working systems and helps us identify potential real issues related to functionality, usability, and accessibility. Your team needs to make every effort to identify this one critical and very important dimension – the UAT tester. The identified UAT tester, with a good understanding, helps achieve the desired results of the project. You can guide the tester with the following dimensions to make their work effective:

- **Testing coverage**: The tester should understand the scope of testing and what gets tested. This means they need to understand and be able to navigate the software system and related tools.
- **Reason for testing**: The tester should understand why they are testing. This means they need to have in-depth knowledge of the business and be able to think and do the testing creatively and effectively, and understand the risks and problems that can be mitigated by effective testing.
- **Understand testing methods and tools**: They can use a combination of various methods, such as black-box, exploratory, and others, depending on what the situation demands. They should use their creativity and be innovative with testing.
- **Evaluation**: To be able to evaluate the end results of testing, they should understand the business requirements and the business priorities. They should be part of the project from the start and involved in defining the acceptance criteria, and be able to confirm what a passing or failed test case means.

> **Note**
>
> Do not choose somebody who is free and available from the business side as a tester just for the sake of doing UAT. You would be better off skipping UAT altogether if this were the case. Another alternative, as a last resort, is that the Business Analyst and a few project SMEs can perform UAT, although it may not be as effective as testing by actual business users. The very purpose of UAT is for your end user to verify and confirm that the solution meets their business needs. If users do not do UAT, you will miss the opportunity to identify issues and get feedback early on. This leads to a cascading effect, and eventually, you run into the risk of poor user adoption.

You should have a diverse group of experts identified as testers from your business verticals. These testers should understand their businesses and how various business functions interact within and outside their business units. They should also understand and be conversant with the software systems and tools. It may so happen that it's your first project release: in this case, identify and train the right individuals who are committed to being the testers on subsequent releases along your roadmap. Retaining the majority of the same business testers helps speed up the testing process.

Typical UAT testers are key stakeholders from each of the functional areas – planning or sales operations teams, Business Analysts (more for informal testing, reproducing errors to identify defects, and retesting test scenarios to fix defects), and training team members.

> **Note**
>
> You may be surprised that you need Business Analysts and training team members to be involved in UAT. I strongly encourage you as a Business Analyst to do so. Just try one time, and you will see the following benefits:
>
> - Business Analysts can do testing quickly and identify and fix issues. Plus, by running the test scripts, they can help fix ambiguous ones. This also helps you to aid business users during their testing and to understand issues and collaborate effectively.
>
> - Training team members will be able to understand the complete process and experience how the users use the system. This helps trainers in preparing or reviewing and fine-tuning training artifacts, as well as during training for end users.

Learning how to help UAT users test effectively

User acceptance testers are like expert samplers. If you can get the right expert with excellent knowledge of the business domain and (to some extent) the software system, that will help the project team, and you will get the right feedback. It's up to the UAT test lead to provide them with the right tools and techniques and define the appropriate scope of testing so that they can complete UAT within the given time and resource constraints. We need to provide the right tools at the right time so that the business testers can do what they are good at and are tasked with doing.

Let us look at some key success factors that help us get testing done effectively:

- **Get the right UAT testers**: Get a diverse group of individuals who are super users, SMEs, business champions, planning team members, and sales operators. Their time, expertise, and business needs are the drivers for successful testing.
- **Involvement from the requirements phase**: The identification of these individuals (at least some of them) should be planned and involved right from the requirements prioritization stage. This helps them understand project priorities and set expectations about why some requirements are in scope and why others are not. They also get involved in understanding the current and proposed business process flows.
- **Walk-through/training**: Before we start UAT, these sets of users need to be trained on how to use the system. Plan to walk them through the entire system end-to-end, even if they may not be testing the entire functionality. This helps them understand how different features are linked and dependent.
- **Help them with navigation**: Provide them with a crash course, including how to log into the system and reset their password. This should include screen features, data views, reports, collaboration features, and print screen features. Make sure to review third-party apps and any integration with pertinent systems. Provide a one-page cheat sheet outlining the most commonly used functions and navigation items.
- **Recurring daily checkpoints**: I always prefer to facilitate two meetings to go through any issues, concerns, and queries. It's always good to share a screen online or through a projector to allow the tester to articulate their concerns or findings better. This also helps other testers see how a specific business user approached testing and their thought process while doing so.
- **Access to systems**: Make sure your tester has access to all the relevant systems that they are supposed to test. For example, say that they are testing account management functionality in Salesforce, and account management utilizes a third-party app such as D&B Hoovers, a KYC system, and an MDM system. Similarly, quote management may

be integrated into CPQ. Access to this system should be made as seamless as possible; if not, a 4-hour test will take days, plus a lot of frustration. Also, make sure users are provided with appropriate access reflecting the security model and not system admin-level access during UAT.

- **Teaching skills needed for testing**: Help with testing with other tools, such as the testing tool, where they may be running the scripts, screenshot tools, and recording tools to capture test evidence that may be needed for later auditing. If they must test on mobile devices, such as an iPad or Chromebook, make sure that you get a few loaned from your IT department and that all apps are made available for testing on these devices.
- **Provide test data**: Providing enough test data for testing, in addition to creating data, will be vital for effective testing. Users should be able to use existing data to make updates and see that the existing data is usable and works with integration, just like new records created by users. This should be in line with production data quality, with scrambled fields wherever you have sensitive MNPI data. A good volume of test data will help with test reports and dashboards, too.
- **Exit criteria**: Help the testers understand when they should mark a test case as passing or failing. The exit criteria should be explained and agreed upon with testers before commencing with UAT. If certain functionality fails even though it meets the exit criteria, but the business SME thinks otherwise, then the exit criteria need to be fixed. They need to understand the rules of testing, and they cannot make up rules while testing.
- **Project team hotline**: For the duration of testing, make sure someone from the project team is available to answer the UAT testers' queries. These could be functionality-related, test script-related, access-related, or anything else related to testing.

> Note
>
> We can never reach a zero-issue stage. So, define what it means when we say testing is completed. The key thing we need to define and understand during the project planning phase is the acceptance criteria.

The bottom line is that UAT testers should understand and agree on what it means to exit UAT. Your project defines the rules around what it means to exit UAT, and there is no set standard or rule. The project team should define and get a consensus on the exit criteria. Here's an example for a typical software project (sample only) – the system functions correctly as proposed, all test scripts or scenarios have been executed, and the following are true:

- There are no critical defects in the core functionality.
- There are no performance issues with either critical or non-critical components. Performance issues, even in non-critical components, will be a drag on the system.
- There are workarounds for defects of high to medium importance where an immediate solution cannot be found.

In this section, we reviewed the importance of identifying the right UAT testers, engaging them early in the project to provide them with the right tools and techniques, and collaborating continuously, which results in helping us get feedback. In the next section, let's discuss what we can do to get feedback from our UAT tester about usability and functionality, and why it is so critical.

Getting feedback on usability

Now, let's explore the usability of the system. Findings around usability, such as simplification, easier navigation, and an intuitive screen flow, are not easy to uncover. We may not have a test script or test scenario for this kind of finding, and if not addressed, it may impact the usability of the system, resulting in low adoption.

By working closely with these UAT testers, you can discover these undefined, undocumented findings. I call these findings because they are not defects in the true sense, nor are they enhancement requests, and we cannot tag them to a specific test script or even a requirement. You can call them anything, but the important thing to note here is that you have to address these for your end users. Make provisions for these kinds of findings and prepare the team beforehand so that you stop bleeding valuable time during the UAT phase. If you understand why they want what they want and how it can improve the user experience, and if it makes sense, take every effort to address them.

Often, testers and business users follow a set of test scripts and continue with their testing, things work as expected, and there are flaws we will probably never find. If the business user who is testing has a deep understanding of the business logic functionality and can empathize with a broad set of end users by considering the following approaches, your end user adoption post-deployment will exceed your expectations:

- A user-centric approach
- A simplified approach to navigation
- A meaningful screen flow or design approach

Let us look at a real-life example: as with other examples, this is simplified a lot, and when I adopted this approach, I could figure out the flaws.

Scenario: *We have a sample account plan where customers need to complete multiple tabs and complete the account plan each year. I simplified this and captured only a few fields per screen and only a few tabs so that it would be easy for you to understand and for me to drive the point across. Most of the fields on the screen are automated (as in, auto-populated based on rules) and let us assume that they can be filled in manually or auto-populated.*

During our SIT phase, our QA team followed the approved test scripts and was able to complete testing without any major issues. It was the same with UAT; when the business users tested everything, it worked like a charm.

Now, let's review this screen by screen:

1. The user logs in to the system and enters the account information in the **ACCOUNT INFO** tab, as shown in *Figure 12.1*. There are required fields, some optional fields, and other automated fields. The user clicks on the **NEXT** button. Assuming the data input is good, no validation errors are visible, and the user is able to successfully navigate to the next screen:

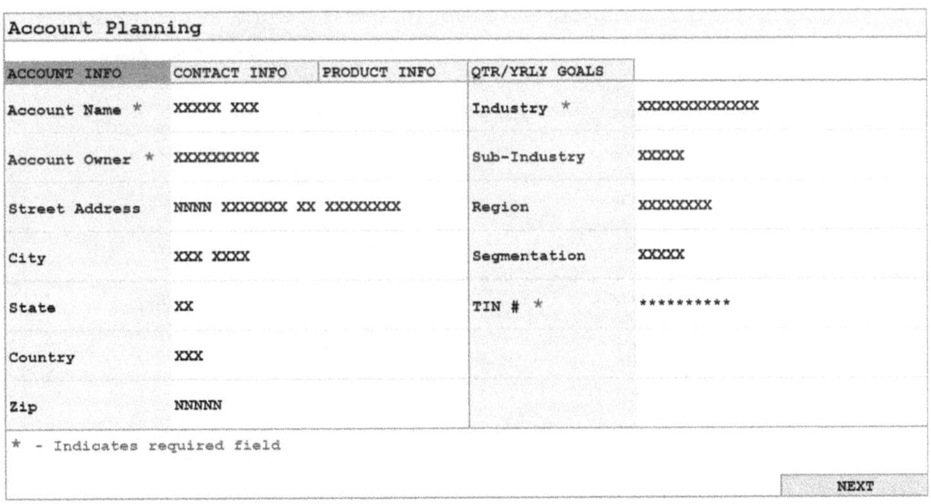

Figure 12.1 – Account Planning – the ACCOUNT INFO tab

2. The user enters the contact info and is able to navigate to the next screen. In case the user wants to go back and fix the previous screen, they have the function to go back by clicking on the **BACK** button:

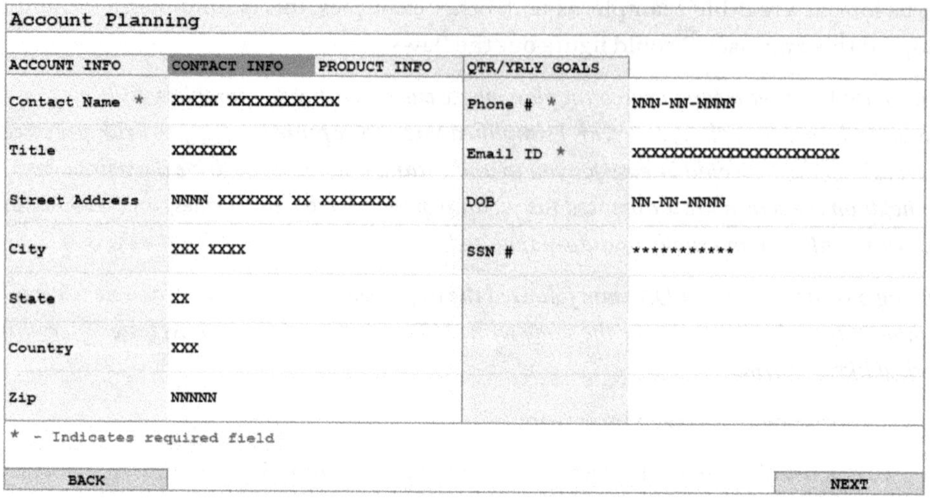

Figure 12.2 – Account Planning – the CONTACT INFO tab

3. The user enters the product info and is able to navigate to the next screen. In case the user wants to go back and fix the previous screen, they have the function to go back by clicking on the **BACK** button. So far, so good, and it works as per the script:

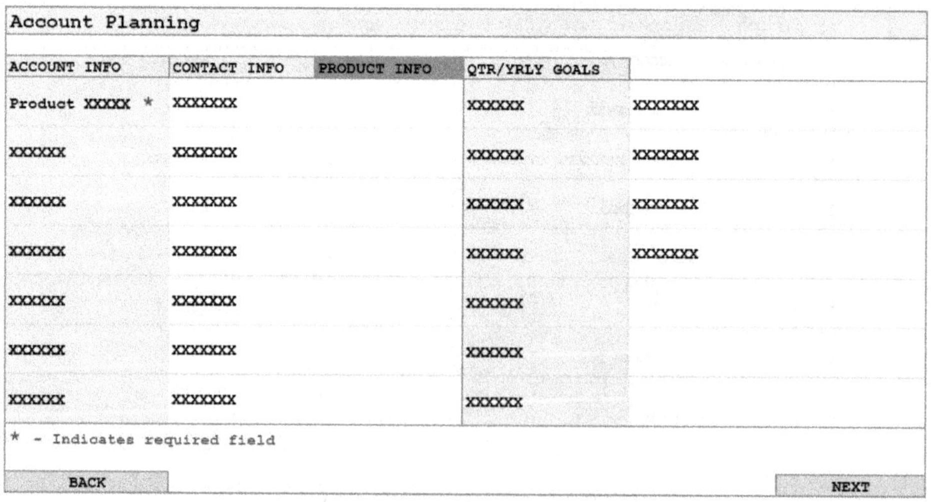

Figure 12.3 – Account Planning – the PRODUCT INFO tab

4. The user enters the quarterly and yearly info and is able to successfully submit the account plan and call it a day:

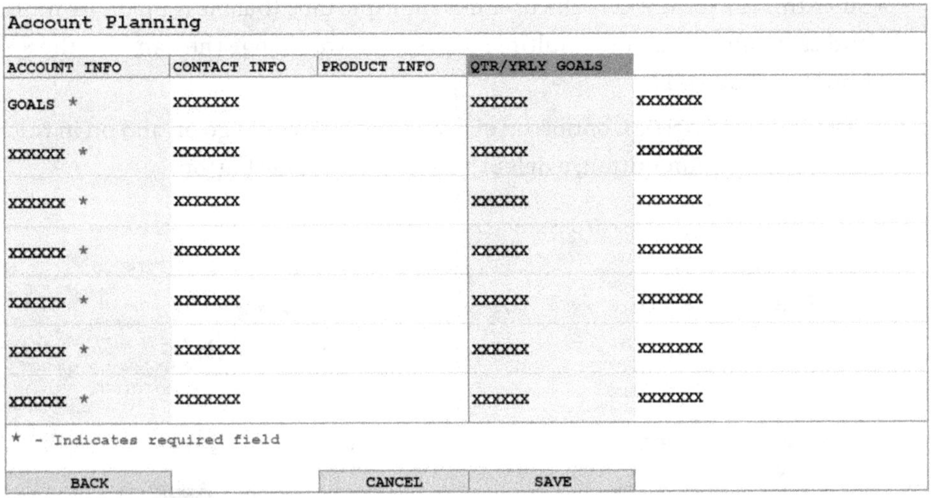

Figure 12.4 – Account Planning – the QTR/YRLY GOALS tab

Take a pause, review these screens, and see whether anything emerges from your observations. I hope you can figure out at least some of them.

Well, we can say UAT for this account planning functionality looks good, and we can sign off, as the user was able to create the plan. Wrong!

Let us take a closer look together and see our findings from the business tester or super user perspective.

Our super user here is the most valuable team member and was able to point out very important features that could save the business user a lot of time, also making them a very happy user.

Let's list a few of them, and this should give you the gist of what I am trying to convey in this example. Here are the flaws observed:

- The user is not able to toggle from one tab to another. In this case, if the user is on the last tab, can they go to the first tab just by selecting the tab?
- Can they save the partially completed version and save it as a draft so that it can be picked up later?
- As per the requirements, the print and email functions are enabled in the menu path (let's assume) – can we have an explicit function at the top of the screen?

- Since this is a form where the user fills multiple tabs (business plans are multiple tabs, and each tab can run into multiple pages), can we change the name on the **SAVE** button to **SUBMIT**?
- Can we add a **CANCEL** option on every screen? We could go on and on in this way with hover help, an edit button, a delete button, and a clone button:

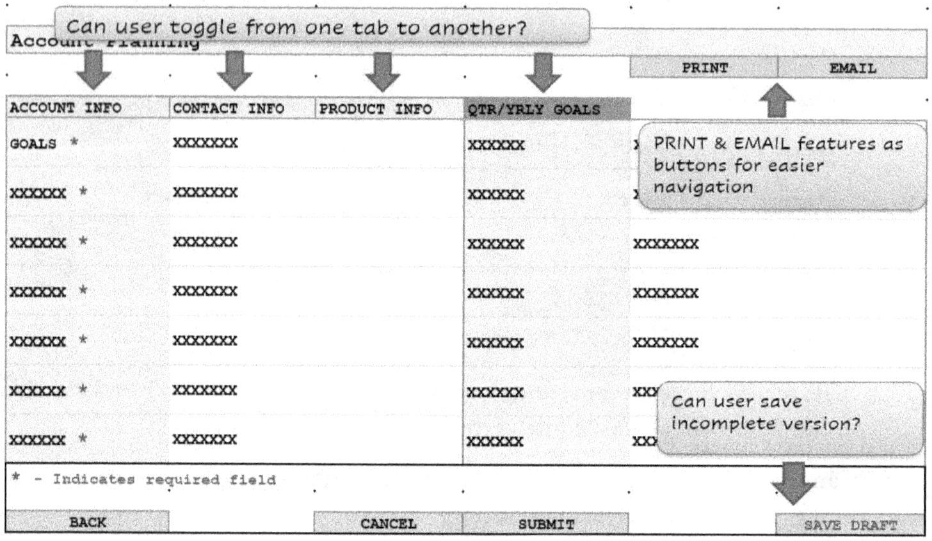

Figure 12.5 – Account Planning – overall feedback for the business user

Your team has designed and developed excellent functionality; the findings here (the flaws) are relatively trivial but make a huge difference to your end users. If we can think like our users and simplify navigation, making screen flows meaningful, we can certainly identify a few of them before the start of UAT by business users. During UAT, if we work with super users and see what they do and how they do it, it will help us deliver an excellent solution for our business users. In the next section, let's discuss the need for the UAT phase and why it is so important.

Note

This approach of testing should not take more than 2 to 4 hours for our example scenario when done by knowledgeable team members. You can see for yourself that spending a few more hours on this within a 4- to 6-month release will add tremendous value and make for a happy customer.

Exploring the need for UAT

We have done so many types of testing—unit testing, systems integration testing, and regression testing. Why one more type of testing? Because this is the only time the business users and the end users will be playing with a production-like system with all the functionality and data. UAT is the last available window for us to make sure that the business requirements are designed, solved, and developed to meet the proposed functional solution. It's not only the functionality but also the look and feel of the screens and the simplicity and ease of navigation for the end user for which we can get feedback.

UAT ensures that we vet and simulate as many scenarios as possible so that the end users will not face the same issues. One critical issue on a large-scale project can impact thousands of users, and this can result in wasted time, resources, and frustrated users.

So, what do we do? Do we just take the SIT scripts and SIT plan and implement the same test scripts by cloning them for UAT? See the *Testing strategy* section from *Chapter 10, Technical and Quality Testing*, for a recap. I have seen many projects adopting this approach, and this chapter helps you understand different approaches by primarily keeping you focused on usability and the user adoption aspects of testing. Who can understand this better than the business user with all the expertise? This provides us with opportunities that can be advantageous to us.

UAT provides us with opportunities such as the following:

- Real users testing the system. Testing resources are from different business areas. They are not from IT, as unit testers and SIT or regression testers are. They have business domain knowledge, and they are the final recipients of the system.
- In addition to following test scripts, business users are encouraged to perform exploratory testing, where testers will come up with innovative and creative scenarios that they can test. This helps us unearth issues that we never thought about earlier.
- Participants from UAT can act as a **single point of contact** (**SPOC**) for the end users within their business units. It helps tremendously, as other business users tend to listen to one of their colleagues from their business unit (rather than someone from the IT production support team). The SPOC can also influence the behavior of the end users and, when managed well, this can result in higher user adoption.
- Since the UAT environment is a clone of the production environment, where you have all the data uploaded, this provides the testers with the ability to preview their future production platform. Since we have large volumes of data, testers can run reporting metrics and dashboards, which can provide us with a general indication of how the system performs. While a full sandbox is ideal for this level of testing, smaller

organizations may opt for a partial copy sandbox due to budget constraints; however, if a partial copy is used, the team must monitor the system extra closely after migrating to production to ensure no data-specific edge cases were missed.

- It provides a great opportunity to check, verify, and validate integrations with other internal or external systems.

By the time we get to UAT, we expect that our QA team will be able to identify as many issues as possible, and retest and close the majority of the identified defects. The Business Analyst did a smoke test and approved the environment for UAT, expecting that, for the most part, the system functions would perform error-free. UAT windows have a much smaller duration than SIT windows. This small window can provide us with so many opportunities, and we have seen some of them.

To truly optimize this critical, short window, we must change how we approach acceptance from the ground up. This is the driving force behind leveraging Agile techniques in the acceptance process.

Leveraging Agile techniques

In the traditional (read: waterfall) lifecycle, acceptance testing is often the final, monumental hurdle, where it can make or delay the release. In an Agile environment, acceptance testing becomes a collaborative, ongoing process, not a final, dreaded event. The core shift moves acceptance testing from a "pass/fail gate" at the end to a "product quality guide" that starts on day one of an iteration. This means we are building quality in, not inspecting a finished product.

When we embrace Agile, we fundamentally change the purpose and timing of acceptance testing. Moving testing activities to the start of the iteration allows the team to identify and resolve potential issues as they arise; it's a strategic advantage that minimizes risk and maximizes alignment. This proactive stance is maintained by focusing on two fundamental shifts in execution:

- **Continuous feedback**: Instead of waiting for a completed feature, we test small, incremental pieces of functionality as soon as they are "done" by the development team. This allows the Product Owner and other stakeholders to provide feedback immediately, while the code is fresh. If something is wrong, the fix is small, cheap, and fast.
- **The power of collaboration**: Acceptance testing is no longer the sole domain of a QA team. It belongs to everyone on the Agile team, especially the Product Owner (defining what is needed), the Developer (implementing how it's built), and the Tester

(challenging how it will be validated). This is the starting point of high-quality acceptance criteria.

Agile techniques to supercharge acceptance testing

Let's explore advanced testing techniques designed to maximize our efficiency.

- **Behavior-Driven Development (BDD)**: This technique is the cornerstone of Agile acceptance testing. It uses a common, readable language (often the Gherkin syntax: Given, When, Then) to define acceptance criteria. This forces stakeholders to clearly articulate the expected behavior of a feature before any code is written. It turns acceptance tests into living documentation that everyone understands. Here's a BDD example using Gherkin syntax:

Salesforce Feature	Acceptance Scenario
Lead Qualification	Automatic conversion of a High-Quality Lead.
Goal	When a Sales Rep marks a lead as "Qualified" and the lead meets a criterion (e.g., has Annual revenue > $100k), the system should automatically create a Contact, Account, and Opportunity.
GIVEN	The Lead record has a Lead Status of Working - Contacted.
AND	The Lead's Annual Revenue field is greater than $100K.
WHEN	The user changes the Lead Status picklist value to Qualified.
THEN	A new Account, Contact, and Opportunity record should be created.
AND	The original Lead record's Is Converted field is set to `True`.

Table 12.1: Lead qualification – example Gherkin syntax

- **Acceptance Test-Driven Development (ATDD)**: Think of this as the Why before the How. The team collectively defines the acceptance tests before the developers start coding. These tests serve as the specification. This means a developer's job is not done simply when the code is complete, but when that code successfully makes the acceptance test pass, thereby ensuring that the team is focused on delivering the ultimate business value from the outset. Here is an example of the ATDD automated flow test:

Salesforce Component	ATDD Approach
Custom Discount Approval Flow	Validate that discount requests over 15% are routed to the Sales Manager approval queue.
Before Code/Flow	The team defines the success condition: "If the Opportunity Discount field is greater than 15%, the record's Approval Status must transition from Draft to Pending Approval."
Development	The Admin builds the flow that checks the discount field and updates Approval Status accordingly.
Test	The automated or manual test runs the scenario: 1. Create a new Opportunity with a Discount of 20%. 2. Save the re-cord. 3. Assert that the record's Approval Status is now Pending Approval.

Table 12.2: Opportunity discount approval flow automation – example of ATDD approach

- **Plan automation**: To achieve that continuous flow and to be truly Agile, acceptance tests must be automated as much as possible. Remember, everything cannot be automated. If it is complex functionality and is new, probably manual testing, both structured and exploratory, is a better option. Tests written using BDD frameworks (such as Cucumber) are designed to be run repeatedly and reliably. Therefore, these automated acceptance tests become the comprehensive Regression Suite, running instantly and repeatedly, providing near-instantaneous feedback and delivering the confidence required for frequent, fast, and successful deployments.

By adopting these techniques, acceptance testing transforms into a proactive, preventative measure that drastically reduces risk, minimizes waste, and ensures the delivered product truly meets the needs of the user. It's about building quality in, not inspecting it afterwards. While this "shift-left" approach is vital for early detection, it must be balanced with a rigorous final gate. Regardless of whether a project follows a traditional or Agile lifecycle, a dedicated User Acceptance Testing (UAT) phase remains essential before production. This ensures that business Subject Matter Experts (SMEs) can validate end-to-end functionality, confirming that the solution performs as intended in real-world scenarios.

Now, let us see how these opportunities can benefit us.

Reviewing the benefits of UAT

There are several benefits to UAT. I will list a few that I find useful:

- Business users get a chance to verify and validate that the software functionality meets the business requirements. In addition to identifying defects, it helps the project get feedback and suggestions from business users. The project team can decide on whether to incorporate the requests in the same release or a future release based on the impact assessment. Following this evaluation, any identified defects are prioritized for action: critical issues are remediated immediately before the production go-live, while minor defects are scheduled for resolution in subsequent releases. To ensure full transparency, these items are documented in a "Known Issues" list, providing users with clear visibility into the system's status and the timeline for upcoming fixes.
- This is our last and only chance to find defects before deploying to the production environment and thus reduce risk. Being knowledgeable about the testing process, they can find defects fast and be able to explain how, when, why, and where they found the defect so that it can be reproduced and fixed faster. If this defect is missed during testing, it may result in different end users from different departments experiencing the same issues after deployment to production. The same issues may be described in different ways, as the end user may not be able to articulate and explain them clearly, so now, in production, there may be 10 or 100 service desk tickets created with different meanings for that one missed UAT issue.
- You are able to identify the behavior of the application from the end user's point of view and ensure that usability is fine-tuned for a better user experience. This is a golden opportunity to get feedback on usability, and you can solicit this from a few users. The sooner we can get this feedback during UAT, the better for us, as we plan to incorporate

this feedback as much as possible into the same release. Remember that this is related to system adoption, and if it were me, I would do my best to make it a great user experience.

- From a technical perspective, identifying issues – whether defect- or usability-related – can be done in a relatively short span since the UAT system is a test environment. Essentially, the project team can work hand in hand with testers and get things fixed and tested faster in the UAT environment. The same issue, if identified in production, must go through the CCB process and all the documentation and approvals, and then wait for the deployment window, which can be weekly or bi-weekly.
- We can ensure the system requirements meet business needs, and by the end of UAT, we can run traceability reports to make sure that, at a minimum, we do not have any open defects for critical and high-priority ones. If there are any open defects, there should be a workaround and a plan to fix the issues immediately during post-deployment. UAT can help us confirm that the software solution design works as proposed and that the software's functionality points to the system requirements and, in turn, fulfills the business needs.
- UAT secures the final, critical buy-in and sign-off from key business stakeholders. At the end of UAT, the official sign-off is a powerful confirmation that the solution meets their needs and they formally accept the risk of proceeding to production. This agreement is essential as it creates shared accountability between the project team and the business, ensuring everyone is aligned on the final delivered product and ready for go-live.

Many more benefits can be identified (please revisit the *Benefits of testing* section from *Chapter 10, Technical and Quality Testing*), and I will leave that up to your imagination and creativity.

Practical tips for success

Let us look at some practical tips that may help you during your UAT phase:

- SMEs and knowledgeable users should verify that the test scenarios or scripts are valid and make sense. If the scripts are confusing or documented incorrectly, such as creating the right scripts for the wrong processes, this will create unwanted defects and lead to fixing and wasting valuable time on useless defects.
- Testers should follow procedures and documentation, but at the same time, be mindful and have control over what they test. As an expert end user, if they find a test script that doesn't fit what they usually do, they need to question it so that it can be amended.
- Test core functionality before getting into secondary functionality.

- Test capabilities and functions to make sure they work before going into variants or edge cases.
- Test for high-impact functionality that may cause major issues in case of failure.
- Test things that are newly added and then test existing ones.
- Test common scenarios first, in accordance with the 80:20 rule. The majority of the time, 20% of common functionality is utilized by 80% of end users, such as creating an opportunity or a quote. So, by testing and fixing issues related to this 20%, you will result in keeping 80% of users with trouble-free functionality.
- Testers should consider broader aspects while testing: product specifications, usability, data quality, requirement problems, and supportability.
- Identify a tester who can think practically, critically, creatively, and innovatively. Challenge them to break the system.
- In addition to testing for explicit functionality, testers need to look for implicit functionality, such as usability aspects that may not be specified but make sense.
- Perform **end-to-end** (**E2E**) testing of each of your scenarios with the handover from one tester to another. As with a relay race, your marketing tester starts the process with lead creation and assignment. Your sales tester picks up the process and converts the opportunity into a quote or order, then your service tester performs the next step in the order processing. This order processing should stimulate order processing and invoice generation, and appropriate notifications and data updates. The complete process should involve all the relevant systems, and your UAT should touch all these touchpoints, starting with the initial data from marketing being used as starting data for your E2E test cases, and ensuring that E2E data simulates real-life data processing in the system.

It's time to summarize what we have learned so far.

Summary

In this chapter, we reviewed the need for formal testing and the importance of acceptance criteria to prove the real needs of our users in a production-like environment. We also saw how leveraging Agile techniques such as BDD and ATDD shifts acceptance testing from a final gate to a continuous, collaborative guide. We saw how UAT plays a key role in building the confidence of users, preparing the system for deployment, and getting ready for a rollout.

After reading this chapter, you should have a good idea of why the right UAT testers are critical for testing and how you can find the right ones and equip them with the right tools so that they can do UAT effectively and provide us with valuable feedback for addressing any problems, so that we can reduce post-production issues and save time and resources.

We have completed our UAT and resolved all our concerns, and now it is time to prepare for deployment to the production system. We need to keep the entire user community informed about the upcoming go-live, and they need to be trained on how to use the system, as well as where they need to reach out for help. In the next chapter, we will discuss effective communication strategies, knowledge management artifacts, and other tools so that they can get acclimatized to the new software system quickly.

Questions

1. Try to recollect a few testing types that are useful during the UAT phase.
2. Name some important testing activities.

Further reading

- *User Acceptance Testing*, published by BCS, The Chartered Institute for IT

Get this book's PDF version and more

Scan the QR code (or go to `packtpub.com/unlock`). Search for this book by name, confirm the edition, and then follow the steps on the page.

UNLOCK NOW

Note: Keep your invoice handy. Purchases made directly from Packt don't require an invoice.

13

Communication and Knowledge Management

In the previous chapter, we discussed **user acceptance testing** (**UAT**) and why it is crucial for a successful go-live, improving user adoption, and gaining trust by working with business testers. We saw the benefits of business users performing testing on real-life business end-to-end scenarios. With UAT, we saw how to ensure that the new functionality does exactly what it is intended to do and meets the business requirements.

In this chapter, we will discuss aspects of communication and knowledge management, especially focused on end users. We will not talk about project management-related communication: we will leave this to the project management team. Here, our focus is on end user communication to make sure that they are well-prepared and informed about the new software features. To be able to do that, we need to plan for end user communication and knowledge management artifacts related to the usage of the new system functions:

- Communication with our end users who will be using new features and functions related to the following:
    - Planning around training schedules
    - The availability and accessibility of knowledge artifacts
    - Support during initial go-live phases
    - Post-production support
- Knowledge management is to be planned, developed, and kept ready, specifically focused on various knowledge artifacts that are needed to enable and help users ramp up knowledge on the new functions, features, and usage of the software system

We will discuss the following topics around communication and knowledge management:

- End user communication
- Different knowledge management types
- The accessibility of knowledge artifacts
- The benefits of communication and knowledge management
- Practical tips for success

Let's explore and see what makes for effective end user communication in the next section.

End user communication

Communication in a project is vital, and the project team needs to understand that, to achieve project goals, we need to ensure to do this effectively. This can be done only if we establish standard communication processes and procedures.

End user communication typically should start during the testing phase of the project. This helps provide advance notice to the end user that changes are on the way, and how they will benefit and help them with their job at the organization. Initial communication should be very high-level, outlining the functionality of different modules with key benefits. Periodically providing the status highlight with target dates creates excitement and interest.

I have seen many projects fail due to insufficient communication, let alone it lacking effectiveness. Thoughtful and well-planned communication based on user groups, culture, and expertise levels helps us mitigate risk. For this, we need to have a good communication strategy and implement it effectively. Let's look at project-level communication at a high level.

Effective communication is essential for any project's success; without it, the right hand doesn't know what the left hand is doing. This leads to misunderstandings, duplicated work, confusion, frustration, and ultimately a loss of trust. Project communication isn't a one-time task; it must be planned and delivered strategically to reinforce understanding and manage expectations. It's much like baking a cake: the right balance matters, because too much or too little never works. Use the matrix below as a high-level guide to shape your communication approach and tailor the strategy to fit your organizational culture.

Communication Element	Key Strategy and Deliverable
Message Source Strategy	Use the right voice. Leadership sends high-level messages that reinforce the project vision, strategic importance, and organizational commitment to the Salesforce implementation. Managers and project leaders send operational messages focused on what teams need to do, such as training, process changes, deadlines, and day-to-day expectations.
Message Timing	Message timing ensures communications are delivered at the right moment, such as kick-off and major milestones, to maximize clarity and adoption. Well-timed messages keep transparency, reduce confusion, and reinforce expected actions, giving stakeholders the information they need exactly when they need it.
Content Tailoring	Segment the audience. Message timing should align to each audience segment, delivering updates when they are most relevant to their role and upcoming responsibilities. By tailoring when and what each group receives, we can reduce noise, improve clarity, and drive timely action across the project.

Communication Element	Key Strategy and Deliverable
Feedback Loop	Make communication two-way by creating simple, accessible feedback channels—such as Q&A sessions, surveys, or team forums—so users can share questions and concerns. Acting on feedback quickly builds trust and improves adoption, showing teams their voices directly shape the solution.
Stakeholder Benefit Core Message	Focus on WIIFM by clearly highlighting how the change benefits the organization, the team, and each user. When people understand what's in it for them, adoption increases and resistance drops significantly.

Table 13.1: Communication alignment matrix

Planning communication, just like all other project activities, is key. For a typical Salesforce project release, I usually consider the following important parameters:

- **Channels of communication**: Remember that one size does not fit all, and it varies by organization. We need to drive the message across multiple channels until it reaches our intended audience. Let's see a few channels that I have found useful:
    - **Email communication**: This is the best way to communicate with a larger audience. Drafting a simple, well-formatted email highlighting key features of the project and sending it to the group at a set frequency, such as daily or weekly, will help keep your end users updated about project information.
    - **Video clips**: A short 3- to 5-minute clip highlighting the key features and functions with software system screenshots will provide a glimpse of what's coming. This can be posted on your company website with a dedicated page for project updates.
    - **Collaboration site**: From within your company network, you can use collaboration tools such as Slack, Confluence, Teams, or Chatter (or any collaboration tool at your organization) to create groups and post updates and feature functions at a regular frequency. This helps with effective collaboration through end users interacting and providing comments. When managed well,

this helps adjust your communication style and prepares for your end user training artifacts.

- **Salesforce In-App Guidance**: In-App Guidance acts as a high-impact, "just-in-time" communication channel by delivering real-time prompts and walk-throughs directly within the user's active workflow. It replaces easily ignored emails and bulky manuals with contextual, actionable alerts that ensure critical updates and training are seen exactly when they matter most. By leveraging targeted messaging based on specific user profiles, you can drive immediate feature adoption and streamline onboarding without the typical digital noise. It effectively transforms your org into a living training environment.
- **Posters**: These are old-school, but if placed in strategic places such as break rooms, water coolers, or next to elevators, they will draw attention and curiosity. This information helps users to search for details that point to your video clips and collaboration site or the project site. If you have a TV monitor that displays company news throughout your company, see whether you can use it to showcase your project too.

- **Frequency**: Too much or too little communication is ineffective. You need the right frequency based on your audience and what works best in your context. With emails, I would say send the details weekly at the same time every week. As with video clips and collaboration sites, try to publish them at a set frequency so that you can develop a cadence for your users and make it a ritual for them. The best time to put up those posters is during the weekend (or on Monday morning before employees come into work). Anything new catches everyone's attention, and it is up to you to make that poster really enticing.
- **Identify user groups**: We need to identify and curate the knowledge artifacts based on the user base. As an example, users in the back office who use the system a lot may prefer to have knowledge artifacts documented with step-by-step instructions. User roles, such as sales analysts and service analysts, may prefer to have one-page reference sheets.
- **Communication delivery**: What I mean here is what medium do we use for communicating with end users? The Business Analysts or project managers can draft the communication, but it needs to go through the business sponsor or the key stakeholders. Communication should be tailored in such a way that it comes from these key people to have the maximum impact. I would also recommend that it is forwarded to their groups by the lead stakeholder or leaders for better reach. Make sure you identify and create the groups beforehand so that it gets easier for the key person who relays the message.

- **Champions of communication**: Identify team members who are passionate about the new system and functionality and who really want this to be successful. These champions will be your conduits who can help with great user adoption. When communication comes from these champions, it is more likely that their team members will trust this person and give it a try. We need to identify and onboard them as early as possible in the project, right from the elicitation of requirements. If they are one of your stakeholders, this would be even better, as they will understand the progression of the business needs from end to end. These champions should be picked from respective business units and should be one to two team members from each unit. In addition, you should always seek help from the project sponsor and key stakeholders at the leadership level to make communication more impactful.
- **Standardized templates**: Like all other project artifacts, these messages should be consistent and should look the same. Basically, create a brand for your project, and when someone sees the header, they should know that it is from your project.

> Note
>
> Create a theme for your project if it is allowed. It will create the branding for your project release. I am fortunate that this was allowed on many of my past projects. We used a logo pretty much everywhere things were related to the project. This builds team camaraderie and belongingness.

- **Feedback**: Communication is a two-way street. You need to listen very attentively and provide avenues for your users to provide feedback, raise concerns, or make suggestions. You may not be able to fix it in that release, but it will certainly help you make improvements in future releases. By being attentive, you can gain their trust and make them more attentive.

> Note
>
> We are not talking about change management communication. This communication is based on how to use the new software functionality and where to get help with usage.

In the next section, let's look at knowledge management types.

Different knowledge management types

In short, **knowledge management** is making sure the information is readily available. It can be in any form; the key takeaway is that the end users should be able to access knowledge artifacts when needed.

There are two main types of knowledge:

- **Explicit knowledge**: This knowledge can be documented and is relatively easy to obtain
- **Tacit knowledge**: This knowledge is know-how and is difficult to identify and capture

Let's discuss each in detail.

Explicit knowledge

These artifacts can be any one of the following. Based on the user base and their role, you can package a combination of relevant documents based on their job function:

- **Standard operating practices**: A set of written, step-by-step instructions detailing how a routine activity must be consistently performed to maintain efficiency and quality.
- **Functional specifications**: A document like our FSD, defining what a system or product must do to satisfy user and business needs.
- **Business process flows**: Visual diagrams such as our "as-is" and "to-be" process flows, illustrating the sequence of activities, decision points, and actors involved in completing a business task.
- **Step-by-step instructions**: Simple, sequential directions for accomplishing a specific task or workflow.
- **Video training**: Audiovisual content, such as a Webex or Zoom training recording, to demonstrate processes, system usage, or concepts for end users. These capture recordings of meetings, training sessions, or decisions for asynchronous review and reference.
- **Cheat sheets**: Concise, summarized reference guides providing key information or shortcuts for immediate use.
- **Lessons learned documents**: Structured summaries detailing what went well, what could be improved, and specific recommendations from past projects.
- **All your project planning artifacts**: The comprehensive set of documents, such as project charters, schedules, budgets, risk registers, and so on, used to manage and execute a project.

- **Test scripts, use cases, user stories, the RTM, and so on**: Documentation defining how a system should behave, how to verify it works, and linking requirements to tests.
- **FAQ documents**: A collection of answers to the most common or frequently asked questions on a given topic or system.

Knowledge documents are living documents and need to be updated periodically to make them current and relevant. If the users are internal to the organization, it is better to provide them access to all project-related documents if it is acceptable to share as per your company guidelines. More information is good so that users can get curious and explore other areas, but at the same time, it may add confusion too. Find the right balance that you feel adds the most value in your context.

Tacit knowledge

This is the knowledge of how the everyday business operates—the 5W1H (who, why, what, when, where, and how). These artifacts need to be thoroughly reviewed by your SMEs before publishing them to your users.

Let's take a look at a few good sources where we can find this tacit knowledge. Paying attention to these project artifacts and taking the time to understand them helps a lot:

- **Best practices**: These can be specific to your organization or in general to the industry.
- **Lessons learned**: The most valuable type of documentation, which helps add value to your future projects by adopting what worked well and avoiding risk by avoiding or mitigating things that pose risks.
- **Problem reports/root cause analysis**: This artifact helps us with similar problems encountered in the future, which can be resolved quickly or altogether avoided.
- **Sessions/meetings**: Minutes from brainstorming sessions or workshops.
- **Issues/suggestions list**: These are requests originating from experts and super users who will help us with their deep knowledge and aid us in future implementations.
- **Product support issues list and resolutions**: This captures the unwritten, experiential insights gained by support teams from consistently resolving unique customer issues.
- **User forums**: This is where users can tell us what works well and what their pain points are. Since these are live sessions, you and the team get an opportunity to understand and elicit the needs and problems.
- **Blogs**: Business blogs help us understand the business side of the house and help us build functionality.

- **Internal communities**: Collaboration groups via Teams, Chatter, and other internal group chat tools help with great ideas and suggestions.
- **Tips and tricks (including workarounds)**: These can be formal documents, but most of the time are discussed informally. They can be workarounds too. Make a note when you hear someone informally share these tips and tricks, and document them.

> Tip
>
> Start focusing on explicit knowledge, as it is easy to create, maintain, and standardize. By having a good knowledge artifact, most user issues can be addressed easily. As for tacit knowledge, leave it to the experts in each area, who can be consulted as needed. Progressively try to document and make these available to the rest of the team.

So far, we have explored knowledge types. Next, let's see how these artifacts can be made easily accessible to our users.

Knowledge artifacts accessibility

In this section, we will discuss accessibility to knowledge artifacts and tools that you use so that your users can easily retrieve them. Knowledge management deals with compiling, organizing, accessing, and circulating information. You plan, collect, compile, organize, and communicate to your users where and how to access knowledge artifacts. Let's see a few good places where we can house these artifacts. There is so much software available on the market. Use types that are relevant to your organization. I will discuss some of them that I have found useful. Keep one of them centralized and sync up the artifacts to other systems, as different users may be comfortable using one or more of the systems of their choice:

- **Confluence**: A great tool and very effective if you use an Agile approach to your project, it will help with having all your project-related documents, as well as knowledge artifacts, in one single location.
- **Salesforce**: I prefer Salesforce content management for housing artifacts and then using Chatter to disseminate links to Chatter groups. Users are able to access knowledge artifacts from the Salesforce system itself, making it more productive.
- **Slack**: It is another excellent collaboration tool that can be used to store and share all your knowledge artifacts.

  Some sample Salesforce knowledge artifact sites are shown here:

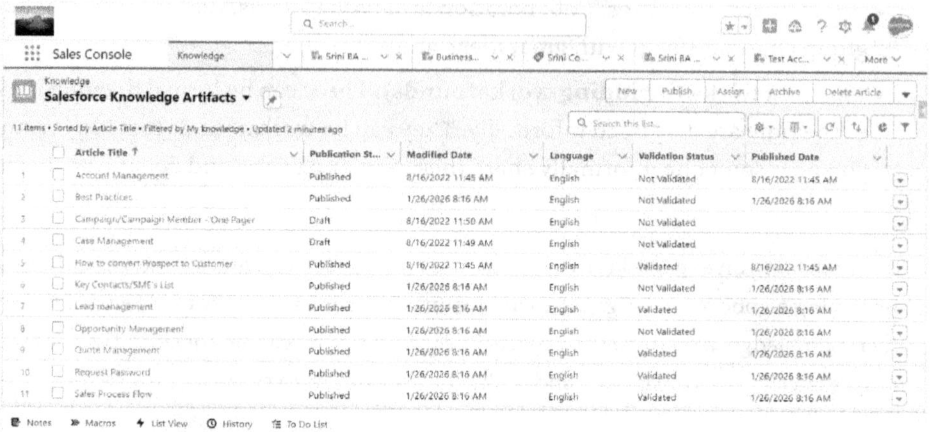

Figure 13.1 – Salesforce knowledge artifacts in Salesforce (sample)

- **SharePoint/Microsoft and Teams/OneDrive**: These are other excellent tools from Microsoft. If you are using Outlook, these tools are seamlessly integrated and help with notifications and communications.

A sample Salesforce knowledge repository on OneDrive is shown here:

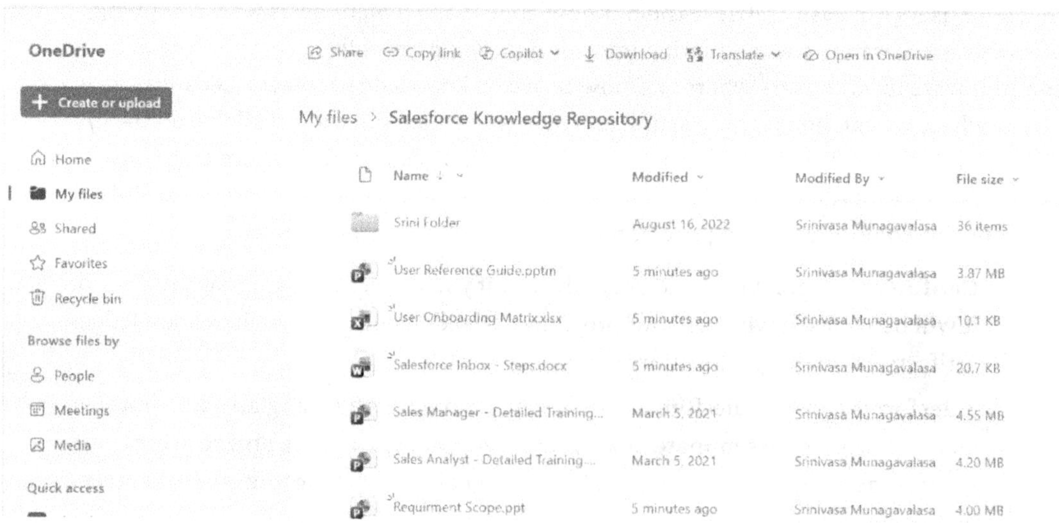

Figure 13.2 – Salesforce knowledge repository on OneDrive (sample)

No matter what tool you use, make sure the user can find artifacts with ease by naming each artifact with a unique and meaningful title, keywords, and tags. This helps users find documents in the search results effectively. Additionally, utilize version control features to ensure users are always accessing the most current iteration, effectively eliminating the

"Final_Final_v2" confusion. This establishes a reliable single source of truth while keeping the history of the document organized and out of the way of daily operations.

Let us look at a few benefits in the next section.

Benefits of communication and knowledge management

Effective communication ensures productive outcomes, and it saves time, resources, and unnecessary frustration.

Ongoing communication with stakeholders, end users, and project team members keeps everyone aware and sets expectations. Some of the benefits are as follows:

- Reduced process time, as end users have the necessary knowledge artifacts at their disposal: Access to ready knowledge allows users to complete tasks quickly without delays from searching or asking.
- Increased productivity, as the user can now spend more time doing business and less time using technology: Efficient processes and clear guides minimize time spent navigating systems or troubleshooting technical issues.
- Expertise gained by users: Consistent exposure to documentation and shared knowledge builds user confidence and system mastery over time.
- Reduces user frustration: Clear expectations and readily available solutions prevent confusion, errors, and the resulting stress.
- Increased communication and collaboration: Shared understanding of processes and goals facilitates smoother interaction across teams.
- Improved user adoption: Users are more likely to utilize a new system or process when they feel supported and understand its purpose and function.
- Aids in faster decision making: Easily accessible, reliable information and clear process flows provide the data needed for quick and informed choices.
- Faster ramp-up (new users): Structured knowledge and documentation significantly shorten the time required for new employees to become fully functional.

Practical tips for success

Let us look at some practical tips around communication and knowledge management to help your end user get ready for the next phase.

Here are some of the practical tips that can help you in your project implementations:

- Communicating clearly and regularly helps foster effective messaging. It provides status updates and honest assessments that build confidence and trustworthiness.
- Tailor your communication with empathy, understanding, and perspective so that the recipient gets the intended communication.
- Simple, clear, crisp communication ensures that the audience gets the intended message by minimizing uncertainty, misunderstanding, and ambiguity.
- Communication enables and facilitates change. Change has to be articulated.
- Welcome feedback, address concerns, and make changes to communication.
- Information should reach those in need.
- Pick appropriate channels of communication, scope, frequency, and methods that work better for your project.
- Keep knowledge artifacts current and updated on an ongoing basis.
- You need champions who are passionate and driven and who can be the medium for effective communication.
- Follow a standard communication model or models. Use visuals as much as possible.
- Make sure the message is received by the recipient.
- Select communication methods that best fit your communication needs.
- Do not send all types of communication to everyone. Users will be drowned in the information, and they may not even pay attention.
- Global implementations necessitate professional translation to ensure clarity and cultural relevance across different regions. Utilize high-quality translation tools for the initial heavy lifting, but always have a native team member verify the final output to ensure the context remains intact.

It's time to conclude the chapter.

Summary

In this chapter, we reviewed the need for good end-user communication and strategies around knowledge management. We need to ensure our communication is concise, clear, with a purpose, structured for coherence, comprehensive, and culturally aware. Frame your communication in such a way that the intended message is understood at the other end. Provide a channel through which the end user can reach out for further clarification.

Effective knowledge management helps lower costs and drive productivity. Investing time and resources upfront through knowledge management activities helps organizations mitigate risk by making the knowledge available when it is needed.

Managing knowledge in a central location will avoid redundancies and version mismatches. Your information can be managed in a single location and disseminated via customized links on various knowledge channels to users. This way, any changes to the artifact can be reflected at one location to keep the information fresh.

To sum up, for knowledge management to be effective, it needs to be up to date, communicated promptly, and accessible to end users.

So far, we have created excitement by communicating with the end user about the upcoming project. In the next chapter, we will cover in detail how to create great training material and short video links for user training. We will highlight the advantages of facilitating in-person or virtual training and what you should and should not cover in this training.

Questions

1. List some examples of formal communication.
2. Give some examples of informal communication.

Get this book's PDF version and more

Scan the QR code (or go to `packtpub.com/unlock`). Search for this book by name, confirm the edition, and then follow the steps on the page.

UNLOCK NOW

Note: Keep your invoice handy. Purchases made directly from Packt don't require an invoice.

14

End-User Training

In the previous chapter, we established that clear communication and centralized knowledge management form the pillars of a successful project foundation. We explored how to mitigate risk and drive productivity by ensuring that information remains current, accessible, and well-structured. Having now generated awareness and excitement among our end users, the next step is to bridge the gap between interest and proficiency.

In this chapter, we focus on the practical execution of end-user training through the creation of high-impact training materials and concise, digestible video content. We will examine the strategic advantages of delivering both in-person and virtual training sessions to maximize engagement across the organization. By the end of this chapter, you will have a clear roadmap for converting initial project momentum into the hands-on competence required for long-term success.

End-user training is as important as all other training: it plays a vital role in the successful adoption of the new functionality by your end users. Our goal here is to train our users so that they can understand the core system functionality, cross-functional integrations, and the overall process flows, connections, and functional dependencies.

In this chapter, we will discuss planning and executing effective training. Training provides us with an opportunity to help users with upcoming changes and help reduce stress. Well-planned communication and effectively delivered training, coupled with well-orchestrated post-go-live super care, help end users get comfortable with new system features.

For any activity to be successful, it needs to be planned. The project team should lay out the details of what they plan to do and how they plan to do it.

In this chapter, we will discuss the following topics around end-user training:

- Planning for training
- Preparing for training

- Setting up the training environment
- Reviewing types of training materials
- Understanding the importance of in-person or live training
- Facilitating a training session
- Benefits of end-user training
- Practical tips for success

Planning for training

Planning for training involves various team members coordinating multiple activities independently and bringing them all together before we deliver our training sessions.

Training isn't merely an instructional event; you can use this as an impactful **change management tool**. It provides a structured environment where users transition from knowing about the change to understanding and practicing the change. Well-structured training directly addresses user anxiety by transforming abstract concepts (the new system) into concrete, navigable steps (how they perform their job). By clearly demonstrating what is changing, how it works, and **what is in it for them** (**WIIFM**), we help reduce the primary driver of resistance: the fear of the unknown. The training environment provides the final, essential platform to reinforce the strategic reasons for the change, tying the new processes back to the business benefits and organizational vision. Knowing this will help you with planning and executing your training more effectively.

We need to put together a training plan that encompasses, at a minimum, the following aspects:

- Be cognizant of our end users—who they are, where they are located, what their job function is, and how we will deliver the training.
- Identify your super users who can act as our trainers and trusted partners. It is like training the trainers, and they will be the main point of contact for their business unit and the go-to person for the users.
- Understand the scope of training—what functions and processes need to be included in the training?
- Choose the training medium—how do we plan to do the training, and what methods do we adopt?
- Plan the training schedule—the dates, the duration, and the number of sessions based on user groups and user roles.

- Prepare the training material—what kind of material do we plan to provide to end users?
- Check training accessibility—how can users access training artifacts, and where do we house them for ease of access?
- Review training sign-off and what it means when we say training is complete.

Let us look at a sample training schedule based on user groups:

Session ID	User Groups	Duration	Countries	MM/DD/YY	MM/DD/YY	MM/DD/YY	MM/DD/YY	MM/DD/YY	MM/DD/YY	MM/DD/YY	MM/DD/YY	MM/DD/YY	MM/DD/YY	MM/DD/YY	MM/DD/YY
CRM - 01	Sales Analyst- Session 1	2 Hrs	Asia												
CRM - 02	Sales Analyst- Session 2	2 Hrs	Asia												
CRM - 03	Service Analyst- Session 1	2 Hrs	Asia												
CRM - 04	Service Analyst- Session 2	2 Hrs	Asia												
CRM - 05	Sales Manager	2 Hrs	Asia												
CRM - 06	Service Managers	2 Hrs	Asia												
CRM - 07	Planning Division	2 Hrs	Asia												
CRM - 08	Marketing	90 Mins	Asia												
CRM - 09	Legal/Compliance	90 Mins	Asia												
CRM - 10	Production Support	90 Mins	Asia												
CRM - 11	Sales Analyst- Session 1	2 Hrs	Americas												
CRM - 12	Sales Analyst- Session 2	2 Hrs	Americas												
CRM - 13	Sales Analyst- Session 3	2 Hrs	Americas												
CRM - 14	Service Analyst- Session 1	2 Hrs	Americas												
CRM - 15	Service Analyst- Session 2	2 Hrs	Americas												
CRM - 16	Service Analyst- Session 3	2 Hrs	Americas												
CRM - 17	Sales Manager	2 Hrs	Americas												
CRM - 18	Service Managers	2 Hrs	Americas												
CRM - 19	Planning Division	2 Hrs	Americas												
CRM - 20	Marketing	90 Mins	Americas												
CRM - 21	Legal/Compliance	90 Mins	Americas												
CRM - 22	Production Support	90 Mins	Americas												

Figure 14.1 – Sample training schedule for Asia and the Americas' user groups

This schedule helps users see an overall training schedule, and they also can appreciate that it is not just their group but a larger part of their organization that is involved, which helps them take it seriously.

Let us look at some key features from this sample schedule:

- A unique session ID so that, later, we can tag the recorded session links. It is also useful to take note of who attends which session and how many participants attend each of these sessions.
- Multiple sessions for larger groups, such as sales analysts and service analysts.
- Staggered dates so that if some team members are busy during a specific time, they can attend the other session.

Publishing this type of training schedule beforehand gives the users advance notice. Also, if a sales manager from Asia cannot make the session, for example, they can plan to attend the Americas session. Later, they can review the recorded Asia session.

Management and stakeholders get an overview of the schedule.

The next steps are to add more details and granularity of session details and time zones for each of the countries. I have simplified the following example matrix:

Americas - Training Sessions											
Session ID	User Groups	Duration	Countries	Facilitator	Attendees	Time Schedule					
						US	Canada	Mexico	Brazil	Chile	Paraguay
CRM - 11	Sales Analyst- Session 1	2 Hrs	Americas	********	30	DD-MMM HH:MM AM	DD-MMM HH:MM AM	DD-MMM HH:MM AM	DD-MMM HH:MM AM	DD-MMM HH:MM AM	DD-MMM HH:MM AM
CRM - 12	Sales Analyst- Session 2	2 Hrs	Americas	********	30	DD-MMM HH:MM AM	DD-MMM HH:MM AM	DD-MMM HH:MM AM	DD-MMM HH:MM AM	DD-MMM HH:MM AM	DD-MMM HH:MM AM
CRM - 13	Sales Analyst- Session 3	2 Hrs	Americas	********	25	DD-MMM HH:MM AM	DD-MMM HH:MM AM	DD-MMM HH:MM AM	DD-MMM HH:MM AM	DD-MMM HH:MM AM	DD-MMM HH:MM AM
CRM - 14	Service Analyst- Session 1	2 Hrs	Americas	********	30	DD-MMM HH:MM AM	DD-MMM HH:MM AM	DD-MMM HH:MM AM	DD-MMM HH:MM AM	DD-MMM HH:MM AM	DD-MMM HH:MM AM
CRM - 15	Service Analyst- Session 2	2 Hrs	Americas	********	30	DD-MMM HH:MM AM	DD-MMM HH:MM AM	DD-MMM HH:MM AM	DD-MMM HH:MM AM	DD-MMM HH:MM AM	DD-MMM HH:MM AM
CRM - 16	Service Analyst- Session 3	2 Hrs	Americas	********	10	DD-MMM HH:MM AM	DD-MMM HH:MM AM	DD-MMM HH:MM AM	DD-MMM HH:MM AM	DD-MMM HH:MM AM	DD-MMM HH:MM AM
CRM - 17	Sales Manager	2 Hrs	Americas	********	20	DD-MMM HH:MM AM	DD-MMM HH:MM AM	DD-MMM HH:MM AM	DD-MMM HH:MM AM	DD-MMM HH:MM AM	DD-MMM HH:MM AM
CRM - 18	Service Managers	2 Hrs	Americas	********	10	DD-MMM HH:MM AM	DD-MMM HH:MM AM	DD-MMM HH:MM AM	DD-MMM HH:MM AM	DD-MMM HH:MM AM	DD-MMM HH:MM AM
CRM - 19	Planning Division	2 Hrs	Americas	********	5	DD-MMM HH:MM AM	DD-MMM HH:MM AM	DD-MMM HH:MM AM	DD-MMM HH:MM AM	DD-MMM HH:MM AM	DD-MMM HH:MM AM
CRM - 20	Marketing	90 Mins	Americas	********	15	DD-MMM HH:MM AM	DD-MMM HH:MM AM	DD-MMM HH:MM AM	DD-MMM HH:MM AM	DD-MMM HH:MM AM	DD-MMM HH:MM AM
CRM - 21	Legal/Compliance	90 Mins	Americas	********	12	DD-MMM HH:MM AM	DD-MMM HH:MM AM	DD-MMM HH:MM AM	DD-MMM HH:MM AM	DD-MMM HH:MM AM	DD-MMM HH:MM AM
CRM - 22	Production Support	90 Mins	Americas	********	6	DD-MMM HH:MM AM	DD-MMM HH:MM AM	DD-MMM HH:MM AM	DD-MMM HH:MM AM	DD-MMM HH:MM AM	DD-MMM HH:MM AM

Asia - Training Sessions											
Session ID	User Groups	Duration	Countries	Facilitator	Attendees	Time Schedule					
						US	Japan	Singapore	India	Philippines	Vietnam
CRM - 01	Sales Analyst- Session 1	2 Hrs	Asia	********	60	DD-MMM HH:MM AM	DD-MMM HH:MM AM	DD-MMM HH:MM AM	DD-MMM HH:MM AM	DD-MMM HH:MM AM	DD-MMM HH:MM AM
CRM - 02	Sales Analyst- Session 2	2 Hrs	Asia	********	60	DD-MMM HH:MM AM	DD-MMM HH:MM AM	DD-MMM HH:MM AM	DD-MMM HH:MM AM	DD-MMM HH:MM AM	DD-MMM HH:MM AM
CRM - 03	Service Analyst- Session 1	2 Hrs	Asia	********	50	DD-MMM HH:MM AM	DD-MMM HH:MM AM	DD-MMM HH:MM AM	DD-MMM HH:MM AM	DD-MMM HH:MM AM	DD-MMM HH:MM AM
CRM - 04	Service Analyst- Session 2	2 Hrs	Asia	********	50	DD-MMM HH:MM AM	DD-MMM HH:MM AM	DD-MMM HH:MM AM	DD-MMM HH:MM AM	DD-MMM HH:MM AM	DD-MMM HH:MM AM
CRM - 05	Sales Manager	2 Hrs	Asia	********	10	DD-MMM HH:MM AM	DD-MMM HH:MM AM	DD-MMM HH:MM AM	DD-MMM HH:MM AM	DD-MMM HH:MM AM	DD-MMM HH:MM AM
CRM - 06	Service Managers	2 Hrs	Asia	********	6	DD-MMM HH:MM AM	DD-MMM HH:MM AM	DD-MMM HH:MM AM	DD-MMM HH:MM AM	DD-MMM HH:MM AM	DD-MMM HH:MM AM
CRM - 07	Planning Division	2 Hrs	Asia	********	5	DD-MMM HH:MM AM	DD-MMM HH:MM AM	DD-MMM HH:MM AM	DD-MMM HH:MM AM	DD-MMM HH:MM AM	DD-MMM HH:MM AM
CRM - 08	Marketing	90 Mins	Asia	********	12	DD-MMM HH:MM AM	DD-MMM HH:MM AM	DD-MMM HH:MM AM	DD-MMM HH:MM AM	DD-MMM HH:MM AM	DD-MMM HH:MM AM
CRM - 09	Legal/Compliance	90 Mins	Asia	********	10	DD-MMM HH:MM AM	DD-MMM HH:MM AM	DD-MMM HH:MM AM	DD-MMM HH:MM AM	DD-MMM HH:MM AM	DD-MMM HH:MM AM
CRM - 10	Production Support	90 Mins	Asia	********	6	DD-MMM HH:MM AM	DD-MMM HH:MM AM	DD-MMM HH:MM AM	DD-MMM HH:MM AM	DD-MMM HH:MM AM	DD-MMM HH:MM AM

Figure 14.2 – Detailed training schedules by country

If you capture the training schedule at this level, it helps you with the following:

- Scheduling more sessions based on time zones. You cannot expect users to join training sessions during off-hours. This will help you plan training timings better.
- How many sessions do you need to facilitate for each user group? In our example, for the Americas, we have 12 sessions, whereas for Asia, we have only 10 sessions. Based on the number of attendees, we can schedule the session accordingly. In my case, I feel training may not be very effective if the number of attendees crosses 30. Based on your user base, it helps you plan how many sessions you would like to facilitate.

This level of detail also helps us see that we are covering all countries in scope. It is a good artifact for your training sign-off.

Now that the training planning is successfully completed, let us start our preparation in the following section.

Preparing for training

To deliver effective training, we need to prepare for all that goes into delivering the training. It takes many days and a good number of resources to prepare for the training. Let's look at some of them:

- A stable test environment is needed for training with valid data. The system should have the latest configuration, and any external apps connected to the system need to be checked off as functional (note that it may not be possible to enable all apps and interfaces working with the test environment). Make sure to perform a comprehensive mock run-through in the training environment to confirm that all workflows and data points function as intended. A smooth session is critical; you only get one chance to make a strong first impression.

- UAT should be close to complete with no critical issues. It's better if it can be done after UAT completion, but usually, projects cannot wait that long.
- Based on the grouping of users, some user groups may need more thorough training, where they should be able to get hands-on experience.
- Collaborate with key stakeholders and leaders to encourage their teams to attend and take training sessions seriously – even better if they are mandated.
- Plan to have the training decks ready so that users can use them for reference and take notes.
- It is highly recommended that you start with relevant business process flows at a high level so that end users understand the context of the business flow and how it relates to the new functionality.
- Keep SMEs available to respond to queries.

In addition, make sure the users also have access to tools and systems during the training. As an example, if you plan to do training via Teams, WebEx, or Zoom, make sure users have access to these video tools and can dial in successfully.

> **Tip**
>
> In all my project training, I make it a point to do the training in real time in a training environment with realistic test data. It always flows from system login to general navigation and specific functions. For me to be able to do this, I need to have a very good training environment. Let's look at what makes a good training environment.

Setting up the training environment

The training environment is very important for the trainer to provide effective training to end users. Think of the times when you are receiving or providing training, and the system may not be stable, or you may not have the required data or access. This affects the end user's focus and understanding of what they are learning.

These kinds of disruptions are completely avoidable, and the following points will help us with this:

- The training environment must be built with the latest code base and metadata.
- Trainers should create training data prior to training sessions (if needed, with the help of a Business Analyst).

- Each trainer should have their own set of user profiles created for their training sessions. Prior to kickoff, ensure that the sandbox environment has been refreshed and that all access profiles are accurately mapped to reflect real-world permissions.
- Valid sample data should be preloaded when showing reports and dashboard functionality.
- Trainer access should be verified and confirmed. For example, the trainer should be able to access the system from the training location and share the screen with users.
- If users are allowed to experiment in the training environment, make sure someone is available to support them.
- Plan to provide access to connected systems and any external apps where feasible. This helps trainers demonstrate end-to-end scenarios seamlessly. For example, by providing access to the D&B app in the training environment, we will be able to show users how to sync customer information from D&B into Salesforce.

There can be numerous other points that may be relevant to your project; the idea I am trying to convey here is that the training system has all functionalities and integrations with relevant and good-quality data. It should mirror your "to-be" production system. Before training, try to create a few end-to-end scenarios to make sure everything is properly connected and works seamlessly.

> Note
>
> Even with a good amount of preparation, some functionalities may not work. It has happened many times to me. By creating and keeping these end-to-end scenarios at hand beforehand, you will be able to show them to the users.

We have the training environment ready and have looked at the training materials that we need so that the users can follow our training. In the following section, we will look at the types of training material that we can develop. Based on the type of project, you may have to create more than one.

Reviewing types of training materials

I will keep this very brief. You do not need overly elaborate or complex formatting to create training materials. They can be as simple as a Word document with screenshots. Let's see some common types of training materials that we all can create:

- PowerPoint or PDF deck with detailed, step-by-step instructions. This will inform and instruct the users step by step.

- Recorded training session by user role, function, or module.
- Quick reference guide. This can be a Word document or a PDF file.
- Training manual for instructor-led training.
- Job aid. This is a simple, short, one- to two-page instruction document categorized by function, so that users can get the right information in the right format to do their job.
- Computer-based training or e-learning.
- Handouts.

We highlighted some training material types, and you can find many excellent paid training software systems that can help you with developing high-level training materials. Feel free to Google it.

> Note
>
> With the Salesforce enablement (formerly myTrailhead) site, you can publish your company-specific knowledge content on the Trailhead learning platform. It helps you deliver relevant content to the right user at the right time. In addition, from Trailhead, your users can access world-class knowledge and best practices.

In the following section, I will highlight why we need live training. In-person training is not always feasible, more so now than ever before. Let's look at and understand why it is important to facilitate and deliver live training (in-person or via web meeting) where you can interact with the end users.

Understanding the importance of in-person or live training

Many training methods can be used, depending on different factors. Choosing the right method is important for training to be effective. In this section, I would like to focus on why I find in-person or live training beneficial for typical medium- to high-complexity projects and beyond. Based on the profile of your end users and project size, you can use other methods, too. Let's look at some of the important factors that I find useful and use to justify conducting a live training session:

- It is led by an instructor presenting to a live audience. You will be able to see the end users, share your screen with them, and interact with them.
- Users can ask questions in real time. These will be actual conversations.
- It's a good opportunity for other attendees to listen to other people's queries and interact with the trainer, as well as other team members.

- The trainer can modulate training based on user engagement. Based on the interaction and how users are engaged, the session can be managed better.
- Complex topics are easy to articulate and can be demonstrated in the training system by sharing the screen and functionality. Visually showing a real scenario in the system makes it easier to understand and helps the users point out issues, if there are any.
- It can be recorded for users to replay later. Listening to the recorded session they already attended will help sync information better.

There are many other benefits of in-person or live training when done well. In the following section, let us see how to facilitate this live training session.

Facilitating a training session

Training should be tailored and facilitated as if we are telling a story with a purpose. Planning and creating the right kind of story will engage your users, and you can connect with them in such a way and influence them to understand and use the system the way it is intended to be used.

In our case, when we train the users, we ensure that they get a holistic view of the complete business process with the functionality. In our example, it can start from logging in to the system until they complete the interaction with the system. Let's see an example with the following sample steps:

- **User login**: This includes the steps for accessing the system via URL or app, resetting the password, and so on.
- **General system navigation steps**:
    - **Lead management**: A service analyst may not care much about lead management, but covering this topic briefly during training will help them understand the overall flow.
- **Converting leads to accounts and contacts**:
    - **Account and contact management**: Including integration with third-party apps
    - **Opportunity and quote management**: Integrations with other systems
    - **Case management**: A sales analyst may not care much about cases the way that a service analyst does – tailor your training to make this topic heavy for the service team and lighter for other teams.
    - **Reports and analytics**: This needs to be covered for all users. Every user needs access to some form of a report based on their job function.

Each time they access the system, it should remind them of the story you told them, rather than just another training session.

For this to happen, you need to plan it early. Make sure you include the following activities or tasks during your planning activities around training:

- **Set learning objectives**: Be very clear on what you want your users to take away from your training session.
- **Develop a story**: Storytelling engages your users and, at the same time, drives the points. One size will never fit all. Tailor your story based on the user type.
- **Plan to make it interactive, encouraging questions and discussions**: Training should be interactive, and users should be asking questions during the training and not waiting until the end of the session. You should not have a separate Q&A session at the end. It needs to be integral to your training, and users should have an option to speak up during the session.
- **Speak with purpose**: Facilitators should understand the purpose, prepare, and be very confident. Confidence is very infectious, and confidence comes with good understanding, knowledge, and preparation.
- **Make your training visual**: Try to do a screen share of the system functionality as much as possible. Start with process flows to help your users understand the complete functionality at a high level before getting into more details.
- **Be prepared**: Understand the training material and the system functionality end-to-end completely. Go through project artifacts, training material, and the training system a few times.
- **SME availability**: Keep a few SMEs available during the training session to answer any business-specific questions. It is natural that the training team may not be able to answer all queries; in such events, take it offline or get back to them later (as in, parking lot items).
- **Establish and communicate training ground rules**: For example, users need to focus without distractions, as it is not the place for discussing out-of-scope or design-related discussions.
- **Feedback**: Get feedback immediately after training. It can be as simple as a 2-minute feedback around what went well and why. What needs improvement and why? Getting instant feedback is always relevant, and it will help your team to fine-tune and adjust future training.

> **Note**
>
> Facilitate and manage your training session in such a way that makes it interactive and engaging. Apply the 80:20 rule. You get to explain the functionality and the processes 80% of the time, and your users get to ask questions 20% of the time. Encourage active participation at the same time, keeping a tab on the time spent on user interactions.

See the following sample training matrix. I use this matrix to plan my training session delivery:

Session Topics/Agenda	User Role							
	Sales Analyst	Service Analyst	Sales Manager	Service Managers	Planning Division	Marketing	Legal/Compliance	Production Support
General Navigation * Apps, Tabs, List View Controls and so on	✓	✓	✓	✓	✓	✓	✓	✓
Lead Management * Lead Functionality * Integrations with Marketing tools	✓	(✓)	✓	(✓)	(✓)	✓	(✓)	✓
Campaign Management * Campaign Functionality * Integration to third party apps	(✓)	(✓)	(✓)	(✓)	(✓)	✓	(✓)	✓
Account Management * Account Functionality * Integration with data enrichment tools	✓	✓	✓	✓	(✓)	(✓)	✓	✓
Contact Management * Contact Functionality * Integration with data enrichment tools	✓	✓	✓	✓	(✓)	(✓)	(✓)	✓
Event Management * Customer Interactions	✓	(✓)	✓	✓	(✓)	✓	(✓)	✓
Opportunity Management * Opportunity Functionality * Opportunity Integrations	✓	(✓)	✓	(✓)	✓	(✓)	(✓)	✓
Quote Management * Quote Functionality * Quote Approval Flow	✓	(✓)	✓	(✓)	✓	(✓)	(✓)	✓
Reports/Analytics * Salesforce Reports/Dashboards * Other Analytic tools	(✓)	(✓)	✓	(✓)	✓	✓	✓	✓
Case Management * Case Functionality * Case Approvals	(✓)	✓	(✓)	✓	(✓)	(✓)	✓	✓

Figure 14.3 – A sample end-user training coverage matrix

The training guide contains all the functionalities and is usually common and consistent for all user groups. When delivering the training, I use the same set of end-to-end scenarios and focus on in-depth details based on the user role.

As an example, for one specific project scenario, my approach is different for each of the roles:

- For the sales analyst and sales manager roles, I go light on campaign management and case management. The focus mostly goes in depth on the details around the account, contacts, opportunities, and quote management, as this is their focus area and job function.
- Service analysts and service managers care more about the account, contacts, interaction with customers, and case management.

- Similarly, marketing users care more about leads and campaign management, and the focus of my training is more detailed based on this job function.
- When it comes to production support, I tend to cover all areas at a faster pace, as they are already conversant with different software systems.

In a nutshell, this simple matrix tells me what functions I need to cover for each of the user role groups and at what level.

Let's see some of the very common training methods:

- Individual hands-on, which is most effective but very expensive. This is usually done post-production if a user runs into too many issues, and the cause may be anything from network issues to understanding functionality.
- Instructor-led training for small groups where users perform tasks in a classroom setting. This is usually done for a small group of back-office users who use the system extensively to perform backend work.
- Seminar-style training, where a trainer displays and walks through functionality on a live screen, demoing how to perform the tasks to users. This is my preferred style, along with many of my other colleagues at different organizations.
- Computer-based or web-based training for users to complete the training on their own.
- Training decks or guides, such as a document outlining step-by-step instructions with visual illustrations.

I found that seminar-style training with a training deck or guide works very effectively. We record the seminars and provide the link to the recording and transcripts so that users can refer to the training as needed.

Benefits of end-user training

Let's take a look at some key benefits of well-planned and well-executed user training:

- Effective training builds confidence among users, as training helps them see the step-by-step functionality from start to finish.
- It helps reduce post-production queries or inquiries.
- It helps users see the practical benefits of their daily activities by understanding the purpose of the functionality.
- End users get opportunities to ask questions, get clarifications, and interact with the group.
- Training helps users see that the project and business are investing time and resources. Users sense trust and feel supported.

- Job aids such as microlearning tools (e.g., FAQs, short videos, and cheat sheets) help users self-service most of the issues.
- Making comprehensive training artifacts available to users and making them available when they need them saves time for the users, as well as your support team.

Practical tips for success

Based on my experience with managing or facilitating training sessions, here are a few tips that can add value and streamline your training processes:

- Communicate clear training goals – learning objectives.
- Encourage end-user feedback – pulse or valuable innovative ideas.
- To make training smooth, plan end-user training early and do not leave end users for last.
- Curate training based on roles by assessing the end-user needs.
- If your training budget is tight, use seminar-based training with pre-recorded training and share it with end users. You can circulate this recorded session with users and solicit Q&A via group collaboration sites, such as Teams or Salesforce Chatter.
- Keep training artifacts current, as you may need them for retraining newly onboarded users.
- Make sure your training users get details during training on how to access the system. This includes system login URLs or desktop icons, as well as resources for resetting passwords. Also, provide useful links and contact information in case they have queries or need help.
- Make training sessions engaging, user-friendly, and interactive for them to be impactful.
- Highlight the benefits of the new system functionality and how it simplifies their work. In short, what do they gain by using the system compared to the current system or functionality?
- Create awareness of what is available and how it benefits them. This includes simple things such as list views (e.g., Kanban and Split View in Salesforce), creating charts from Salesforce reports, or subscribing to dashboards to be delivered via email.
- Training materials should be made available on demand to your end users. They should be available in many forms and from many devices.

- The trainer should have the relevant skills and experience with the software application. They should know exactly what they are teaching and why they are teaching it.
- Create a short video of screen recordings (via videos and micro videos) that will help you create a visual representation of a single process – for example, how to create prospects using the D&B app or how to approve quotes. Also, make use of tools such as Salesforce In-App Guidance or training tools that can provide users with context-based help.
- Expand on the role of the identified super users as the first line of sustained training support post-go-live, focusing on their ongoing mentorship and knowledge transfer duties.
- For continued success, your knowledge base should be an easily searchable repository for all training materials (decks, recordings, job aids, FAQs, quick reference guides, and so on).

We can keep adding to this list on and on. Let's end this chapter here and summarize it.

Summary

In this chapter, we started with the activities and tasks to consider during planning to train your end users. Next, we reviewed the various activities that go into training preparation. Then, we discussed aspects of why we need a good training environment and various types of training materials that supplement and reinforce our training sessions. By now, you must have a good idea of why live training is more impactful and how to facilitate it. We saw a few good examples and explored how they can aid us in ensuring that we cover all areas of the functionality for all our users. Finally, we concluded the chapter by understanding the benefits of training and a few practical tips that you can take into consideration for your project.

In the next chapter, we will cover the details on why post-go-live support is so critical and how user forms help Business Analysts get feedback. We will discuss in detail how regular user forums are designed in a way to help end users continuously learn about and understand the system better. Project teams can also understand pain points and get valuable insight into how to improve the system usage and thus improve user adoption.

Questions

1. List some advantages of synchronous training.
2. List some advantages of asynchronous training.

Get this book's PDF version and more

Scan the QR code (or go to `packtpub.com/unlock`). Search for this book by name, confirm the edition, and then follow the steps on the page.

UNLOCK NOW

Note: Keep your invoice handy. Purchases made directly from Packt don't require an invoice.

15

Post-Production Support and Super Care

In the previous chapter, we successfully completed our end user training. With this, we have completed all the project activities and got the go-ahead to go live with the new functionality. Our team did a phenomenal job, right from understanding business requirements to developing and deploying a great solution that meets the business needs. We took our time, planned, executed training, and made sure the team was aware of new features and functions. We also made sure that they were upskilled with all the tools and tricks on how to navigate and use the system. Finally, the day we were waiting for arrived, and we implemented and deployed the new system (features and functions), which enabled access to the software system for our users.

Now, what's next?

I have seen many projects celebrate and disband the project team within a week or two after going live. This is where all the problems start. For users to get adjusted to the system functionality, they need to practice a few times, and during practice, they need help and support. This is crucial for any project, and spending a few weeks during this period can help tremendously in making savvy users who can navigate the system functions with expertise. This automatically leads to excellent user adoption.

Ask yourself these key questions, and you will understand why production support is critical to any project implementation:

- Do our end users know when they can start using the new system?
- How can they access the new system and its features?
- Who can they reach out to if they need help?

We will cover the following topics in this chapter to address these queries:

- Super care
- Production support
- User forums
- Delivery cadence
- Benefits of production support
- User Engagement & Activity Monitoring
- Practical tips for success

Supporting users after the go-live event consists of two parts:

- **Super care**: Short period after go-live with an enhanced support model by the project and support team. This is the stabilization period for your project, and the issues can be human- and/or system-related. There is usually a super care period after every release.
- **Production and maintenance support**: Ongoing support for maintaining and managing the software system till the end of its life. Support systems are relatively stable systems where user issues and queries are addressed according to predefined and approved **service-level agreements** (**SLAs**). There will be some spikes here and there, and this is the reason why we need to define SLAs.

Let's take a deep dive and explore super care in the next section.

Super care

The **super care** period is where you support your end users immediately after the go-live event. This is to ensure that the end users get all kinds of support in any shape or form, which enables them to perform their tasks on the newly enhanced system. The super care period is usually for 4 weeks (up to 6 weeks for very large projects), starting immediately after the go-live event.

To make super care effective, the following are some of the considerations:

- Super care should be planned well in advance as part of your project planning.
- The right resources need to be secured to support this team. This includes any cross-functional teams, **identity and access management** (**IAM**) teams, network teams, and so on.
- Proper communication needs to be established a few weeks before the super care starts. End users should know how, where, and who they can reach out to for help.
- Open communication channels so that your users can access real-time information and timely help.

- Facilitate at least two status meetings every day during super care, where end users and key stakeholders can dial in and discuss recurring issues and their pain points.
- Publish and communicate common recurring themes (including usability issues) and a list of known issues so that users are aware and do not report the same issues. Disclosing non-critical issues and workarounds in advance of go-live ensures a smoother transition and faster triage.
- Keep one person in charge of the inventory of all the issues to analyze and group common themes, so that they can be addressed as a group.
- Solve common recurring issues as soon as possible, as that will cut down your call volumes drastically by almost 60–80%.
- Issues can be usability-related too; make sure that you create a simple cheat sheet and communicate to all end users the issues and steps to resolve them.
- Save all your communication-related documents and resolutions in one shared folder where everyone can view and see the status in real time. Publish status reports twice daily with ETAs for submitted issues.
- CAB members should be part of the super care, and they should meet at least twice a day to review and approve or reject requests.
- Keep an eye out and understand whether it is truly an issue or a new requirement. Park all new requirements during the super care period unless it is a *priority 1* issue that may be impacting a large part of the user base. You can revisit them and prioritize them once super care ends.
- Set up a video call where you can share the screen with users, and, as needed, the user can share their screen with you for better understanding.
- Your user issues may not be related to the system that you implemented. It may be that your user, for some reason, may not be able to access the software system or the functionality. We need to make sure the super care team addresses and resolves the issues by collaborating with the right team and not deflecting the issue to another team.
- Involving and educating the production support team from the early phases of the project ensures that they have a complete understanding of the process, design, testing issues, and access to knowledge artifacts, including known issues with workarounds. This will help them get a good grasp of the system to be able to confidently support the application.
- Define and agree on production support SLAs. Your organization may have defined SLAs organization-wide. If not, create one and get an agreement from the stakeholders.

SLAs need to be agreed on by both sides—business stakeholders and the production support leads.

- Engage super users and make sure they are fully engaged, as they are the voice of the end users from their business unit, and they play a key role in driving user adoption.

Let us review one of the approaches. This will provide you with some guidance to get the gist of things for consideration in your projects.

For all of our projects of any size, we always ensure that we have a super care period. It all depends on the size of the project, and it can vary from 1 week for simple projects to 6 weeks for complex projects. Let us consider a medium to complex project and see what we did during our super care period:

- We started our super care planning right from the project planning phase. We secured and allocated time for team members to work on super care activities, and identified the right resources, skill sets, and tools required. There will be a lot of pushback as these activities come with a project cost and need to be planned and secured well in advance.
- We started communicating with end users about the super care agenda and what they could expect during the super care period.
- Then, during the super care period, we scheduled twice-daily status meetings: one in the morning and the other in the afternoon. We invited all respective super users to join this call and all users who had something to report – either an issue, clarification, or query – to hop on this call. This is the place where discussing one specific user's issue can automatically resolve other users' similar issues. All other users with no issues are welcome to join, but they rarely do.
- We usually book a room called the war room and staff the room with key team members who are instrumental in resolving the issues. These resources are available during working hours (and beyond as needed). We also open a WebEx or Teams meeting for our remote users from other locations and regions to join. Team members in the office or on web calls can hop on and off as needed.
- Our team tries to understand the users' issues/queries/concerns as much as possible, and we always display and share the live screen so that everyone is on the same page. Sometimes, we even ask end users to share their screens and show us how to reproduce the issue:

A simple example will prove why we need to do this. In our case, we implemented Salesforce for the EMEA region. One specific set of users had an issue accessing Salesforce, and this happened only when users accessed it from that specific location. When the user was granted admin access and when our tech team logged on as the user, they were able to access it successfully. Hence, none of us could reproduce the issue even after following the right steps. So, along with a team of experts, we requested the user to share their screen so that our team could see exactly what was happening. It took about an hour, and finally, one of our team members asked the user to check for the TLS protocol in their browser settings, and we found out that the user had the wrong flag checked. After checking the right flag, the end user was able to access the system. We found this out from another set of users who were having the same issues. Without the ability to share screens and view and analyze the issues in real time, it would have taken forever to identify this issue.

- We publish status reports and known issues lists on collaboration sites such as Confluence or Teams so that all our end users are aware of or updated with the latest news and events.

Chronologically, these are the events that take place during the six weeks of super care:

- **First and second week of super care**: During the first two weeks, we see many users having issues accessing the system or the right functionality. This could be because of the following:
    - **Users do not have the right Salesforce URL, or they do not remember their password**: We can resolve this by creating a two-page document showing step-by-step instructions, including how to reset the password by clicking on the **Forgot password** link. If you enable SSO, this will resolve the login issue, but they may still have an issue with what URL to access. In the case of SSO, it is always good to provide instructions on how to create a desktop icon or how to bookmark an SSO link.
    - **Users with incorrect access to the Salesforce system**: There can be many factors. They may be assigned an incorrect role and/or profile. It can be related to missing permission sets, or it can be missing team members in public groups. One example is that our legal team is unable to see cases for approval. When a user creates a case and submits it, cases are routed and assigned to a specific queue based on the business unit and country. As legal team members are not added to the queue, they are not able to view cases for approval or rejection.
    - **Users with third-party app issues**: Many users have issues with usability when trying to access a third-party application, such as trying to sync up customer/contact data from D&B. So, we walk them through the process and create a quick two- or three-page quick reference guide for all users (we made a short video clip, too). Similarly, when users try to use secondary features such as converting a prospect to a customer on account records, they need to add a KYC number and a few other details. Providing a cheat sheet will resolve issues

quickly. Once users do these activities a few times, such as creating a few customer records, it becomes second nature, and they do not need those reference materials anymore.

- **Users with generic queries/concerns/complaints**: We get lots of advice, suggestions, and criticism from users, and that is very common. Communicate and reinforce that this system is built for efficiency, and there is some learning involved. Make a note of all those users who give both positive and negative feedback, and capture them in a document. You will find valuable information and some very good ideas that can help with future releases or enhancements. We will also get lots of enhancement requests from users, forcing us to get them implemented ASAP. One of the senior team members should work with project sponsors to address them and add them to a future product backlog. At the same time, communicate the same to all the end users. This communication should come from sponsors or critical stakeholders to be impactful. We need to manage the noise and address true business user issues that are relevant to the project scope.
- **User- and system-related issues**: Any such issues, when reported, should be captured as a ticket for traceability. For the first few weeks, one of your team members or the super users should help create the service tickets.

- **Third and fourth weeks of super care**: We saw more advanced secondary issues such as approval flows, opportunity and quote calculations, or issues with integrations. These need the involvement of SMEs and the technical team. Most of them take time to develop and obviously need thorough testing. We need to prioritize and then plan to deploy them accordingly based on the availability of resources. Again, any *priority 1* issues should be addressed ASAP, and for other priorities, devise a workaround and place them in your product backlog for future prioritization.

  Users will start creating and running reports, and we will see issues around creating and modifying reports, report filters, report downloads, and report schedules. The same will be true for team dashboards. One common issue most often seen in Salesforce reporting is that the users are not able to see custom fields while creating reports. Make sure custom fields are added when creating custom report types. This is a very simple task, but I found team members running around and wasting time trying to categorize it as an access issue.
- **Last few weeks of super care**: Issues encountered before slowing down and issues related to reconciliation, such as month-end or quarter-end, will pop up. These are advanced issues and might be better siloed to the planning or sales operation team. You

may have to work with the team and help them fix the reports, dashboards, and analytics:

  - Try to help a few users who have issues navigating the application for any reason. See whether the team can have one-on-one or small-group sessions and help them work on the system while the project SME follows along.
  - Start requesting and enforcing that users create service tickets. Without a ticket, work should not be started, and you need to be disciplined and bold enough to enforce this.
  - Start involving your production support team and let them start handling and routing the tickets. They need to work with the project team and understand the functionality so that they get a smooth transition. They need to clearly understand that they are the ones who are going to handle these issues in a week or so.

- **Last week of super care**: You should not see any more common issues. You may come across some edge case issues (the one-off scenario kind) that either your team or the production support team can handle. During this period, work on closing the super care and fully transitioning to production support with an SLA in effect. Until now, we implemented high-priority and common issues in tight, small windows with approval from CAB. We did this so that end users did not lose traction and interest. This period is like an internship period, where we try to make the interns comfortable and help them navigate smoothly and understand how and where to find help when needed. Now, it is time for them to start working independently.

Now that we have successfully completed super care and transitioned future tasks to the production support team, in the next section, we will look at what production support means and what makes good production support.

Production support

Production support is an ongoing activity, and if users are using a software system, there will be issues with the system. Imagine this in the same way as maintaining your car or your central air conditioning unit. You do not know when you will run into issues, and you need someone to take care of them as soon as possible. In addition, there are preventive maintenance activities involved to keep your equipment running smoothly. This is where the production support team comes into play. There are usually three levels of production support: simple data updates and password resets are performed by level 1 support; troubleshooting user errors that can be user- or system-related, and fixing minor bugs, is done by level 2 support; and finally, all advanced-level activities that need **root cause analysis** (**RCA**) are assigned to level 3.

The common tasks of a typical production support team are listed next, and I have provided a small set of examples. The list can go on and on forever:

- **Periodic maintenance**:
  - **Quarterly and annual planning maintenance activities**: Changes to default values—as an example, the fed rates in basis points are managed as metadata, and the interest rate margin field on opportunity is tied to the fed rate. Any time the fed rate is changed, the custom metadata needs to be adjusted.
  - **Annual and semi-annual territory management updates and forecast management updates**: Updates to quote approval routing rules. For example, volume discounts vary periodically, or the level of approval may change.
  - **Re-org changes**: Many times, there may be a company re-org where you have to make changes to data ownership, role hierarchy, sharing rules, workflows, and so on.
- **Bugs and issues with functionality**:
  - Users run into issues such as being unable to save or modify data. These are typical bugs in the code that might affect some users. It can also relate to data.
  - Some users do not have access to certain fields or records. This may be related to the fact that they changed teams and their access has not been updated accordingly.
  - Users can view individual records but are not able to see reports or dashboards. This may be due to a lack of access to the report or dashboard folders.
- **Data maintenance**:
  - Users create duplicate data, resulting in skewed reports.

  - Users are not able to create records, as the system prompts them about a duplicate record that they cannot see.
  - Ownership changes as team members move to another department or leave the firm.
  - Schedule report updates.
  - De-dupe activities to clean up accounts and contacts.
- **Minor enhancement requests**:
  - Request to add or remove picklist values.
  - Request to add new fields or change field types.
  - Add or remove team members from workflow notifications or approvals.
  - Request to create new report types.
  - Request with reports and dashboards.
- **Release management**:
  - Ensure that Salesforce release maintenance (three times a year) is tested and that the system is error-free by the production release date.
  - Also, ensure that all third-party apps are compliant with their own releases as well as the Salesforce release.

If the system is not periodically maintained to fulfill the business needs, it will create a lot of confusion and will impact usability and adoption. For this to be effective, we need to set some ground rules and rules of engagement. The project team needs to plan and ensure that there is a support team available so that support can go smoothly as desired. All software projects should ensure that there will be an ongoing cost of maintenance after the go-live event, and budgets need to be made available to staff production support resources.

Let us see activities that can make production support effective:

- Define SLAs based on the priority that is calculated based on impact and urgency. Your organization may already have defined SLAs for all your applications. You can reuse them. The point I am trying to make is to set expectations for business users. A well-documented, agreed-upon, and communicated SLA will keep everyone transparent.
- Staff the production support team with the right number of team members with the right skills. If you are implementing Salesforce CRM, make sure you have at least Salesforce admin-level skill set team members.
- Production support and the project team need to work hand in hand to understand and make sure there is no conflict with code and release management.

- The project team should involve production support team members with the projects, and their involvement, at least from the UAT phase, will help them come up to speed.
- Business analysts should include all the production support team members during user forums.
- Project artifacts, especially the design documents and training material, should always be available to the production support team.
- The production support team should always follow the same cadence when making changes to the application (SIT > UAT > Production route).
- Production support needs to look out and get involved outside Salesforce and other CRM user communities to understand the latest trends and best practices.
- The production support team can prepare the data for upload, but before uploading, the respective business users making the requests should review the final file and approve it for loading into UAT for validation. On business approval in UAT, this data can be loaded into production.
- The team should look to simplify and innovate in a way that benefits all users and not just take orders. They should say no to users if it does not add value, at least to a small group.
- Set up campfires, brown bags, or other forms of knowledge-sharing sessions to educate users. This will be a good place for you to understand users' needs. This session should be more informal and educational.
- The production support team should have a weekly call with business stakeholders and provide status and walkthroughs.
- The release should always be planned and published. Here is an example:
    - Small changes, such as mass data updates or picklist additions, are done weekly every Friday at 6 p.m. EST (3 p.m. PST), excluding the last Friday of the month.
    - Any minor enhancements, such as adding new flows or Apex triggers, are done monthly at 9 p.m. EST (6 p.m. PST) on the last Friday of every month. *Priority 1* releases can happen anytime with approval from CAB.
- Any system changes shall be approved by CAB, and the project SME should be one of the CAB team members.
- Always make a backup, or even better, use a version control tool. It can be specific code, such as Apex classes, triggers, or object data. In the case that things go wrong, you can revert. This is usually captured in your CAB artifact, but just in case it is missing from there, a backup is useful.

In addition to these activities, the production support team should actively engage super users and business SMEs to help prioritize issues. Support team members must be knowledgeable, and the transition plan should be clearly defined and well-executed. This preparation ensures that the team is operationally ready to manage all production support activities. Production support leads should also provide periodic status reports and maintain consistent communication with all users in scope.

A successful transition to production support depends on the support team's early and continuous involvement throughout the project lifecycle. Embedding support members within the project team builds ownership and deep technical understanding, while structured knowledge transfer and clearly defined support deliverables eliminate dependency on hyper-care. Treating the handover to operational support as a formal milestone, rather than an afterthought, significantly reduces post-launch risk and establishes a foundation for stable, long-term operations.

> Note
>
> Organizations tend to provide staff production support with relatively junior members assuming they are for routine tasks, and the team's job is to keep the lights on. Staff in the support team need at least one experienced, knowledgeable senior-level team member, and the rest of the support team can be junior team members.
>
> I recommend that all team members work on production support activities at least for a short period to really understand and get a feel for them. For junior team members, this is the place to find opportunities to learn and grow.

To make production support effective, I would like to carve out a section for user forums, as I found this to be an excellent conduit for establishing rapport with business users and being their trusted advisor. Let's look at what is involved and what made it useful to me.

User forums

The final and arguably most critical topic covered in this chapter is the role of user forums. User forums provide a structured platform for collaboration, knowledge sharing, and continuous feedback, enabling users to learn from one another while giving the organization valuable insights into adoption challenges and opportunities for improvement.

User forums are periodic meetings with your SMEs, SPOCs, end users, and key production support team members to establish open and honest communication, share knowledge and understanding of their existing pain points, and get real-time feedback from the participants.

The user forum session should be about 30 to 45 minutes. These sessions are primarily for education and information, and should be purely voluntary. When managed well, you will see excellent participation, as they are more informal in nature. These meetings give you a pulse on what the adoption would look like. This does not replace the production support status meeting or other official meetings.

Before even going into the user forums, I would like to explain why and how they helped me during my multiple implementations with many organizations to achieve high levels of user adoption. It takes some time to form and run a productive user forum.

I started this user forum to improve user adoption. Before this, we implemented multiple projects successfully, and systems were adopted well for the first few months, but then adoption declined. As long as you have multiple releases, users tend to use the system well, as the enhancements are rolled up into those releases and taken care of by the project teams. Once the project roadmap is completed, we need to have a proper cadence to understand the business pain points they have, while at the same time keeping them aligned with the latest and greatest features to enable them to do things in an efficient way.

User forums' key considerations and requirements are as follows:

- Identify one to two passionate team members from each business unit and make them the SPOC for that business unit.
- All requests are funneled through this team and prioritized along with other SPOCs from other business units during these user forums.
- Another important area is to focus on data to ensure it is current and relevant. We create many reports and dashboards to make sure key fields are maintained and dupes are eliminated. To keep data complete, we enabled workflow reminders and implemented validation rules.
- Share your users' list of development items planned to be released so that they are aware of what functionality to expect. Show them in the system and walk through them to get early feedback.
- Talk to them about the items that will be addressed in the next 2 to 4 weeks. This helps with reprioritizing as needed and for all SPOCs to come to a common understanding and agreement.
- Take a topic and walk them through it in the system. It can be as simple as going through existing account management or quote management processes to refresh their memory on a new topic that is about to be released to create excitement.
- Discuss pain points and recurring issues that the team should be working on to address them.

- Working sessions to help team members make use of existing tools, such as creating list view controls, reports, dashboards, and so on.
- Forums should be held typically every 2 weeks. For a global project, you may need to divide the session into groups, and forums should be facilitated by different team members, with each team member facilitating one or two groups.
- Typical forum time should be about 30 to 45 minutes, and the business users who attend should get some value out of it. To start with, you will see only a handful of them joining. As it grows and if the business users get value, you will see larger numbers joining these forums.
- Most importantly, user forums help build trust. Trust builds confidence. Confidence builds user adoption.
- By creating a company-wide dashboard for each business unit, all users can see how their business unit is performing compared to other business units. This helps drive healthy competition.
- User forums should optimally be facilitated by team members who know the business processes as well as the software system, with considerable experience facilitating meetings and workshops.

Now that you know the considerations for an effective user forum, let us look at what you should plan and cover during that short, bimonthly session.

Topics to cover during the user forum

A typical user forum, as noted earlier, should not run for more than 30 to 45 minutes. A typical agenda for this meeting would look like this:

- Enhancements and bug fixes demo (10 mins): Features/functions planned for production deployment
- Discuss existing pain points (8 to 10 mins): Common issues faced by your users
- Knowledge session (12 to 15 mins): Pick one topic that was requested by team members
- Q&A session (10 mins)
- Feedback (2 mins): Ask participants what went well/where it needs improvements
- Summary and conclusion (1 min)

End users can benefit only when action is taken. A user forum is one such avenue where you can generate opportunities to improve and enhance superior service. If you do not have user forums set up yet, you still can enhance the end user experience in the following ways:

- Periodic brown bag sessions to go over interesting topics for a wide range of users. You can invite cross-functional teams, too.

- Create collaboration groups and share information and knowledge tips.
- Enhance the application by implementing simple automation tasks such as auto notifications, reminders, enforcing validation rules, and so on.
- Encourage active collaboration on internal and external sites.
- Deliver quick wins – easy-to-implement requests during each support release. This way, you always deliver something, and the user will see continuous delivery.
- Establish data governance, as data is the lifeblood of any organization. Spending time to keep the data pristine will help your end user and their manager with accurate metrics and reports that can aid in decision-making.
- Continuous knowledge sharing and training to your end users in one form or another keeps them up to date.

User forums provide us with a valuable exchange of information and create a good rapport with users. To be able to deliver what is promised, we need to inform users about how the activities are planned and when they are going to be delivered. Let us see that in the next section.

Delivery cadence

Delivery cadence helps maintain sanity when managing expectations with your users during your production support activities. Publish the delivery cadence and communicate how requests are prioritized, scoped for production release, tested, and deployed.

Some of the key advantages of a well-planned delivery cadence are as follows:

- Establishes a predictable delivery cadence – scope of work and time duration between deliveries
- Enables better planning and cross-functional coordination
- Manages scope creeps and last-minute new work additions
- Helps balance and plan work better
- Fine-tunes and adjusts delivery cadence that fits your organization

The sample delivery cadence calendar is planned a year in advance. Again, this is planning, and a few releases may be cancelled due to quarter-end or year-end maintenance activities.

The following figure shows a sample delivery cadence. Publishing this kind of schedule well in advance helps manage expectations with your users.

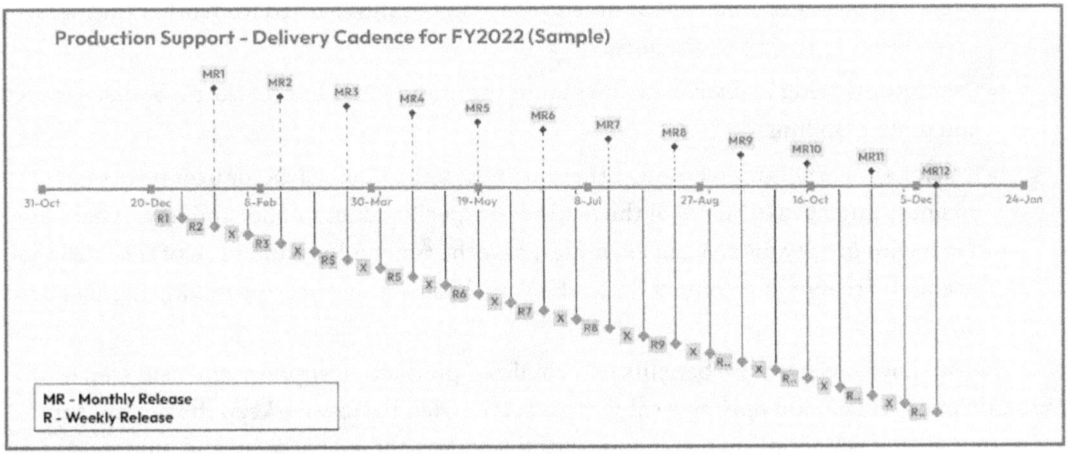

Figure 15.1 – Production support: delivery cadence for FY2022 (sample)

Let's review some key benefits of production support in the next section.

Benefits of production support

Now, let's look at some benefits that we can get from productive production support and user forums. The user forum is where we collaborate and share knowledge with business users, and aids us in making production support more effective:

- Users stay current and understand the best way to use the system and accomplish their work.
- User forums provide a continuous communication channel between end users, SPOCs, and the production support teams.
- Keep everything transparent as the issues are understood and resolved based on the published SLAs.
- Users can discuss the pain point and get their requests prioritized collectively.
- Identifying SPOCs from each business unit helps team members from that business unit approach and get guidance from SPOCs, which will be more productive and effective.
- Engaging and working with business stakeholders helps keep the data clean. Good quality data helps the team with effective reporting and management, with timely decision-making.
- Providing an overview of specific topics and best practices helps team members reinforce their knowledge and helps make them savvy users.

- Users and business units will be able to see many things learned from other business units based on their performance.
- User forums bring in diverse business unit users and provide a platform for discussion and understanding.
- It helps spread adoption among other business units if one SPOC or user from one business unit speaks highly of the features of specific functionality and how it benefited them with quality data. As an example, I saw the tremendous adoption of the D&B tool to enrich account and contact data when one business unit started talking highly about this tool.

Now that we have reviewed the benefits of formalized production support, the next step is to maintain engagement and optimize value. This section details how we keep the momentum going by utilizing key adoption metrics to proactively monitor user activity and guide continuous improvement.

User engagement and activity monitoring

We will also delve into **adoption analytics**, illustrating how key stakeholders can monitor business performance and gain the essential visibility needed to make data-driven decisions about our adoption strategy. This analytical approach is an ongoing, iterative activity that must be adjusted as the business evolves. Accurately measuring user adoption is critical to maximizing the return on our Salesforce project investments.

This section focuses on the key analytics that reveal how effectively users engage with the platform, enabling us to identify high-performing champions, target users who require additional support (laggards), and prioritize opportunities for system optimization.

We will now review the most important metrics that I found effective:

- **Login frequency and active users**: This measurement is the foundational metric for adoption, indicating whether users have successfully integrated Salesforce into their daily workflow. A low frequency serves as the primary red flag for potential adoption failure. Monitor via standard Salesforce Reports (e.g., *Login History Report*) and platform monitoring tools:
    - Login frequency and active users: daily, weekly, or monthly active users
    - Login patterns by role or business unit
    - Users who haven't logged in for 30, 60, or 90 days

- **Record creation volume and data integrity**: High record creation volume confirms user trust in Salesforce as the system of record. Conversely, incomplete or inaccurate records immediately signal process friction or a lack of user proficiency:
    - **Standard reports**: Use *Opportunities by Created Date* and similar reports, grouped by owner
    - **Custom report types**: Join users with opportunities, cases, or accounts to see creation patterns
    - **Dashboard charts**: Create bar charts showing records created per user per month
    - **Field audit**: Enable **Field History Tracking** on critical fields to monitor completion
- **Feature utilization/depth of engagement**: This metric demonstrates that users are leveraging Salesforce capabilities beyond basic data entry. Deeper feature adoption is directly correlated with achieving the platform's intended **return on investment (ROI)**:
    - Reports and dashboards usage
    - List views created and used
    - Chatter posts and comments
    - Mobile app usage
    - Custom app usage
    - Search queries performed
- **Workflow and process completion rates**: These metrics validate that users are following established, optimized workflows. Deviations, such as slow opportunity stage progression or prolonged case resolution times, reveal points of system struggle or process abandonment:
    - Opportunity history reports
    - Case age SLA reports
    - Task reports
    - Flow analytics
- **Integrated adoption dashboard**: Final decision-making is supported by a consolidated dashboard that combines the preceding metrics, specifically tracking the following:
    - Records created trend: month, quarter, and fiscal year by object

  - Field completion percentages on key objects
  - Data quality score (combination of completeness, accuracy, and timeliness)

These adoption analytics and resulting insights are the foundation for a continuous improvement cycle. They enable the team to fine-tune training and communication efforts, and provide the definitive, data-backed business case for future system optimization, **user experience** (**UX**) improvements, or automation features for the next development sprint or enhancement release.

In the upcoming section, let's explore practical tips before we conclude this chapter.

Practical tips for success

Let us check some practical tips that I found useful:

- Identify the right SPOCs. They should ideally be the business users who are involved as SMEs in the project right from the planning phase.
- Staff your production support team with at least a few certified Salesforce admins/developers.
- Do not get discouraged if not many users join the user forums. Keep meeting key members and their managers individually and encourage them to attend the forums.
- Always publish the agenda beforehand. Send it a day before the session so that it works as a notification tool too. If you enabled Chatter in Salesforce, send the agenda via Chatter.
- There should be at least one takeaway, and it should add value to the attendee. Ask them what topic they would like to see in the next session.
- Always sends minutes with recorded session links attached to all attendees. Keep the minutes nice and short.
- Recognize and thank team members who went above and beyond. User forums and collaboration sites are places that help spread recognition.

Let's end with our last set of practical tips for success and summarize this chapter.

Summary

In this chapter, we covered details on why post-go-live support is so critical and how user forums help the production support team, as well as the project team, get feedback. We saw the benefits of how regular user forums are designed, tailored, and facilitated in a way that meets your end users' needs, helps the end user to continuously learn and understand the system better, and achieves the desired level of user adoption. Good adoption implies that we truly understood the business needs during our elicitation activity. We designed and developed the right solution, tested the system, and trained the end users well. Finally, we created and followed a sound production support plan. Production support should be planned and executed just like a project, with the right set of resources, keeping it lively. Putting the right effort and securing resources upfront for production support requirements helps the production support team run the business effectively and efficiently.

Your project involves multiple sprints, but your production support is one big marathon. Keep it going smoothly and steadily.

Questions

1. What is the role of production support?
2. Name a few systems you can use to track production support issues.
3. How many levels of production support are there?

Get this book's PDF version and more

Scan the QR code (or go to `packtpub.com/unlock`). Search for this book by name, confirm the edition, and then follow the steps on the page.

UNLOCK NOW

Note: Keep your invoice handy. Purchases made directly from Packt don't require an invoice.

16

The Salesforce Productivity Tool Kit

In the last chapter, we discussed super care and user adoption features to educate users on everything available in the system that they can use to support business activities and increase overall productivity.

This chapter focuses on how we can achieve operational excellence. There are many wonderful tools, such as inline editing, guided workflows, and intelligent analytics, available in Salesforce that we can leverage to maintain sustained adoption. As Business Analysts, our role is to bridge the gap between technology and efficiency; this requires us to be both aware of these tools and skilled in their configuration.

We will cover the following topics in this chapter:

- Efficiency and maintenance
- Automation and guided work
- Guided selling and sales processes
- Intelligence and adoption
- Future state

There are many tools that are available to us, and I will review some of these in more detail so that you get an idea of what these tools are and how they can be used for our benefit. Note that some features are available only in the Enterprise and/or Unlimited editions. I encourage you to explore these features and functionalities using Trailhead Developer Editions.

Efficiency and maintenance

Efficiency and maintenance are essential for maximizing the value of Salesforce and supporting operational excellence. By implementing targeted tools and processes, organizations can streamline workflows and enhance the overall management of their data. Some of them that we can quickly enable are as follows:

- Inline editing in list views and reports
- Restriction rules
- Scoping rules

These solutions focus on reducing manual effort, minimizing errors, and ensuring that data remains accurate and accessible for decision-making. Streamlined workflows help teams complete tasks more quickly, while robust data management practices maintain the integrity of information across the system. Together, these improvements contribute to a more productive and resilient environment, empowering users to work efficiently and confidently as business needs evolve. Let's look at them in detail.

- **Inline editing in list views and reports**: Inline editing empowers users to modify fields directly within a list of records, such as a list view or a report run page, without navigating to the detailed record page. This capability significantly enhances efficiency, especially when performing mass updates or conducting data clean-up activities. For example, if users need to update the stage or close date for multiple opportunities, they can efficiently make these changes from a single screen instead of accessing each opportunity record.
- **Restriction rules**: Restriction rules are a powerful security feature, letting admins prevent specific users from accessing certain records. These rules prevent any access granted via other mechanisms, such as **Organization-wide defaults**, **sharing rules**, or **role hierarchy**. These rules act as a final filter, reducing the number of records returned in list views, reports, lookups, or related lists. This approach enhances compliance and ensures that record visibility can be precisely tailored. For instance, access to particular opportunity records can be restricted for designated groups of team members based on a specified flag. Also, if you are implementing a financial service cloud, you can implement **Compliant Data Sharing** in **Financial Service Cloud** (**FSC**) to ensure documents containing **Material Non-Public Information** (**MNPI**) are only accessible to authorized team members. Set role-based permissions to restrict access to your deal team, ensuring confidentiality. In the past, to achieve this same functionality, we had to develop complex Apex logic. Up until restriction rules, Salesforce's sharing model was

to incrementally give access and not selectively remove anything already given. See *Figure 16.1* for a sample rule that restricts access to records based on specific criteria.

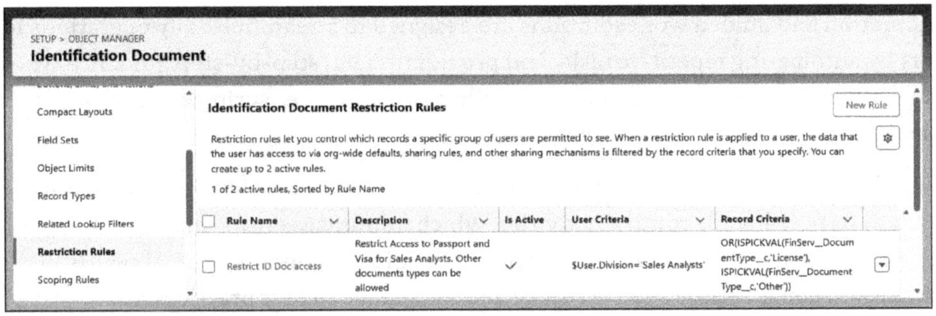

Figure 16.1 – Sample restriction rule configuration

- **Scoping rules**: Scoping rules offer a way to control which records most users see by default when accessing an object, such as in list views or reports, without altering their underlying access rights. By setting a more focused and relevant default view on an object's home page and in reports, users are directed toward the most pertinent records. Scoping rules do not restrict access but instead help users focus on information that is most relevant to their roles and daily tasks.

With an understanding of efficiency tools, let's discuss solutions that automate routine tasks and provide structured guidance to users in the next section. See *Figure 16.2* for a sample **Scoping Rules** screen. The configuration for **Scoping Rules** looks similar to **Restriction Rules**.

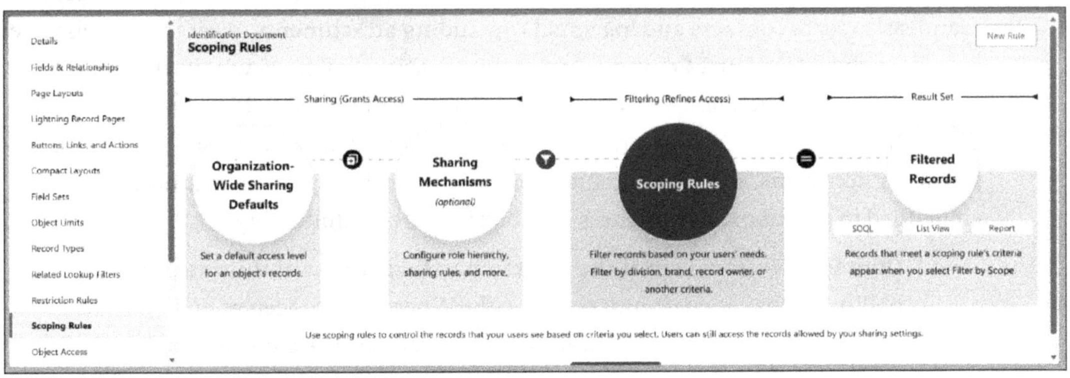

Figure 16.2: Scoping Rules screen in Salesforce

Automation and guided work

Automation and guided work solutions are designed to streamline daily operations for end users by automating repetitive tasks and providing clear, step-by-step guidance. These features help users navigate complex workflows with ease, ensuring consistency and reducing manual effort across the organization.

By implementation of automated processes, not just your users but your admins can also rely on the system to handle routine activities, which minimizes errors and saves time. Structured guidance supports users by presenting prompts or instructions at critical points in their workflow, leading to improved accuracy and adherence to best practices. Let's take a look at some automation and guided tools in Salesforce.

- Salesforce Inbox integration with Outlook
- Instant contact creation
- Streamlined activity logging
- Screen flows for multi-record creation

Overall, these enhancements contribute to increased productivity, allowing users to focus on higher-value activities while maintaining compliance and efficiency within the Salesforce environment. Let's explore them in more detail.

- **Salesforce Inbox integration with Outlook**: Salesforce Inbox integration with Microsoft Outlook delivers significant productivity enhancements by enabling users to seamlessly create contacts and log emails, including attachments, directly to Salesforce records such as Accounts, Contacts, and Opportunities—all from within their email client. When users activate Salesforce Outlook integration and hold a Salesforce Inbox license, Microsoft Outlook is transformed into an advanced extension of Salesforce, providing access to CRM data and functionality through a dynamic side panel embedded in the inbox. Key features of Inbox include the following:
    - **Contact creation**: One of the most impactful features of this integration is the ability to create new contacts on the fly. When a user receives an email from a sender whose address does not exist in Salesforce, the Salesforce side panel proactively prompts the user to create a new record. The system streamlines the process by intelligently extracting and pre-filling key fields such as **Email**, **First Name**, and **Last Name** based on information from the Outlook email signature

or contact card. This automation significantly reduces the time required for data entry and ensures that valuable contacts are captured efficiently.

- **Streamlined activity logging**: In addition to contact creation, integration offers a streamlined approach to logging emails and attachments. Users can utilize the log email feature to ensure all essential customer communications are recorded against the appropriate CRM (usually attached to accounts or contacts) records. The system automatically suggests matching Salesforce records, allowing users to simply select the relevant records and choose **Save** or **Log**. By default, when emails are logged to Salesforce, their attachments are also saved as files and linked to the corresponding Salesforce records. Also, users have the flexibility to associate emails and attachments with multiple accounts, contacts, and Opportunities as needed. For example, if a customer sends an email with important attachments, users can upload both the email and its attachments to the appropriate Salesforce records with a single click, ensuring that all critical information is captured and easily accessible within the CRM.

> Note
>
> You can visit the following link to understand how to set up Salesforce Inbox: `https://packt.link/y6Q1g`.

- **Screen flows for multi-record creation**: As we know, **Salesforce Flow** is a powerful declarative no-code tool that lets us create automations, forms, and guided user experiences. We can make use of these flows to gain efficiency. As an example, screen flows are designed to guide users through a series of screens, collecting relevant information, executing logic, and creating or updating records within Salesforce. Unlike standard record creation pages, screen flows offer a superior approach when users are required to handle complex, repetitive, or highly guided data-entry tasks. For scenarios where multiple records need to be created in a single session—such as capturing several tasks or contacts—screen flows utilize collection variables and loops combined with decision elements. This methodology allows users to efficiently enter information for multiple entities without navigating away from the flow. For example, during a client meeting, a user can quickly create records for all meeting attendees from a single screen. The flow can be configured to capture only the essential details, such as first name, last name, and email address. Once these core pieces of information are entered into Salesforce, users have the flexibility to update any additional attendee details at a later time as needed.

Guided selling and sales processes

Guided selling in Salesforce helps sales users navigate complex sales motions by embedding structure and guidance directly into their daily workflow. Instead of relying on external training materials or individual experience, guided selling uses Salesforce-native capabilities to standardize how opportunities progress and what actions are expected at each stage. Sales Processes and Sales Paths play a foundational role in this approach by defining the sales journey and providing in-context direction that improves consistency, data quality, and overall productivity. While they do not fully automate decision-making, they establish the framework on which more advanced guided selling capabilities can be built.

Let us look at some key aspects of how Sales Processes and Sales Paths contribute to guided selling, along with practical Salesforce examples:

- **Sales Processes define the structure**: A well-defined Sales Process establishes consistent Opportunity stages and aligns sales execution with business strategy. For example, a Salesforce Opportunity sales process may define stages such as Qualification, Discovery, Proposal, and Negotiation, ensuring every sales rep progresses deals using the same lifecycle and stage definitions across regions.
- **Sales Paths provide in-context guidance**: The Sales Path builds on the Sales Process by highlighting key fields, best practices, and success criteria at each stage. For instance, at the Proposal stage, the Sales Path can surface required fields such as **Amount** and **Close Date** while displaying tips on proposal preparation and links to approved pricing or proposal templates.
- **Foundational guided selling capability**: A Sales Path represents entry-level guided selling by guiding sales behavior rather than decisions. A newly onboarded sales rep can rely on the Sales Path to understand what information must be captured and what activities are expected at each stage without referring to external documentation.
- **Clear separation between guidance and decisions**: While the Sales Path explains what needs to be done, it does not actively guide choices. For example, the Sales Path may instruct a rep to validate customer requirements during Discovery, but a screen flow is needed to ask qualifying questions and recommend the appropriate product or solution based on customer inputs.
- **Improved productivity and data quality**: When designed intentionally, Sales Processes and Sales Paths reduce incomplete Opportunities and rework. In Salesforce, validation rules combined with Sales Paths can prevent an Opportunity from moving to

the next stage unless critical fields, such as **Budget** or **Decision Maker**, are populated correctly.

- **Scalable foundation for advanced guided selling**: Sales Processes and Sales Paths create a stable base for more advanced guided selling capabilities. Once the core process is established, organizations can layer in screen flows, dynamic forms, or CPQ-based configuration and pricing guidance without redesigning the underlying sales model.

This approach allows sales teams to spend less time figuring out how to navigate Salesforce and more time focusing on meaningful customer conversations and closing deals.

Intelligence and adoption

Enhancements in this area focus on equipping users with tools and features that facilitate informed decision-making while encouraging the consistent use of best practices. These solutions are designed to integrate smart, actionable insights into the workflow, making it easier for users to adopt efficient ways of working and achieve better outcomes. By promoting intelligent processes and guiding users toward recommended actions, the toolkit supports not only individual productivity but also the overall adoption of optimal business patterns throughout the organization.

Some of them are listed here:

- **Report and dashboard subscription option**: Educating end users on how to subscribe to reports and dashboards is a fundamental step toward self-service analytics. By guiding users through the setup of filters and the scheduling of delivery, **Business Analysts (BAs)** can empower users to receive regularly scheduled snapshots of their key reports and dashboards directly in their inbox. This reduces the burden on BAs to run ad hoc reports and transforms end users from passive data requestors into self-sufficient consumers of standard analytics. The subscription feature is crucial because it enables users to access important data without needing to log into Salesforce or navigate the **Analytics** tab, thereby streamlining their workflow and promoting data-driven decision-making. Based on your subscription, there may be limits on how many reports or dashboards an individual user can subscribe to.
- **Utilizing CRM Analytics for business analysis**: CRM Analytics plays a vital role in advanced business intelligence by combining disparate data sources and leveraging Einstein Discovery for predictive and prescriptive AI insights. This capability extends beyond the limits of standard reporting, allowing organizations to gain deeper insights into their business operations and make more informed decisions based on data-driven

predictions and recommendations. This paid add-on can be particularly valuable for larger implementations and is worth considering during planning.

- **Intelligent list views**: Intelligent list views in Salesforce enhance the standard list view experience by incorporating Einstein Scoring, such as Lead Score and Opportunity Score. These features allow users to filter and prioritize records directly within list views, creating a highly efficient triage-based workflow. By surfacing the most relevant records and insights, users can take immediate and informed action without the need to navigate to separate reports or individual record pages, thereby improving productivity and response times. This feature comes as standard with the Performance and Unlimited editions.
- **In-App Guidance and just-in-time training**: Salesforce's In-App Guidance enables admins to create and display custom, contextual help messages—such as prompts and walk-throughs—directly within the Salesforce Lightning interface. This feature is essential for the adoption of driving features and providing just-in-time training, as guidance is triggered exactly when the user needs it, on the relevant page or component. By delivering training at the moment of need, In-App Guidance significantly boosts user productivity and reduces the reliance on support tickets or external documentation, eliminating wasted time spent searching for training materials. See *Figure 16.3* for an example of In-App Guidance for list view creation.

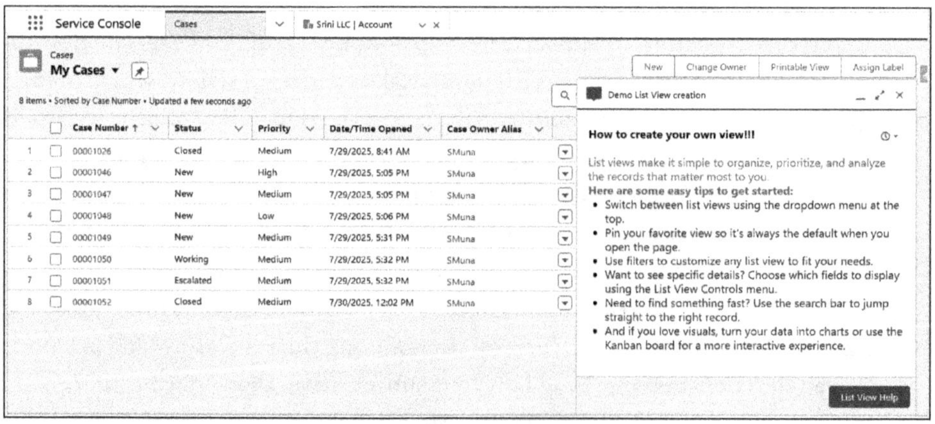

Figure 16.3: In-App Guidance for list view creation

We've explored some of the key tools I use, and there are many other valuable features available that can further enhance user productivity. In the next section, let's take a closer look at the future, particularly with the emergence of Agentic AI capabilities.

Future state

As organizations move toward the next wave of autonomous, goal-driven automation, it is essential to develop a clear strategy for the future state of operations. This involves defining objectives and aligning business processes with advanced automation capabilities, ensuring that systems and teams are prepared to leverage emerging technologies effectively.

In anticipation of these advancements, a focused training plan should be implemented to equip users and administrators with the necessary skills and knowledge. Training initiatives should address the adoption of new automation tools, clarify best practices, and provide hands-on guidance for navigating goal-driven workflows. By preparing users for this transition, organizations can maximize the benefits of automation and foster a culture of continuous improvement. Let's explore how this can be done.

Laying the Groundwork for Advanced Automation with Agentic AI

Salesforce Agentforce introduces an AI-powered assistant designed to support sales teams by automating repetitive tasks. This technology streamlines the sales process, allowing associates to focus on higher-value activities and improving overall efficiency.

- **Agentic AI in Salesforce**: Looking ahead, Agentic AI capabilities in Salesforce will enable self-directed agents to autonomously plan and execute complex, multi-step business objectives. For example, processes such as automated partner accounts and user onboarding with various entitlements or automated complex loan applications can be managed with minimal human intervention. As a result, BAs can shift their focus to governance and defining desired outcomes, rather than manual task execution. **Example 1 – Lead qualification**: Agentic AI can automatically analyze incoming leads, score them based on historical patterns, and enrich missing data from external sources. It doesn't just score—it can autonomously trigger next steps such as assigning high-value leads to senior reps or scheduling follow-up tasks without human intervention.

  Example 2 – Case resolution: Agentic AI can handle repetitive service requests end-to-end. For instance, when a customer reports a password reset issue, the AI can verify identity, trigger the reset process, and confirm resolution—all without an agent touching the case. For complex cases, it can gather context and prepare a summary before routing to a human agent.

- **In-App Guidance for just-in-time training**: To drive adoption of new features and processes, In-App Guidance within Salesforce employs prompts and walk-throughs that provide contextual, just-in-time training. These tools deliver targeted assistance directly within the Salesforce user interface, ensuring users receive the support they need at the moment it is most relevant and facilitating the transition to advanced automation technologies.

- **Context-aware prompts**: AI can analyze what a user is doing in real time—such as creating an Opportunity, updating a case, or configuring a quote—and deliver guidance tailored to that exact action. Instead of generic tips, the AI provides dynamic, role-specific instructions that feel like a personal coach embedded in the app.
- **Adaptive learning paths**: Agentic AI can track user behavior and skill gaps, then adjust the guidance accordingly. For example, if a sales rep repeatedly misses key fields in the Opportunity stage, AI can trigger a micro-training module right inside Salesforce, ensuring they learn without leaving their workflow.
- **Personalized content delivery**: AI can pull from a library of training resources and select the most relevant snippet—video, checklist, or quick guide—based on the user's role, experience level, and current task. This makes training highly efficient and engaging.

Now you are in a position to take advantage of all the **out-of-the-box** (**OOB**) tools available in Salesforce. These tools and features are what make your users keep using the system. With this, let's summarize and conclude this chapter.

Summary

This chapter brings together the Salesforce productivity ecosystem into a cohesive strategy, reinforcing that the ultimate objective of any implementation—from simple inline editing to advanced Agentic AI—is to maximize the value of every user interaction. By thoughtfully leveraging a comprehensive "tool kit," administrators and analysts can reduce friction through bulk-safe Flows, guided screen processes, seamless inbox integrations, intelligent list views, and automated subscriptions. While the technology continues to evolve, the central goal remains unchanged: streamline the user experience so that data is captured efficiently and insights are delivered proactively at the right moment.

Looking ahead, the chapter introduces the shift from traditional automation toward autonomous, goal-driven Agentic AI. Staying competitive requires a mindset of continuous improvement—regularly reviewing seasonal release notes, experimenting in Trailhead environments, and listening carefully to user feedback, especially around "click fatigue." By mastering low-code, declarative capabilities, professionals can translate complex backend logic into intuitive, high-adoption solutions that evolve alongside the Salesforce platform.

In the next chapter, we shift the focus from system capabilities to your professional growth. We will review Business Analyst certification sample questions and explore the diverse career opportunities available to those who master the Salesforce ecosystem.

Questions

1. When moving from traditional automation (such as Flows) to Agentic AI (Agentforce), what is the primary shift in the Business Analyst's strategy?
2. Which component of the "Guided Selling" process acts as an on-demand coach by providing actionable tips, links, and best practices at each specific stage of a deal?
3. Historically, the Salesforce sharing model has been described as "additive." How do Restriction Rules change this paradigm for a Business Analyst?

Get this book's PDF version and more

Scan the QR code (or go to `packtpub.com/unlock`). Search for this book by name, confirm the edition, and then follow the steps on the page.

UNLOCK NOW

Note: Keep your invoice handy. Purchases made directly from Packt don't require an invoice.

17

Salesforce Business Analyst Certification

The **Salesforce Certified Business Analyst** (**BA**) certification is designed for professionals who bridge the gap between business stakeholders and technical teams on Salesforce initiatives. Unlike purely technical Salesforce certifications, this credential emphasizes business analysis skills, customer-centric thinking, and solution alignment rather than configuration or development depth.

This certification validates that a BA can effectively discover business needs, collaborate with stakeholders, document and manage requirements, support solution delivery, and ensure successful user adoption within a Salesforce environment.

The Salesforce BA certification is intended for the following:

- BAs working on Salesforce implementations or enhancements
- Functional consultants who focus on requirements and stakeholder engagement
- Product owners or solution leads involved in Salesforce delivery
- Professionals transitioning into a Salesforce-focused BA role

You are expected to operate confidently in cross-functional teams, acting as trusted advisors who translate business strategy into Salesforce-enabled solutions.

In this chapter, we will cover the following topics:

- Experience prerequisites
- Skills and competencies assessed
- Exam characteristics
- BA certification – sample questions

Let's start with the exam prerequisites, the skills and competencies assessed in the exam, and conclude with a sample set of BA questions and answers.

Experience prerequisites

See details at `https://trailhead.salesforce.com/help?article=Salesforce-Certified-Business-Analyst-Exam-Guide`.

While Salesforce does not enforce mandatory prerequisites, successful candidates typically have the following:

- 2+ years of BA experience, including the following:
  - Leading or owning requirements activities
  - Driving business process improvements
  - Facilitating stakeholder discussions and decision-making
- 2+ years of Salesforce Platform experience, such as the following:
  - Working on Salesforce projects (Sales Cloud, Service Cloud, or related apps)
  - Understanding standard Salesforce capabilities and limitations
  - Participating in Agile or hybrid delivery models

This experience ensures that candidates can answer scenario-based questions grounded in real-world Salesforce implementations.

Skills and competencies assessed

The certification evaluates a candidate's ability across six major competency areas:

- **Customer Discovery**: Candidates must demonstrate the ability to do the following:
  - Understand business strategies, goals, initiatives, and challenges
  - Analyze the current state of a customer's Salesforce environment
  - Identify opportunities and constraints within existing processes and systems
  - Align Salesforce capabilities with business needs
  - Apply a structured implementation lifecycle for planning BA activities

  A strong emphasis is placed on customer-centric discovery, empathy, and understanding the broader business context, not just Salesforce features.
- **Collaboration with Stakeholders**: This domain focuses on how effectively a BA works with people. Candidates are expected to do the following:
  - Identify and analyze key stakeholders across business and technical teams

- Select appropriate elicitation techniques (interviews, workshops, and surveys)
- Manage competing priorities and resolve conflicts
- Facilitate alignment between the current state and the future state
- Act as a trusted advisor and liaison

Success in this area requires communication, facilitation, and negotiation skills rather than technical expertise.

- **Business Process Mapping**: Candidates must show proficiency in the following:
  - Defining the scope of complex business processes
  - Breaking processes into manageable, logical steps
  - Documenting current-state and future-state processes
  - Using process maps to engage stakeholders and uncover gaps
  - Managing process documentation in a version-controlled repository

  The focus is on clarity, scope control, and stakeholder understanding, not on diagramming tools themselves.

- **Requirements Management**: This section assesses the foundational BA discipline. Candidates should be able to do the following:
  - Differentiate between scope, requirements, and user stories.
  - Elicit, analyze, validate, and prioritize requirements
  - Ensure that requirements are clear, testable, and traceable
  - Manage changes using version control and governance practices

  The exam emphasizes business clarity and value, not excessive documentation.

- **User Stories and Acceptance Criteria**: User stories are central to Salesforce delivery, especially in Agile environments. Candidates must demonstrate the following:
  - Understanding user story components (persona, need, and value)
  - Ability to write clear, business-focused acceptance criteria
  - Readiness of stories for development and testing
  - Proper documentation and version control of user stories

  Technical implementation details are intentionally out of scope for this domain.

- **Development Support and User Acceptance**: This domain validates a BA's role beyond requirements. Candidates are expected to do the following:
  - Support solution delivery by clarifying requirements during development
  - Validate completed functionality against acceptance criteria

- ◦ Support and coordinate **user acceptance testing** (**UAT**)
- ◦ Confirm that delivered solutions meet business expectations

The BA is accountable for business validation, not coding or deployment.

Exam characteristics

The Salesforce BA certification exam is designed to evaluate your ability to bridge the gap between business needs and technical solutions. Rather than testing your ability to navigate the **Setup** menu, the exam challenges your critical thinking through the following structure:

- **Question style**: Scenario-based multiple-choice questions
- **Answers**: One or more correct options per question
- **Focus**: Decision-making, prioritization, and application of BA principles
- **Technical depth**: Conceptual Salesforce knowledge, not hands-on configuration

The exam rewards candidates who think like experienced BAs, not administrators or developers.

Preparation expectations:

To excel in the Salesforce BA certification, you must transition from a technical **builder** mindset to a strategic **advisor** role. Your preparation should prioritize the following objectives:

- **Understand Salesforce capabilities at a conceptual level**: Focus on what the platform can do to solve business problems, rather than memorizing specific clicks
- **Practice real-world scenarios involving stakeholders and trade-offs**: Learn how to navigate conflicting priorities and select the path that provides the most value
- **Focus on why a solution is chosen, not how it is built**: Prioritize the business logic and rationale behind architectural decisions
- **Strengthen fundamentals in discovery, requirements, and UAT**: Master the end-to-end lifecycle of a project, from the initial interview to final user acceptance

Hands-on project experience combined with scenario-based practice questions is the most effective preparation strategy.

In the next section, let's take a look at some sample Q&As.

I strongly recommend you sign up for Trailhead and explore the courses. The following are some of the BA-related links:

- `https://trailhead.salesforce.com/help?article=Salesforce-Certified-Business-Analyst-Exam-Guide#about`

- `https://trailhead.salesforce.com/content/learn/modules/business-analyst_skills-strategies`
- `https://trailhead.salesforce.com/content/learn/trails/get-started-as-a-salesforce-business-analyst`
- `https://trailhead.salesforce.com/content/learn/modules/salesforce-business-analyst-certification-prep`

Take a look at the "*How to Register for Salesforce Certification Exam in 2026*" YouTube video on how to register for the exam: `https://www.youtube.com/watch?v=_7cmq28hCqA`.

BA certification—sample questions

This section provides sample multiple-choice questions aligned with BA certification exams, with a strong emphasis on the Salesforce Certified BA syllabus. The questions reflect themes and concepts discussed throughout this book and the referenced certification notes, including customer discovery, stakeholder collaboration, business process mapping, requirements, user stories, and user acceptance testing.

Each question may have one or more correct answers, as explicitly stated. Answers and brief explanations are provided to help reinforce learning and identify knowledge gaps.

1. **Customer discovery**
   Which activities are most appropriate during the customer discovery phase of a Salesforce implementation? (Choose two.)

   a. Configuring validation rules

   b. Understanding business goals and challenges

   c. Analyzing the current Salesforce environment

   d. Writing Apex test classes

   Correct answer: B and C

   Explanation: Customer Discovery focuses on understanding business strategy, challenges, and the current state, including how Salesforce is currently used.

2. **Business analyst role**
   What is a primary responsibility of a business analyst during the **planning phase** of the implementation lifecycle?

   a. Performing unit testing

   b. Defining business analysis activities and approach

c. Migrating legacy data

d. Deploying solutions to production

Correct answer: B

Explanation: During planning, the BA defines how analysis activities will be conducted throughout the project lifecycle.

3. **Stakeholder collaboration**

Which techniques are most effective for eliciting requirements from senior stakeholders? (Choose two.)

a. One-on-one interviews

b. Anonymous surveys

c. Executive workshops

d. Technical code reviews

Correct answer: A and C

Explanation: Interviews and facilitated workshops allow deeper exploration of strategic needs and priorities.

4. **Stakeholder** management

A Business Analyst is facing conflicting priorities from Sales and Service stakeholders. What should the business analyst do first?

a. Escalate the issue directly to the executive sponsor.

b. Document all requests without prioritizing.

c. Facilitate a discussion to align on business value.

d. Defer decisions until development starts.

Correct answer: C

Explanation: The BA acts as a trusted advisor and facilitator to help stakeholders reach consensus based on business value.

5. **Business process mapping**

What is the primary purpose of documenting a **current-state business process**?

a. To design the final solution

b. To identify gaps, inefficiencies, and constraints

c. To create user stories

d. To train end users

Correct answer: B

Explanation: Current-state analysis helps uncover pain points and improvement opportunities before defining the future state.

6. **Process decomposition**
When analyzing a complex business process, what should a business analyst do first?

    a. Automate the entire process
    b. Break the process into manageable subprocesses
    c. Create acceptance criteria
    d. Define test scripts

Correct answer: B

Explanation: Decomposition allows complex processes to be understood, analyzed, and scoped effectively.

7. **Version control**
Why should business processes and requirements be stored in a **version-controlled repository**?

    a. To restrict stakeholder access
    b. To track changes and manage scope
    c. To improve system performance
    d. To replace documentation standards

Correct answer: B

Explanation: Version control ensures traceability, accountability, and controlled scope management.

8. **Scope vs. requirements**
Which statement best describes the difference between **scope** and **requirements**?

    a. Scope defines how the system is built; requirements define what the system must do.
    b. Scope defines boundaries; requirements define what must be delivered.
    c. Scope is optional; requirements are mandatory.
    d. There is no difference.

Correct answer: B

Explanation: Scope sets boundaries, while requirements specify the detailed needs within those boundaries.

9. **Requirements Prioritization**

Which factors should be considered when prioritizing requirements? (Choose three.)

a. Business value

b. Stakeholder urgency

c. Developer preference

d. Risk and dependency

Correct answer: A, B, and D

Explanation: Effective prioritization balances value, urgency, and risk, not personal preferences.

10. **User stories**

Which components are essential in a well-written user story? (Choose two.)

a. Persona or role

b. Technical design

c. Business value

d. Deployment steps

Correct answer: A and C

Explanation: User stories focus on who needs something and why, not how it is technically implemented.

11. **Acceptance criteria**

What is the main purpose of **acceptance criteria**?

a. To define deployment activities

b. To validate that requirements are met

c. To estimate development effort

d. To document system architecture

Correct answer: B

Explanation: Acceptance criteria provide clear conditions for determining whether a requirement has been successfully implemented.

12. **INVEST principle**

Which two attributes of the INVEST model help ensure that user stories are ready for development? (Choose two.)

a. Independent

b. Technical

c. Valuable

d. Exhaustive

Correct answer: A and C

Explanation: Stories should be independent and valuable to deliver incremental business benefits.

13. **Journey Mapping**
What is a key benefit of using a **customer journey map**?

a. It replaces process diagrams.

b. It increases empathy and understanding of customer pain points.

c. It eliminates the need for requirements.

d. It defines system architecture.

Correct answer: B

Explanation: Journey maps visualize customer experiences, emotions, and challenges across touchpoints.

14. **Customer-centric discovery**
Which activity aligns with the **"Be your customer"** step in customer-centric discovery?

a. Reviewing release notes

b. Shadowing users and observing workflows

c. Conducting UAT

d. Writing user stories

Correct answer: B

Explanation: This step focuses on empathy by experiencing the customer's perspective firsthand.

15. **Problem Analysis**
Which questions help analyze a business challenge effectively? (Choose two.)

a. Who is affected?

b. How many developers are available?

c. Why does the issue occur?

d. Which programming language is used?

Correct answer: A and C

Explanation: Root cause analysis focuses on impact and causation, not technical implementation details.

16. **Salesforce capabilities**

    Which Salesforce features can help drive user productivity without custom development? (Choose two.)

    a. Einstein Activity Capture

    b. Apex triggers

    c. Macros

    d. Custom REST APIs

    Correct answer: A and C

    Explanation: These are out-of-the-box features included with Sales Cloud licenses.

17. **Change Enablement**

    What is an effective way to encourage Salesforce adoption after go-live?

    a. Disable unused features

    b. Use in-app guidance prompts

    c. Limit training materials

    d. Rely only on documentation

    Correct answer: B

    Explanation: In-app guidance provides contextual, just-in-time support to users.

18. **User acceptance testing (UAT)**

    What is the primary role of a business analyst during UAT?

    a. Writing code fixes

    b. Validating that solutions meet business requirements

    c. Managing production deployments

    d. Performing performance testing

    Correct answer: B

    Explanation: The BA ensures that the delivered solution aligns with the agreed requirements and business outcomes.

19. **UAT readiness**

    Which artifacts are most critical for successful UAT? (Choose two.)

    a. Approved requirements

b. Acceptance criteria

c. System architecture diagrams

d. Source code repositories

Correct answer: A and B

Explanation: Clear requirements and acceptance criteria form the foundation for effective UAT.

20. **Metrics and success measurement**
Why should metrics be defined during problem analysis?

a. To estimate licensing costs

b. To measure solution impact and success

c. To assign developer tasks

d. To finalize technical design

Correct answer: B

Explanation: Metrics enable objective evaluation of whether business outcomes have been achieved.

21. **Trusted Advisor Role**
What behavior best demonstrates a business analyst acting as a **trusted advisor**?

a. Always agreeing with stakeholders

b. Recommending solutions aligned to business value and constraints

c. Deferring decisions to developers

d. Avoiding conflict discussions

Correct answer: B

Explanation: A trusted advisor provides informed, value-driven guidance, even when trade-offs are required.

22. **Continuous improvement**
Which activity best supports long-term Salesforce success?

a. One-time training session

b. Ignoring user feedback after launch

c. Reviewing adoption metrics and iterating

d. Locking requirements permanently

Correct answer: C

Explanation: Continuous monitoring and iteration ensure sustained value and adoption.

> Note
>
> If you would like to become a holistic BA, try to explore PMI-PBA and IIBA-CBAP.
>
> **PMI-PBA:** `Professional in Business Analysis (PMI-PBA) Certification | PMI`
>
> **IIBA-CBA:** `Senior Business Analysis Certification CBAP® | IIBA®`

Summary

Mastering the Salesforce BA certification requires shifting from a technical builder mindset to a strategic advisor role, prioritizing the *why* behind solutions over the *how* of configuration. By focusing on conceptual platform capabilities, real-world stakeholder trade-offs, and the fundamentals of discovery and UAT, you prove your ability to bridge the gap between business needs and technical execution. This certification serves as a powerful milestone, validating your expertise in delivering value through alignment—a skill set that opens the door to our final chapter, *Career Opportunities and Related BA Roles*, where we will explore how to leverage these credentials into high-impact positions within the ecosystem.

Get this book's PDF version and more

Scan the QR code (or go to `packtpub.com/unlock`). Search for this book by name, confirm the edition, and then follow the steps on the page.

UNLOCK NOW

Note: Keep your invoice handy. Purchases made directly from Packt don't require an invoice.

18

Career Opportunities and Related BA Roles

Throughout this book, the focus has been on building strong business analysis fundamentals while applying them effectively within the Salesforce ecosystem. As you progress in your learning journey, a natural question arises: *What does a career as a Salesforce Business Analyst actually look like, and where can it lead?*

The Salesforce ecosystem offers a wide range of career opportunities for aspiring Business Analysts. Unlike traditional IT environments, Salesforce roles are highly interconnected, allowing professionals to move laterally and vertically based on skills, interests, and experience. This chapter explores the most common career paths for aspiring Salesforce Business Analysts, examines closely related roles, and explains how professionals from adjacent positions—particularly Salesforce Administrators—can successfully transition into BA roles. The intent is to provide clarity, realism, and practical guidance for long-term career growth.

We will cover the following sections in detail in this chapter.

- The Salesforce Business Analyst role in practice
- Common entry points into a Salesforce BA career
- Career progression for Salesforce Business Analysts
- Other related roles in the Salesforce ecosystem
- Skills that enable long-term success
- Practical tips

Let's explore each of these sections.

The Salesforce Business Analyst role in practice

A Salesforce Business Analyst plays a pivotal role in ensuring that business needs are translated into effective, scalable Salesforce solutions. While titles may vary across organizations, the core responsibility remains consistent: acting as the bridge between business stakeholders and delivery teams.

In practice, Salesforce Business Analysts are expected to do the following:

- Understand end-to-end business processes and identify opportunities for improvement
- Elicit, analyze, document, and validate business requirements
- Translate business needs into Salesforce-aligned functional requirements
- Evaluate declarative versus programmatic solution options
- Collaborate closely with business stakeholders, project managers, administrators, developers, architects, and testers
- Support testing, user adoption, and change management activities

What distinguishes a Salesforce Business Analyst from a generalist BA is platform awareness. Salesforce BAs do not operate in abstraction. They understand what the platform can deliver natively, where customization is justified, and how design decisions impact scalability, security, and long-term maintenance. This ability to think simultaneously in business and platform terms is what makes the role both valuable and in demand.

Common entry points into a Salesforce BA career

There is no single prescribed path to becoming a Salesforce Business Analyst. Many professionals enter the role from adjacent positions, such as administrators, developers, and testers, bringing complementary strengths that can be refined over time.

Transition from a traditional BA role

Business Analysts with experience in ERP, CRM, or custom application environments often transition naturally into Salesforce projects. Your BA skills from other domains are mostly transferable. They typically bring strong skills in the following:

- Requirements elicitation and documentation
- Stakeholder communication and facilitation
- Process modeling and gap analysis

However, success in Salesforce requires these professionals to expand their skill set to include the following:

- Salesforce data model and security concepts
- Declarative automation tools such as flows and validation rules
- Awareness of Salesforce limits, release cycles, and best practices

Without this platform knowledge, even experienced BAs may struggle to provide guidance relevant to the solution.

Transition from Salesforce administrator to BA

Salesforce administrators represent one of the most common and effective entry points into the BA role. Administrators already understand how Salesforce works and how users interact with the system. Their strengths often include the following:

- Hands-on configuration experience
- Strong understanding of data, security, and automation
- Exposure to user adoption and support challenges

To move into a Business Analyst role, Administrators must deliberately shift their focus from *solution execution* to *problem definition*. This includes the following:

- Leading discovery conversations rather than responding to requests
- Asking business-focused questions such as why and what outcome is needed
- Documenting requirements and assumptions clearly
- Thinking beyond individual features to end-to-end processes

This transition is less about abandoning technical skills and more about elevating them through structured analysis and strategic thinking.

Transition from business or domain roles

Professionals from sales operations, service operations, marketing operations, or finance often become effective Salesforce Business Analysts because they understand real-world business workflows. Their challenge lies in acquiring enough Salesforce knowledge to translate business needs into platform-aligned solutions. With focused learning and project exposure, this gap can be closed relatively quickly. To ramp up your skills, use **Trailhead** as "zero-cost" training.

Bridging the gap between a business need and a technical solution is a high-value skill set that only grows in demand. As you move beyond the basics of requirements gathering and into the realm of strategic implementation, your opportunities for advancement expand. Here is how that journey typically unfolds.

Career progression for Salesforce BAs

While job titles and responsibilities vary by organization, Salesforce BA careers typically follow a progression that reflects increasing responsibility and influence.

Junior Salesforce BA

At the entry level, the focus is on learning and contribution. Responsibilities may include the following:

- Supporting requirement-gathering activities
- Documenting user stories and acceptance criteria
- Assisting with testing and validation
- Learning Salesforce terminology, features, and delivery practices

Success at this stage depends on attention to detail, willingness to learn, and openness to feedback. To truly excel, keep these three principles in mind:

- **Become a "Why" detective:** Don't just record what a user asks for; dig into why they need it. Understanding the pain point behind the request prevents you from building "faster horses" when the business actually needs a car.
- **Master the art of visualization:** Words can be misinterpreted, but a clear process map rarely is. Use tools such as Lucidchart or Miro to transform messy verbal requirements into clean flowcharts—it's the fastest way to prove you understand the business logic.
- **Build in a sandbox, learn in the UI:** Stay curious about the "Admin" side of the house. Even if you aren't the one clicking the buttons to build the solution, knowing what is possible with "clicks not code" makes you a much more credible bridge between the business and the developers.

Salesforce BA

At the mid-level, Business Analysts operate with greater independence. They are expected to do the following:

- Lead discovery and requirements workshops
- Analyze and optimize business processes
- Recommend Salesforce-native solutions
- Work closely with delivery teams to ensure alignment

This is the stage where Business Analysts begin to influence solution design rather than simply document requirements. The value of a mid-level BA lies in their ability to act as a "value engineer." They don't just ask what the business wants; they challenge stakeholders to simplify their processes before they are automated. By identifying technical debt and advocating for **out-of-the-box (OOTB)** functionality over custom code, they save the organization significant long-term maintenance costs and ensure the platform remains scalable.

- **Develop "consultative confidence"**: Learn to say "no" or "not yet" to stakeholders. Your job is to protect the health of the Salesforce Org by steering the business toward best practices, even when they push for complex customizations.
- **Think in data models**: Start visualizing how a requirement affects the schema builder. Understanding how objects relate to one another (lookup versus master-detail) will help you write requirements that developers can actually implement.
- **Bridge the gap with demos**: Don't wait until the end of a sprint to show progress. Use wireframes or "paper prototyping" to validate requirements early, ensuring that the business and the technical team are always in lockstep.

Senior Salesforce BA

Senior Salesforce Business Analysts take on a more strategic role. They often do the following:

- Guide solution direction across multiple teams or initiatives
- Balance business priorities with architectural considerations
- Mentor junior Business Analysts
- Serve as trusted advisors to stakeholders

At this level, strong judgment, communication, and decision-making skills are just as important as Salesforce expertise. The true value of a senior BA is their "enterprise empathy." They possess the foresight to see how a configuration change in one department—such as Marketing—will ripple through to Finance or Customer Success months down the line. By managing these cross-cloud dependencies and governing the roadmap, they prevent the platform from becoming a "zombie system" of disconnected parts, ensuring that every dollar spent on Salesforce aligns strictly with the company's strategic objectives.

- **Master the art of negotiation**: You will often act as the primary mediator between a demanding business lead and a protective Technical Architect. Your success depends on your ability to negotiate a **Minimum Viable Product (MVP)** that satisfies the immediate business need without compromising the long-term integrity of the system.
- **Prioritize change management**: Even the most elegant technical solution will fail if the end users refuse to adopt it. Spend as much energy on user adoption strategies, communication plans, and training as you do on the technical solution design.
- **Invest in leadership, not just certifications**: While staying current with Salesforce releases is vital, your ability to mentor junior team members and lead a high-stakes

Discovery session with C-suite executives is your greatest differentiator. At this stage, you must learn to sell "business value" rather than just "platform features."

Other related roles in the Salesforce ecosystem

The Salesforce ecosystem includes several roles that overlap significantly with business analysis. Understanding these roles helps aspiring BAs identify alternative or complementary career paths.

Salesforce functional consultant

Functional Consultants focus on translating business requirements into Salesforce solutions, often within specific clouds, such as Sales, Service, or Experience Cloud. In consulting environments, the distinction between a Salesforce BA and a Functional Consultant is often minimal. The difference typically lies in emphasis:

- Business Analysts focus more on discovery, requirements, and process analysis.
- Functional Consultants focus more on solution design and configuration.

Many professionals move between these roles over the course of their careers.

Salesforce product owner

In agile delivery models, Salesforce Business Analysts frequently work alongside—or transition into—Product Owner roles. Product Owners are responsible for backlog prioritization, value delivery, and stakeholder alignment. Strong Business Analysts are well-positioned for this role due to their understanding of both business needs and platform constraints.

Long-term path: Salesforce solution architect

For Business Analysts with strong technical aptitude and broad platform experience, solution architecture represents a natural long-term progression. Architects require a deep understanding of integrations, data strategy, security, and scalability. Many successful Salesforce architects began their careers as Business Analysts.

The journey of a Salesforce Business Analyst is one of constant evolution—from translating requirements as a junior, to optimizing processes as a mid-level professional, and finally steering strategy as a senior leader. Whether you ultimately choose to dive deep into technical architecture or move into executive-level product ownership, the core of your value remains the same: you are the vital bridge between business problems and technology solutions.

Skills that enable long-term success

Successful Salesforce Business Analysts combine foundational BA skills with platform expertise and strong interpersonal capabilities. They often become the "go-to person" or **Subject Matter Expert (SME)** within a project, possessing enough technical literacy to brainstorm with developers and enough business acumen to truly empathize with stakeholders. Long-term success in this space isn't just about memorizing the **Setup** menu; it's about the ability to ask the right questions, spot potential friction before it happens, and translate technical limitations into clear, manageable business outcomes. As the platform grows, the most indispensable BAs are those who stay adaptable and maintain a "process-first" mindset. You can focus on building the following skills:

- Core business analysis skills
  - Requirements elicitation and validation
  - Process modeling and analysis
  - Stakeholder communication and facilitation
  - Documentation and traceability
- Salesforce-specific skills
  - Data model and security understanding
  - Declarative automation capabilities
  - Awareness of platform limits and best practices
  - Ability to evaluate declarative versus programmatic solutions
- Professional and interpersonal skills
  - Clear and concise communication
  - Facilitation and negotiation
  - Adaptability to frequent change
  - Continuous learning mindset
- Most importantly, focus on AI learning
  - **Agentic orchestration**: Shift from documenting human tasks to defining "instructions," "topics," and "guardrails" for autonomous agents using AgentForce.

  - **Data grounding and prompting**: Master prompt engineering and data cloud fundamentals to ensure that AI outputs are grounded in reliable, real-time business context.
  - **Ethical governance**: Champion AI ethics and oversight to identify bias, manage data privacy, and ensure that automated decisions align with human-centered business value.

A career as a Salesforce Business Analyst offers both flexibility and longevity. The role sits at the intersection of business strategy and technology execution, making it critical to successful Salesforce implementations. For aspiring professionals, the ecosystem provides multiple entry points, clear growth paths, and opportunities to evolve into leadership, architecture, or product-focused roles.

By building strong business analysis foundations, developing Salesforce platform expertise, and continuously refining communication and analytical skills, aspiring Salesforce Business Analysts can position themselves for sustained success and meaningful impact within the Salesforce ecosystem.

Practical tips

- **Move from "what" to "why"**: Holistic BAs challenge assumptions, ask value-driven questions, and ensure every requirement supports a business objective.
- **Own the end-to-end lifecycle**: They engage early—before projects are approved—and stay involved through UAT, adoption, and post-implementation measurement.
- **Build cross-disciplinary fluency**: Holistic BAs understand project management, product thinking, and technology concepts, allowing them to communicate effectively across roles.
- **Apply techniques with intent**: Rather than over-documenting, holistic BAs select techniques purposefully, balancing rigor with agility.
- **Think in capabilities, not features**: They focus on long-term business capabilities and outcomes rather than isolated functional requests.
- **From Business Analyst to business partner**: As a partner, influence decisions rather than simply recording them, enable organizational change rather than just delivery, and measure success in outcomes, not outputs.
- **Participate in significant events and groups**: Attend World Tours (they are free), Dreamforce, and join local Trailblazer Community Groups and Salesforce Business Analyst groups.

Summary

In this chapter, we explored the diverse entry points into the Salesforce Business Analyst role and the clear trajectory for long-term growth. We learned how domain experts can leverage their real-world experience to bridge the gap between business needs and platform capabilities, and why a "process-first" mindset is the foundation of success. Finally, we reviewed the progression from junior to senior level, highlighting how increasing your influence—rather than just your technical knowledge—opens doors to specialized roles such as Solution Architect or Product Owner.

As we conclude this journey, remember that being a Salesforce Business Analyst is about more than documenting requirements; it is about architecting solutions that drive real human value. In an era where AI and automation are rapidly redefining the platform, your ability to think critically and translate complex visions into actionable strategy remains your greatest asset. By shifting your focus from simply delivering features to fostering deep business partnerships, you transition from a project participant to a leader in digital transformation. The Salesforce ecosystem is vast and ever evolving, but its true power is only unlocked through the clarity, empathy, and intent you bring to every stakeholder's interaction. Embrace this path with curiosity and conviction, knowing that your work is the essential bridge between a business's current challenges and its future potential.

The path to mastery is ongoing, so keep learning and practicing as you adapt to the ever-evolving world of technology and AI. By shifting your focus from "features" to "business partnership," you will drive lasting transformation for every stakeholder you serve. May your analytical insights lead to innovative solutions, and may your professional journey be filled with meaningful impact.

Good luck with your future business analysis efforts!

Get this book's PDF version and more

Scan the QR code (or go to `packtpub.com/unlock`). Search for this book by name, confirm the edition, and then follow the steps on the page.

UNLOCK NOW

Note: Keep your invoice handy. Purchases made directly from Packt don't require an invoice.

19

Unlock Your Exclusive Benefits

Your copy of this book includes the following exclusive benefits:

Online Exam-Prep Tools

Ace your certification exam with exam-ready online resources

DRM-Free PDF Version

Download DRM-free PDF and ePub copies of this book.

7-Day Packt Library Access

Get 7-day unlimited access to 8,000+ books and videos. No credit card required.

Available for first-time Packt+ trial users only.

Next-Gen Reader Access

Read this book on Packt Reader with progress sync, dark mode and note-taking.

Follow the guide below to unlock them. The process takes only a few minutes and needs to be completed once.

Unlock this Book's Free Benefits in 3 Easy Steps

Step 1

Keep your purchase invoice ready for *Step 3*. If you have a physical copy, scan it using your phone and save it as a PDF, JPG, or PNG.

For more help on finding your invoice, visit `https://www.packtpub.com/en-us/unlock?step=1`.

> Note
>
> **Note**: If you bought this book directly from Packt, no invoice is required. After *Step 2*, you can access your exclusive content right away.

Step 2

Scan the QR code or go to `packtpub.com/unlock`.

On the page that opens (similar to *Figure 19.1* on desktop), search for this book by name and select the correct edition.

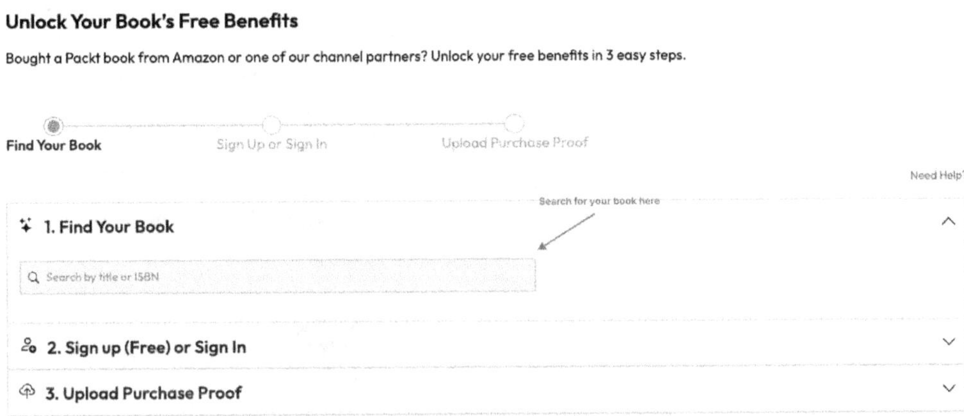

Figure 19.1: Packt unlock landing page on desktop

Step 3

After selecting your book, sign in to your Packt account or create one for free. Then upload your invoice (PDF, PNG, or JPG, up to 10 MB). Follow the on-screen instructions to finish the process.

Need Help

If you get stuck and need help, visit `https://www.packtpub.com/unlock-benefits/help` for a detailed FAQ on how to find your invoices and more. This QR code will take you to the help page.

Note

Note: If you are still facing issues, reach out to `customercare@packt.com`.

<packt>

packtpub.com

Subscribe to our online digital library for full access to over 7,000 books and videos, as well as industry leading tools to help you plan your personal development and advance your career. For more information, please visit our website.

Why subscribe?

- Spend less time learning and more time coding with practical eBooks and Videos from over 4,000 industry professionals
- Improve your learning with Skill Plans built especially for you
- Get a free eBook or video every month
- Fully searchable for easy access to vital information
- Copy and paste, print, and bookmark content

At www.packtpub.com, you can also read a collection of free technical articles, sign up for a range of free newsletters, and receive exclusive discounts and offers on Packt books and eBooks.

Other Books You May Enjoy

If you enjoyed this book, you may be interested in these other books by Packt:

Salesforce End-to-End Implementation Handbook

Kristian Margaryan Jørgensen

ISBN: 9781804613221

- Discover the critical activities in Salesforce implementation
- Address common issues faced in implementing Salesforce
- Explore appropriate delivery methodology
- Understand the importance of a change management strategy
- Govern Salesforce implementation through all its phases
- Gain insights on key activities in the continuous improvement phase
- Leverage customer 360 for analytics, AI and automation

Becoming a Salesforce Certified Technical Architect

Tameem Bahri

ISBN: 9781803239439

- Explore core architectural concepts essential for any Salesforce architect
- Understand Salesforce knowledge domains using practical examples
- Practice creating solutions using scenarios focusing on particular knowledge domains
- Discover key artifacts needed to document and explain an end-to-end solution
- Apply data life cycle management effectively in the Salesforce ecosystem
- Design appropriate enterprise integration interfaces to build your connected solution
- Know what to expect on the day of the review board along with valuable tips and tricks

Salesforce CRM Administration Handbook

Krzysztof Nowacki, Mateusz Twarożek

ISBN: 9781835085691

- Discover strategies to stay up-to-date with Salesforce releases
- Integrate Salesforce products seamlessly to meet diverse business needs
- Explore Sales and Service Cloud and its transformative impact on sales and customer support operations
- Master opportunity management for successful deal closures and pipeline forecasting
- Understand Salesforce Orgs, managing users, settings, and customization
- Explore data import and export methods and data mapping
- Discover best practices, mock tests, and valuable tips and tricks to prepare for Salesforce certification

Packt is searching for authors like you

If you're interested in becoming an author for Packt, please visit `authors.packtpub.com` and apply today. We have worked with thousands of developers and tech professionals, just like you, to help them share their insight with the global tech community. You can make a general application, apply for a specific hot topic that we are recruiting an author for, or submit your own idea.

Share your thoughts

Now you've finished *The Salesforce Business Analysis Playbook*, we'd love to hear your thoughts! Scan the QR code below to go straight to the Amazon review page for this book and share your feedback or leave a review on the site that you purchased it from.

`https://packt.link/r/1806109271`

Your review is important to us and the tech community and will help us make sure we're delivering excellent quality content.

Index

www.ingramcontent.com/pod-product-compliance
Lightning Source LLC
Chambersburg PA
CBHW051832300326
42079CB00008B/41